Warne's

METRIC CONVERSION TABLES

Compiled by Helen Perrin, B.Sc., M.Sc.

Main Sections : LENGTH (including Velocity)   AREA
VOLUME CAPACITY WEIGHT
TEMPERATURE

Frederick Warne

Published by
Frederick Warne & Co Ltd: London
Frederick Warne & Co Inc: New York
1974

ISBN 0 7232 1761 0

Tables computed and set by Comtech Ltd, London
Printed in Great Britain by
William Clowes & Sons Limited
London, Beccles and Colchester

682.10 73

Contents

Introduction

The **Imperial System** of measurement, based on the yard for length and the pound for weight, has been used in the United Kingdom for many centuries. The **Metric System** was founded by the French during the French Revolution. The **Système International d'Unités (International System of Units)** is an extension and refinement of the metric system, finally agreed on at an international conference in 1960. The international symbol for this system is **SI**.

Metric units are related very simply, by factors of ten, for example:

$$1 \text{ kilometre} = 1\ 000 \text{ metres}$$
$$1 \text{ millimetre} = \tfrac{1}{1000} \text{ metre}$$

But the units of the Imperial System are not related in any systematic way, for example:

$$1 \text{ mile} = 1\ 760 \text{ yards}$$
$$1 \text{ foot} = \tfrac{1}{3} \text{ yard}$$

Thus calculations involving them are more involved than those involving metric units.

A metric system which has been used in the past in the United Kingdom for scientific work is the **Centimetre-Gramme-Second** system **(CGS)**, which had the centimetre and gramme as basic units. This system was superseded by one with the metre and kilogramme as basic units, as this simplified scientific measurements considerably, particularly where electrical units were used. This was called the **MKS** system **(Metre-Kilogramme-Second)**, and it led directly to SI.

The United Kingdom decided to adopt SI as the primary system for all measures and weights because almost 90% of the world's population live in countries that use SI, or are committed to use it.

SI Units

There are six **base-units**

quantity	unit	symbol
length	metre	m
mass	kilogramme	kg
time	second	s
electric current	ampere	A
temperature	kelvin	K
luminous intensity	candela	cd

The SI units for plane angle and solid angle, the radian (rad) and steradian (sr) respectively, are called **supplementary units**.

The **derived units** are stated in terms of the base-units; for example, velocity is expressed in metres per second (m/s) and area is measured in square metres (m^2). Some derived units are given special names, for example the unit of energy is the joule (J) (or kg m^2/s^2 in terms of the base-units).

SI Prefixes

prefix	multiplies by	symbol
tera	10^{12}	T
giga	10^9	G
mega	10^6	M
kilo	1 000	k
*****hecto**	100	h
*****deca**	10	da

prefix	divides by	symbol
*****deci**	10	d
*****centi**	100	c
milli	1 000	m
micro	10^6	μ
nano	10^9	n
pico	10^{12}	p
femto	10^{15}	f
atto	10^{18}	a

Examples:

$$1 \text{ MJ} = 1\ 000\ 000 \text{ J}$$
$$1 \text{ km} = 1\ 000 \text{ m}$$
$$1 \text{ mm} = 0{\cdot}001 \text{ m}$$

The use of these prefixes is to be avoided if possible.
Multiples of units are normally restricted to steps of a thousand, and fractions to steps of a thousandth. (The centimetre, however, is expected to be widely used in non-technical spheres.)

US Units

The basic units of the yard and the pound have been identical in the United States and the United Kingdom since 1963. Multiples and subdivisions of the yard and the pound are the same in both countries except for the hundred-weight and the ton (see *Weight* section). The US and UK units of capacity also differ (see *Capacity* section).

By international agreement the United Kingdom, Europe and most other countries use the spellings *metre, litre* and *kilogramme*. In North America the spellings are *meter, liter* and *kilogram*.

Use of the Tables

It is hoped that in each table the range covered will suffice for most needs. When a conversion value cannot be directly obtained, break the figure down to a point where each component does occur in the table, then the total of the separate converted values gives the required conversion.

Example: 1 234·5 ft does not appear in Table 3.
But 1 234·5 ft = (1 000+230+4·5) ft
$$= (304·800+70·104+1·372) \text{ m}$$
$$= 376·276 \text{ m}$$
For very large values, or fractional parts, it may be necessary to adjust available values. If the upper limit of a table is 1 000: to convert 9 000, take the value for 900 and multiply by 10. Similarly if the lower limit is 0·1, to convert 0·003, take the value for 0·3 and divide by 100.

Length

SI base-unit: **metre** (m)

The **metre** was originally defined as being one ten-millionth part of the distance from the North Pole to the equator at sea-level through Paris. Later its length was fixed by international agreement as the distance between two marks on a bar of platinum and iridium, which was kept in Paris. In 1960, it was more precisely defined as 1 650 763·73 wavelengths of the orange light given off by the gas krypton-86.

Imperial to SI

1 inch (in)			=**25·4** mm
1 foot (ft)	=	12 in	=**0·304 8** m
1 yard (yd)	= $\begin{cases} \end{cases}$	36 in 3 ft	=**0·914 4** m
1 chain	=	22 yd	=**20·116 8** m
1 furlong (fur)	= $\begin{cases} \end{cases}$	220 yd 10 ch	=**0·201 168** km
1 mile	= $\begin{cases} \end{cases}$	1 760 yd 80 ch 8 fur	=1·609 34 km

(Conversion factor in **bold type** indicates exact value.)

SI to Imperial

1 millimetre (mm)	=	0·039 370 1 in
1 centimetre (cm)	=	0·393 701 in
1 metre (m)	= $\begin{cases} \end{cases}$	39·370 1 in 3·280 8 ft 1·093 61 yd
1 kilometre (km)	= $\begin{cases} \end{cases}$	0·621 371 mile 1 093·61 yd

Nautical Measure

1 fathom (fm) =	6·08 ft	=1·853 2 m
1 nautical mile= $\begin{cases} \end{cases}$	1 000 fm 6 080 ft	=1·853 2 km

(1 international nautical mile=1·852 km)

VELOCITY

1 mile/h=1·609 km/h	1 km/h=0·621 4 mile/h
1 ft/s =0·304 8 m/s	1 m/s =3·281 ft/s

Thus to convert feet per second to metres per second, the table converting feet to metres can be used. Similarly the corresponding *Length* table can be used to convert mile/h, m/s, km/h, etc.

in	mm	in	mm	in	mm	in	mm
1/16	1·588	9¼	234·950	21¼	539·750	33¼	844·550
1/8	3·175	9½	241·300	21½	546·100	33½	850·900
3/16	4·763	9¾	247·650	21¾	552·450	33¾	857·250
1/4	6·350	10	254·000	22	558·800	34	863·600
5/16	7·938	10¼	260·350	22¼	565·150	34¼	869·950
3/8	9·525	10½	266·700	22½	571·500	34½	876·300
7/16	11·113	10¾	273·050	22¾	577·850	34¾	882·650
1/2	12·700	11	279·400	23	584·200	35	889·000
9/16	14·288	11¼	285·750	23¼	590·550	35¼	895·350
5/8	15·875	11½	292·100	23½	596·900	35½	901·700
11/16	17·463	11¾	298·450	23¾	603·250	35¾	908·050
3/4	19·050	12	304·800	24	609·600	36	914·400
13/16	20·638	12¼	311·150	24¼	615·950	37	939·800
7/8	22·225	12½	317·500	24½	622·300	38	965·200
15/16	23·813	12¾	323·850	24¾	628·650	39	990·600
1	25·400	13	330·200	25	635·000	40	1 016·000
1¼	31·750	13¼	336·550	25¼	641·350	41	1 041·400
1½	38·100	13½	342·900	25½	647·700	42	1 066·800
1¾	44·450	13¾	349·250	25¾	654·050	43	1 092·200
2	50·800	14	355·600	26	660·400	44	1 117·600
						45	1 143·000
2¼	57·150	14¼	361·950	26¼	666·750	46	1 168·400
2½	63·500	14½	368·300	26½	673·100	47	1 193·800
2¾	69·850	14¾	374·650	26¾	679·450	48	1 219·200
3	76·200	15	381·000	27	685·800	49	1 244·600
3¼	82·550	15¼	387·350	27¼	692·150	50	1 270·000
3½	88·900	15½	393·700	27½	698·500		
3¾	95·250	15¾	400·050	27¾	704·850	51	1 295·400
4	101·600	16	406·400	28	711·200	52	1 320·800
						53	1 346·200
4¼	107·950	16¼	412·750	28¼	717·550	54	1 371·600
4½	114·300	16½	419·100	28½	723·900	55	1 397·000
4¾	120·650	16¾	425·450	28¾	730·250		
5	127·000	17	431·800	29	736·600	56	1 422·400
						57	1 447·800
5¼	133·350	17¼	438·150	29¼	742·950	58	1 473·200
5½	139·700	17½	444·500	29½	749·300	59	1 498·600
5¾	146·050	17¾	450·850	29¾	755·650	60	1 524·000
6	152·400	18	457·200	30	762·000		
						61	1 549·400
6¼	158·750	18¼	463·550	30¼	768·350	62	1 574·800
6½	165·100	18½	469·900	30½	774·700	63	1 600·200
6¾	171·450	18¾	476·250	30¾	781·050	64	1 625·600
7	177·800	19	482·600	31	787·400	65	1 651·000
7¼	184·150	19¼	488·950	31¼	793·750	66	1 676·400
7½	190·500	19½	495·300	31½	800·100	67	1 701·800
7¾	196·850	19¾	501·650	31¾	806·450	68	1 727·200
8	203·200	20	508·000	32	812·800	69	1 752·600
						70	1 778·000
8¼	209·550	20¼	514·350	32¼	819·150		
8½	215·900	20½	520·700	32½	825·500	71	1 803·400
8¾	222·250	20¾	527·050	32¾	831·850	72	1 828·800
9	228·600	21	533·400	33	838·200		

Note: For *centimetres*, instead of *millimetres*, move the decimal point in the given mm value one place to the left.

ft	in	cm	ft	in	cm	ft	in	cm
	1	2·54	4	1	124·46	8	1	246·38
	2	5·08	4	2	127·00	8	2	248·92
	3	7·62	4	3	129·54	8	3	251·46
	4	10·16	4	4	132·08	8	4	254·00
	5	12·70	4	5	134·62	8	5	256·54
	6	15·24	4	6	137·16	8	6	259·08
	7	17·78	4	7	139·70	8	7	261·62
	8	20·32	4	8	142·24	8	8	264·16
	9	22·86	4	9	144·78	8	9	266·70
	10	25·40	4	10	147·32	8	10	269·24
	11	27·94	4	11	149·86	8	11	271·78
1	0	30·48	5	0	152·40	9	0	274·32
1	1	33·02	5	1	154·94	9	1	276·86
1	2	35·56	5	2	157·48	9	2	279·40
1	3	38·10	5	3	160·02	9	3	281·94
1	4	40·64	5	4	162·56	9	4	284·48
1	5	43·18	5	5	165·10	9	5	287·02
1	6	45·72	5	6	167·64	9	6	289·56
1	7	48·26	5	7	170·18	9	7	292·10
1	8	50·80	5	8	172·72	9	8	294·64
1	9	53·34	5	9	175·26	9	9	297·18
1	10	55·88	5	10	177·80	9	10	299·72
1	11	58·42	5	11	180·34	9	11	302·26
2	0	60·96	6	0	182·88	10	0	304·80
2	1	63·50	6	1	185·42	10	1	307·34
2	2	66·04	6	2	187·96	10	2	309·88
2	3	68·58	6	3	190·50	10	3	312·42
2	4	71·12	6	4	193·04	10	4	314·96
2	5	73·66	6	5	195·58	10	5	317·50
2	6	76·20	6	6	198·12	10	6	320·04
2	7	78·74	6	7	200·66	10	7	322·58
2	8	81·28	6	8	203·20	10	8	325·12
2	9	83·82	6	9	205·74	10	9	327·66
2	10	86·36	6	10	208·28	10	10	330·20
2	11	88·90	6	11	210·82	10	11	332·74
3	0	91·44	7	0	213·36	11	0	335·28
3	1	93·98	7	1	215·90	11	1	337·82
3	2	96·52	7	2	218·44	11	2	340·36
3	3	99·06	7	3	220·98	11	3	342·90
3	4	101·60	7	4	223·52	11	4	345·44
3	5	104·14	7	5	226·06	11	5	347·98
3	6	106·68	7	6	228·60	11	6	350·52
3	7	109·22	7	7	231·14	11	7	353·06
3	8	111·76	7	8	233·68	11	8	355·60
3	9	114·30	7	9	236·22	11	9	358·14
3	10	116·84	7	10	238·76	11	10	360·68
3	11	119·38	7	11	241·30	11	11	363·22
4	0	121·92	8	0	243·84	12	0	365·76

ft	m	ft	m	ft	m	ft	m
½	0.1524	26	7.9248	76	23.1648	126	38.4048
1	0.3048	27	8.2296	77	23.4696	127	38.7096
1½	0.4572	28	8.5344	78	23.7744	128	39.0144
2	0.6096	29	8.8392	79	24.0792	129	39.3192
2½	0.7620	30	9.1440	80	24.3840	130	39.6240
3	0.9144						
3½	1.0668	31	9.4488	81	24.6888	131	39.9288
4	1.2192	32	9.7536	82	24.9936	132	40.2336
4½	1.3716	33	10.0584	83	25.2984	133	40.5384
5	1.5240	34	10.3632	84	25.6032	134	40.8432
		35	10.6680	85	25.9080	135	41.1480
5½	1.6764						
6	1.8288	36	10.9728	86	26.2128	136	41.4528
6½	1.9812	37	11.2776	87	26.5176	137	41.7576
7	2.1336	38	11.5824	88	26.8224	138	42.0624
7½	2.2860	39	11.8872	89	27.1272	139	42.3672
8	2.4384	40	12.1920	90	27.4320	140	42.6720
8½	2.5908						
9	2.7432	41	12.4968	91	27.7368	141	42.9768
9½	2.8956	42	12.8016	92	28.0416	142	43.2816
10	3.0480	43	13.1064	93	28.3464	143	43.5864
		44	13.4112	94	28.6512	144	43.8912
10½	3.2004	45	13.7160	95	28.9560	145	44.1960
11	3.3528						
11½	3.5052	46	14.0208	96	29.2608	146	44.5008
12	3.6576	47	14.3256	97	29.5656	147	44.8056
12½	3.8100	48	14.6304	98	29.8704	148	45.1104
13	3.9624	49	14.9352	99	30.1752	149	45.4152
13½	4.1148	50	15.2400	100	30.4800	150	45.7200
14	4.2672						
14½	4.4196	51	15.5448	101	30.7848	151	46.0248
15	4.5720	52	15.8496	102	31.0896	152	46.3296
		53	16.1544	103	31.3944	153	46.6344
15½	4.7244	54	16.4592	104	31.6992	154	46.9392
16	4.8768	55	16.7640	105	32.0040	155	47.2440
16½	5.0292						
17	5.1816	56	17.0688	106	32.3088	156	47.5488
17½	5.3340	57	17.3736	107	32.6136	157	47.8536
18	5.4864	58	17.6784	108	32.9184	158	48.1584
18½	5.6388	59	17.9832	109	33.2232	159	48.4632
19	5.7912	60	18.2880	110	33.5280	160	48.7680
19½	5.9436						
20	6.0960	61	18.5928	111	33.8328	161	49.0728
		62	18.8976	112	34.1376	162	49.3776
20½	6.2484	63	19.2024	113	34.4424	163	49.6824
21	6.4008	64	19.5072	114	34.7472	164	49.9872
21½	6.5532	65	19.8120	115	35.0520	165	50.2920
22	6.7056						
22½	6.8580	66	20.1168	116	35.3568	166	50.5968
23	7.0104	67	20.4216	117	35.6616	167	50.9016
23½	7.1628	68	20.7264	118	35.9664	168	51.2064
24	7.3152	69	21.0312	119	36.2712	169	51.5112
24½	7.4676	70	21.3360	120	36.5760	170	51.8160
25	7.6200						
		71	21.6408	121	36.8808	171	52.1208
		72	21.9456	122	37.1856	172	52.4256
		73	22.2504	123	37.4904	173	52.7304
		74	22.5552	124	37.7952	174	53.0352
		75	22.8600	125	38.1000	175	53.3400

ft	m	ft	m	ft	m	ft	m
176	53·6148	330	100·5840	580	176·7840	830	252·9840
177	53·9496	335	102·1080	585	178·3080	835	254·5080
178	54·2544	340	103·6320	590	179·8320	840	256·0320
179	54·5592	345	105·1560	595	181·3560	845	257·5560
180	54·8640	350	106·6800	600	182·8800	850	259·0800
181	55·1688	355	108·2040	605	184·4040	855	260·6040
182	55·4736	360	109·7280	610	185·9280	860	262·1280
183	55·7784	365	111·2520	615	187·4520	865	263·6520
184	56·0832	370	112·7760	620	188·9760	870	265·1760
185	56·3880	375	114·3000	625	190·5000	875	266·7000
186	56·6928	380	115·8240	630	192·0240	880	268·2240
187	56·9976	385	117·3480	635	193·5480	885	269·7480
188	57·3024	390	118·8720	640	195·0720	890	271·2720
189	57·6072	395	120·3960	645	196·5960	895	272·7960
190	57·9120	400	121·9200	650	198·1200	900	274·3200
191	58·2168	405	123·4440	655	199·6440	905	275·8440
192	58·5216	410	124·9680	660	201·1680	910	277·3680
193	58·8264	415	126·4920	665	202·6920	915	278·8920
194	59·1312	420	128·0160	670	204·2160	920	280·4160
195	59·4360	425	129·5400	675	205·7400	925	281·9400
196	59·7408	430	131·0640	680	207·2640	930	283·4640
197	60·0456	435	132·5880	685	208·7880	935	284·9880
198	60·3504	440	134·1120	690	210·3120	940	286·5120
199	60·6552	445	135·6360	695	211·8360	945	288·0360
200	60·9600	450	137·1600	700	213·3600	950	289·5600
205	62·4840	455	138·6840	705	214·8840	955	291·0840
210	64·0080	460	140·2080	710	216·4080	960	292·6080
215	65·5320	465	141·7320	715	217·9320	965	294·1320
220	67·0560	470	143·2560	720	219·4560	970	295·6560
225	68·5800	475	144·7800	725	220·9800	975	297·1800
230	70·1040	480	146·3040	730	222·5040	980	298·7040
235	71·6280	485	147·8280	735	224·0280	985	300·2280
240	73·1520	490	149·3520	740	225·5520	990	301·7520
245	74·6760	495	150·8760	745	227·0760	995	303·2760
250	76·2000	500	152·4000	750	228·6000	1 000	304·8000
255	77·7240	505	153·9240	755	230·1240	2 000	609·6
260	79·2480	510	155·4480	760	231·6480	3 000	914·4
265	80·7720	515	156·9720	765	233·1720	4 000	1 219·2
270	82·2960	520	158·4960	770	234·6960	5 000	1 524·0
275	83·8200	525	160·0200	775	236·2200	6 000	1 828·8
						7 000	2 133·6
280	85·3440	530	161·5440	780	237·7440	8 000	2 438·4
285	86·8680	535	163·0680	785	239·2680	9 000	2 743·2
290	88·3920	540	164·5920	790	240·7920		
295	89·9160	545	166·1160	795	242·3160	10 000	3 048·0
300	91·4400	550	167·6400	800	243·8400	15 000	4 572·0
						20 000	6 096·0
						25 000	7 620·0
305	92·9640	555	169·1640	805	245·3640	30 000	9 144·0
310	94·4880	560	170·6880	810	246·8880	35 000	10 668·0
315	96·0120	565	172·2120	815	248·4120	40 000	12 192·0
320	97·5360	570	173·7360	820	249·9360	45 000	13 716·0
325	99·0600	575	175·2600	825	251·4600	50 000	15 240·0

yd	m	yd	m	yd	m	yd	m
1/8	0.1143	11	10.0584	61	55.7784	111	101.4984
1/4	0.2286	12	10.9728	62	56.6928	112	102.4128
3/8	0.3429	13	11.8872	63	57.6072	113	103.3272
1/2	0.4572	14	12.8016	64	58.5216	114	104.2416
5/8	0.5715	15	13.7160	65	59.4360	115	105.1560
3/4	0.6858						
7/8	0.8001	16	14.6304	66	60.3504	116	106.0704
1	0.9144	17	15.5448	67	61.2648	117	106.9848
		18	16.4592	68	62.1792	118	107.8992
1 1/8	1.0287	19	17.3736	69	63.0936	119	108.8136
1 1/4	1.1430	20	18.2880	70	64.0080	120	109.7280
1 3/8	1.2573						
1 1/2	1.3716	21	19.2024	71	64.9224	121	110.6424
1 5/8	1.4859	22	20.1168	72	65.8368	122	111.5568
1 3/4	1.6002	23	21.0312	73	66.7512	123	112.4712
1 7/8	1.7145	24	21.9456	74	67.6656	124	113.3856
2	1.8288	25	22.8600	75	68.5800	125	114.3000
2 1/8	1.9431	26	23.7744	76	69.4944	126	115.2144
2 1/4	2.0574	27	24.6888	77	70.4088	127	116.1288
2 3/8	2.1717	28	25.6032	78	71.3232	128	117.0432
2 1/2	2.2860	29	26.5176	79	72.2376	129	117.9576
2 5/8	2.4003	30	27.4320	80	73.1520	130	118.8720
2 3/4	2.5146						
2 7/8	2.6289	31	28.3464	81	74.0664	131	119.7864
3	2.7432	32	29.2608	82	74.9808	132	120.7008
		33	30.1752	83	75.8952	133	121.6152
3 1/8	2.8575	34	31.0896	84	76.8096	134	122.5296
3 1/4	2.9718	35	32.0040	85	77.7240	135	123.4440
3 3/8	3.0861						
3 1/2	3.2004	36	32.9184	86	78.6384	136	124.3584
3 5/8	3.3147	37	33.8328	87	79.5528	137	125.2728
3 3/4	3.4290	38	34.7472	88	80.4672	138	126.1872
3 7/8	3.5433	39	35.6616	89	81.3816	139	127.1016
4	3.6576	40	36.5760	90	82.2960	140	128.0160
4 1/8	3.7719	41	37.4904	91	83.2104	141	128.9304
4 1/4	3.8862	42	38.4048	92	84.1248	142	129.8448
4 3/8	4.0005	43	39.3192	93	85.0392	143	130.7592
4 1/2	4.1148	44	40.2336	94	85.9536	144	131.6736
4 5/8	4.2291	45	41.1480	95	86.8680	145	132.5880
4 3/4	4.3434						
4 7/8	4.4577	46	42.0624	96	87.7824	146	133.5024
5	4.5720	47	42.9768	97	88.6968	147	134.4168
		48	43.8912	98	89.6112	148	135.3312
5 1/8	4.6863	49	44.8056	99	90.5256	149	136.2456
5 1/4	4.8006	50	45.7200	100	91.4400	150	137.1600
5 3/8	4.9149						
5 1/2	5.0292	51	46.6344	101	92.3544	151	138.0744
5 5/8	5.1435	52	47.5488	102	93.2688	152	138.9888
5 3/4	5.2578	53	48.4632	103	94.1832	153	139.9032
5 7/8	5.3721	54	49.3776	104	95.0976	154	140.8176
6	5.4864	55	50.2920	105	96.0120	155	141.7320
7	6.4008	56	51.2064	106	96.9264	156	142.6464
8	7.3152	57	52.1208	107	97.8408	157	143.5608
9	8.2296	58	53.0352	108	98.7552	158	144.4752
10	9.1440	59	53.9496	109	99.6696	159	145.3896
		60	54.8640	110	100.5840	160	146.3040

yd	m	yd	m	yd	m	yd	m
161	147·2184	211	192·9384	261	238·6584	311	284·3784
162	148·1328	212	193·8528	262	239·5728	312	285·2928
163	149·0472	213	194·7672	263	240·4872	313	286·2072
164	149·9616	214	195·6816	264	241·4016	314	287·1216
165	150·8760	215	196·5960	265	242·3160	315	288·0360
166	151·7904	216	197·5104	266	243·2304	316	288·9504
167	152·7048	217	198·4248	267	244·1448	317	289·8648
168	153·6192	218	199·3392	268	245·0592	318	290·7792
169	154·5336	219	200·2536	269	245·9736	319	291·6936
170	155·4480	220	201·1680	270	246·8880	320	292·6080
171	156·3624	221	202·0824	271	247·8024	321	293·5224
172	157·2768	222	202·9968	272	248·7168	322	294·4368
173	158·1912	223	203·9112	273	249·6312	323	295·3512
174	159·1056	224	204·8256	274	250·5456	324	296·2656
175	160·0200	225	205·7400	275	251·4600	325	297·1800
176	160·9344	226	206·6544	276	252·3744	326	298·0944
177	161·8488	227	207·5688	277	253·2888	327	299·0088
178	162·7632	228	208·4832	278	254·2032	328	299·9232
179	163·6776	229	209·3976	279	255·1176	329	300·8376
180	164·5920	230	210·3120	280	256·0320	330	301·7520
181	165·5064	231	211·2264	281	256·9464	331	302·6664
182	166·4208	232	212·1408	282	257·8608	332	303·5808
183	167·3352	233	213·0552	283	258·7752	333	304·4952
184	168·2496	234	213·9696	284	259·6896	334	305·4096
185	169·1640	235	214·8840	285	260·6040	335	306·3240
186	170·0784	236	215·7984	286	261·5184	336	307·2384
187	170·9928	237	216·7128	287	262·4328	337	308·1528
188	171·9072	238	217·6272	288	263·3472	338	309·0672
189	172·8216	239	218·5416	289	264·2616	339	309·9816
190	173·7360	240	219·4560	290	265·1760	340	310·8960
191	174·6504	241	220·3704	291	266·0904	341	311·8104
192	175·5648	242	221·2848	292	267·0048	342	312·7248
193	176·4792	243	222·1992	293	267·9192	343	313·6392
194	177·3936	244	223·1136	294	268·8336	344	314·5536
195	178·3080	245	224·0280	295	269·7480	345	315·4680
196	179·2224	246	224·9424	296	270·6624	346	316·3824
197	180·1368	247	225·8568	297	271·5768	347	317·2968
198	181·0512	248	226·7712	298	272·4912	348	318·2112
199	181·9656	249	227·6856	299	273·4056	349	319·1256
200	182·8800	250	228·6000	300	274·3200	350	320·0400
201	183·7944	251	229·5144	301	275·2344	351	320·9544
202	184·7088	252	230·4288	302	276·1488	352	321·8688
203	185·6232	253	231·3432	303	277·0632	353	322·7832
204	186·5376	254	232·2576	304	277·9776	354	323·6976
205	187·4520	255	233·1720	305	278·8920	355	324·6120
206	188·3664	256	234·0864	306	279·8064	356	325·5264
207	189·2808	257	235·0008	307	280·7208	357	326·4408
208	190·1952	258	235·9152	308	281·6352	358	327·3552
209	191·1096	259	236·8296	309	282·5496	359	328·2696
210	192·0240	260	237·7440	310	283·4640	360	329·1840

yd	m	yd	m	yd	m	yd	m
361	330·0984	411	375·8184	461	421·5384	555	507·4920
362	331·0128	412	376·7328	462	422·4528	560	512·0640
363	331·9272	413	377·6472	463	423·3672	565	516·6360
364	332·8416	414	378·5616	464	424·2816	570	521·2080
365	333·7560	415	379·4760	465	425·1960	575	525·7800
366	334·6704	416	380·3904	466	426·1104	580	530·3520
367	335·5848	417	381·3048	467	427·0248	585	534·9240
368	336·4992	418	382·2192	468	427·9392	590	539·4960
369	337·4136	419	383·1336	469	428·8536	595	544·0680
370	338·3280	420	384·0480	470	429·7680	600	548·6400
371	339·2424	421	384·9624	471	430·6824	605	553·2120
372	340·1568	422	385·8768	472	431·5968	610	557·7840
373	341·0712	423	386·7912	473	432·5112	615	562·3560
374	341·9856	424	387·7056	474	433·4256	620	566·9280
375	342·9000	425	388·6200	475	434·3400	625	571·5000
376	343·8144	426	389·5344	476	435·2544	630	576·0720
377	344·7288	427	390·4488	477	436·1688	635	580·6440
378	345·6432	428	391·3632	478	437·0832	640	585·2160
379	346·5576	429	392·2776	479	437·9976	645	589·7880
380	347·4720	430	393·1920	480	438·9120	650	594·3600
381	348·3864	431	394·1064	481	439·8264	655	598·9320
382	349·3008	432	395·0208	482	440·7408	660	603·5040
383	350·2152	433	395·9352	483	441·6552	665	608·0760
384	351·1296	434	396·8496	484	442·5696	670	612·6480
385	352·0440	435	397·7640	485	443·4840	675	617·2200
386	352·9584	436	398·6784	486	444·3984	680	621·7920
387	353·8728	437	399·5928	487	445·3128	685	626·3640
388	354·7872	438	400·5072	488	446·2272	690	630·9360
389	355·7016	439	401·4216	489	447·1416	695	635·5080
390	356·6160	440	402·3360	490	448·0560	700	640·0800
391	357·5304	441	403·2504	491	448·9704	705	644·6520
392	358·4448	442	404·1648	492	449·8848	710	649·2240
393	359·3592	443	405·0792	493	450·7992	715	653·7960
394	360·2736	444	405·9936	494	451·7136	720	658·3680
395	361·1880	445	406·9080	495	452·6280	725	662·9400
396	362·1024	446	407·8224	496	453·5424	730	667·5120
397	363·0168	447	408·7368	497	454·4568	735	672·0840
398	363·9312	448	409·6512	498	455·3712	740	676·6560
399	364·8456	449	410·5656	499	456·2856	745	681·2280
400	365·7600	450	411·4800	500	457·2000	750	685·8000
401	366·6744	451	412·3944	505	461·7720	755	690·3720
402	367·5888	452	413·3088	510	466·3440	760	694·9440
403	368·5032	453	414·2232	515	470·9160	765	699·5160
404	369·4176	454	415·1376	520	475·4880	770	704·0880
405	370·3320	455	416·0520	525	480·0600	775	708·6600
406	371·2464	456	416·9664	530	484·6320	780	713·2320
407	372·1608	457	417·8808	535	489·2040	785	717·8040
408	373·0752	458	418·7952	540	493·7760	790	722·3760
409	373·9896	459	419·7096	545	498·3480	795	726·9480
410	374·9040	460	420·6240	550	502·9200	800	731·5200

yd	m	yd	m	yd	m	yd	m
805	736·0920	1 550	1 417·32	4 050	3 703·32	6 600	6 035·04
810	740·6640	1 600	1 463·04	4 100	3 749·04	6 700	6 126·48
815	745·2360	1 650	1 508·76	4 150	3 794·76	6 800	6 217·92
820	749·8080	1 700	1 554·48	4 200	3 840·48	6 900	6 309·36
825	754·3800	1 750	1 600·20	4 250	3 886·20	7 000	6 400·80
830	758·9520	1 800	1 645·92	4 300	3 931·92	7 100	6 492·24
835	763·5240	1 850	1 691·64	4 350	3 977·64	7 200	6 583·68
840	768·0960	1 900	1 737·36	4 400	4 023·36	7 300	6 675·12
845	772·6680	1 950	1 783·08	4 450	4 069·08	7 400	6 766·56
850	777·2400	2 000	1 828·80	4 500	4 114·80	7 500	6 858·00
855	781·8120	2 050	1 874·52	4 550	4 160·52	7 600	6 949·44
860	786·3840	2 100	1 920·24	4 600	4 206·24	7 700	7 040·88
865	790·9560	2 150	1 965·96	4 650	4 251·96	7 800	7 132·32
870	795·5280	2 200	2 011·68	4 700	4 297·68	7 900	7 223·76
875	800·1000	2 250	2 057·40	4 750	4 343·40	8 000	7 315·20
880	804·6720	2 300	2 103·12	4 800	4 389·12	8 100	7 406·64
885	809·2440	2 350	2 148·84	4 850	4 434·84	8 200	7 498·08
890	813·8160	2 400	2 194·56	4 900	4 480·56	8 300	7 589·52
895	818·3880	2 450	2 240·28	4 950	4 526·28	8 400	7 680·96
900	822·9600	2 500	2 286·00	5 000	4 572·00	8 500	7 772·40
905	827·5320	2 550	2 331·72	5 050	4 617·72	8 600	7 863·84
910	832·1040	2 600	2 377·44	5 100	4 663·44	8 700	7 955·28
915	836·6760	2 650	2 423·16	5 150	4 709·16	8 800	8 046·72
920	841·2480	2 700	2 468·88	5 200	4 754·88	8 900	8 138·16
925	845·8200	2 750	2 514·60	5 250	4 800·60	9 000	8 229·60
930	850·3920	2 800	2 560·32	5 300	4 846·32	9 100	8 321·04
935	854·9640	2 850	2 606·04	5 350	4 892·04	9 200	8 412·48
940	859·5360	2 900	2 651·76	5 400	4 937·76	9 300	8 503·92
945	864·1080	2 950	2 697·48	5 450	4 983·48	9 400	8 595·36
950	868·6800	3 000	2 743·20	5 500	5 029·20	9 500	8 686·80
955	873·2520	3 050	2 788·92	5 550	5 074·92	9 600	8 778·24
960	877·8240	3 100	2 834·64	5 600	5 120·64	9 700	8 869·68
965	882·3960	3 150	2 880·36	5 650	5 166·36	9 800	8 961·12
970	886·9680	3 200	2 926·08	5 700	5 212·08	9 900	9 052·56
975	891·5400	3 250	2 971·80	5 750	5 257·80	10 000	9 144·00
980	896·1120	3 300	3 017·52	5 800	5 303·52	11 000	10 058·40
985	900·6840	3 350	3 063·24	5 850	5 349·24	12 000	10 972·80
990	905·2560	3 400	3 108·96	5 900	5 394·96	13 000	11 887·20
995	909·8280	3 450	3 154·68	5 950	5 440·68	14 000	12 801·60
1 000	914·4000	3 500	3 200·40	6 000	5 486·40	15 000	13 716·00
1 050	960·1200	3 550	3 246·12	6 050	5 532·12	16 000	14 630·40
1 100	1 005·8400	3 600	3 291·84	6 100	5 577·84	17 000	15 544·80
1 150	1 051·5600	3 650	3 337·56	6 150	5 623·56	18 000	16 459·20
1 200	1 097·2800	3 700	3 383·28	6 200	5 669·28	19 000	17 373·60
1 250	1 143·0000	3 750	3 429·00	6 250	5 715·00	20 000	18 288·00
1 300	1 188·7200	3 800	3 474·72	6 300	5 760·72	21 000	19 202·40
1 350	1 234·4400	3 850	3 520·44	6 350	5 806·44	22 000	20 116·80
1 400	1 280·1600	3 900	3 566·16	6 400	5 852·16	23 000	21 031·20
1 450	1 325·8800	3 950	3 611·88	6 450	5 897·88	24 000	21 945·60
1 500	1 371·6000	4 000	3 657·60	6 500	5 943·60	25 000	22 860·00

miles	km	miles	km	miles	km	miles	km
1/8	0.2012	11	17.7028	61	98.1700	111	178.6372
1/4	0.4023	12	19.3121	62	99.7793	112	180.2465
3/8	0.6035	13	20.9215	63	101.3887	113	181.8559
1/2	0.8047	14	22.5308	64	102.9980	114	183.4652
5/8	1.0058	15	24.1402	65	104.6074	115	185.0746
3/4	1.2070						
7/8	1.4082	16	25.7495	66	106.2167	116	186.6839
1	1.6093	17	27.3588	67	107.8260	117	188.2932
		18	28.9682	68	109.4354	118	189.9026
1 1/8	1.8105	19	30.5775	69	111.0447	119	191.5119
1 1/4	2.0117	20	32.1869	70	112.6541	120	193.1213
1 3/8	2.2128						
1 1/2	2.4140	21	33.7962	71	114.2634	121	194.7306
1 5/8	2.6152	22	35.4056	72	115.8728	122	196.3400
1 3/4	2.8164	23	37.0149	73	117.4821	123	197.9493
1 7/8	3.0175	24	38.6243	74	119.0915	124	199.5587
2	3.2187	25	40.2336	75	120.7008	125	201.1680
2 1/8	3.4199	26	41.8429	76	122.3101	126	202.7773
2 1/4	3.6210	27	43.4523	77	123.9195	127	204.3867
2 3/8	3.8222	28	45.0616	78	125.5288	128	205.9960
2 1/2	4.0234	29	46.6710	79	127.1382	129	207.6054
2 5/8	4.2245	30	48.2803	80	128.7475	130	209.2147
2 3/4	4.4257						
2 7/8	4.6269	31	49.8897	81	130.3569	131	210.8241
3	4.8280	32	51.4990	82	131.9662	132	212.4334
		33	53.1084	83	133.5756	133	214.0428
3 1/8	5.0292	34	54.7177	84	135.1849	134	215.6521
3 1/4	5.2304	35	56.3270	85	136.7942	135	217.2614
3 3/8	5.4315						
3 1/2	5.6327	36	57.9364	86	138.4036	136	218.8708
3 5/8	5.8339	37	59.5457	87	140.0129	137	220.4801
3 3/4	6.0350	38	61.1551	88	141.6223	138	222.0895
3 7/8	6.2362	39	62.7644	89	143.2316	139	223.6988
4	6.4374	40	64.3738	90	144.8410	140	225.3082
4 1/8	6.6385	41	65.9831	91	146.4503	141	226.9175
4 1/4	6.8397	42	67.5924	92	148.0596	142	228.5268
4 3/8	7.0409	43	69.2018	93	149.6690	143	230.1362
4 1/2	7.2420	44	70.8111	94	151.2783	144	231.7455
4 5/8	7.4432	45	72.4205	95	152.8877	145	233.3549
4 3/4	7.6444						
4 7/8	7.8456	46	74.0298	96	154.4970	146	234.9642
5	8.0467	47	75.6392	97	156.1064	147	236.5736
		48	77.2485	98	157.7157	148	238.1829
5 1/8	8.2479	49	78.8579	99	159.3251	149	239.7923
5 1/4	8.4491	50	80.4672	100	160.9344	150	241.4016
5 3/8	8.6502						
5 1/2	8.8514	51	82.0765	101	162.5437	151	243.0109
5 5/8	9.0526	52	83.6859	102	164.1531	152	244.6203
5 3/4	9.2537	53	85.2952	103	165.7624	153	246.2296
5 7/8	9.4549	54	86.9046	104	167.3718	154	247.8390
6	9.6561	55	88.5139	105	168.9811	155	249.4483
7	11.2654	56	90.1233	106	170.5905	156	251.0577
8	12.8748	57	91.7326	107	172.1998	157	252.6670
9	14.4841	58	93.3420	108	173.8092	158	254.2764
10	16.0934	59	94.9513	109	175.4185	159	255.8857
		60	96.5606	110	177.0278	160	257.4950

miles	km	miles	km	miles	km	miles	km
161	259·104	211	339·572	261	420·039	311	500·506
162	260·714	212	341·181	262	421·648	312	502·115
163	262·323	213	342·790	263	423·257	313	503·725
164	263·932	214	344·400	264	424·867	314	505·334
165	265·542	215	346·009	265	426·476	315	506·943
166	267·151	216	347·618	266	428·086	316	508·553
167	268·760	217	349·228	267	429·695	317	510·162
168	270·370	218	350·837	268	431·304	318	511·771
169	271·979	219	352·446	269	432·914	319	513·381
170	273·588	220	354·056	270	434·523	320	514·990
171	275·198	221	355·665	271	436·132	321	516·599
172	276·807	222	357·274	272	437·742	322	518·209
173	278·417	223	358·884	273	439·351	323	519·818
174	280·026	224	360·493	274	440·960	324	521·427
175	281·635	225	362·102	275	442·570	325	523·037
176	283·245	226	363·712	276	444·179	326	524·646
177	284·854	227	365·321	277	445·788	327	526·255
178	286·463	228	366·930	278	447·398	328	527·865
179	288·073	229	368·540	279	449·007	329	529·474
180	289·682	230	370·149	280	450·616	330	531·084
181	291·291	231	371·758	281	452·226	331	532·693
182	292·901	232	373·368	282	453·835	332	534·302
183	294·510	233	374·977	283	455·444	333	535·912
184	296·119	234	376·586	284	457·054	334	537·521
185	297·729	235	378·196	285	458·663	335	539·130
186	299·338	236	379·805	286	460·272	336	540·740
187	300·947	237	381·415	287	461·882	337	542·349
188	302·557	238	383·024	288	463·491	338	543·958
189	304·166	239	384·633	289	465·100	339	545·568
190	305·775	240	386·243	290	466·710	340	547·177
191	307·385	241	387·852	291	468·319	341	548·786
192	308·994	242	389·461	292	469·928	342	550·396
193	310·603	243	391·071	293	471·538	343	552·005
194	312·213	244	392·680	294	473·147	344	553·614
195	313·822	245	394·289	295	474·756	345	555·224
196	315·431	246	395·899	296	476·366	346	556·833
197	317·041	247	397·508	297	477·975	347	558·442
198	318·650	248	399·117	298	479·585	348	560·052
199	320·259	249	400·727	299	481·194	349	561·661
200	321·869	250	402·336	300	482·803	350	563·270
201	323·478	251	403·945	301	484·413	351	564·880
202	325·087	252	405·555	302	486·022	352	566·489
203	326·697	253	407·164	303	487·631	353	568·098
204	328·306	254	408·773	304	489·241	354	569·708
205	329·916	255	410·383	305	490·850	355	571·317
206	331·525	256	411·992	306	492·459	356	572·926
207	333·134	257	413·601	307	494·069	357	574·536
208	334·744	258	415·211	308	495·678	358	576·145
209	336·353	259	416·820	309	497·287	359	577·754
210	337·962	260	418·429	310	498·897	360	579·364

miles	km	miles	km	miles	km	miles	km
361	580·973	411	661·440	461	741·908	555	893·186
362	582·583	412	663·050	462	743·517	560	901·233
363	584·192	413	664·659	463	745·126	565	909·279
364	585·801	414	666·268	464	746·736	570	917·326
365	587·411	415	667·878	465	748·345	575	925·373
366	589·020	416	669·487	466	749·954	580	933·420
367	590·629	417	671·096	467	751·564	585	941·466
368	592·239	418	672·706	468	753·173	590	949·513
369	593·848	419	674·315	469	754·782	595	957·560
370	595·457	420	675·924	470	756·392	600	965·606
371	597·067	421	677·534	471	758·001	605	973·653
372	598·676	422	679·143	472	759·610	610	981·700
373	600·285	423	680·753	473	761·220	615	989·747
374	601·895	424	682·362	474	762·829	620	997·793
375	603·504	425	683·971	475	764·438	625	1 005·840
376	605·113	426	685·581	476	766·048	630	1 013·887
377	606·723	427	687·190	477	767·657	635	1 021·933
378	608·332	428	688·799	478	769·266	640	1 029·980
379	609·941	429	690·409	479	770·876	645	1 038·027
380	611·551	430	692·018	480	772·485	650	1 046·074
381	613·160	431	693·627	481	774·094	655	1 054·120
382	614·769	432	695·237	482	775·704	660	1 062·167
383	616·379	433	696·846	483	777·313	665	1 070·214
384	617·988	434	698·455	484	778·922	670	1 078·260
385	619·597	435	700·065	485	780·532	675	1 086·307
386	621·207	436	701·674	486	782·141	680	1 094·354
387	622·816	437	703·283	487	783·751	685	1 102·401
388	624·425	438	704·893	488	785·360	690	1 110·447
389	626·035	439	706·502	489	786·969	695	1 118·494
390	627·644	440	708·111	490	788·579	700	1 126·541
391	629·254	441	709·721	491	790·188	705	1 134·588
392	630·863	442	711·330	492	791·797	710	1 142·634
393	632·472	443	712·939	493	793·407	715	1 150·681
394	634·082	444	714·549	494	795·016	720	1 158·728
395	635·691	445	716·158	495	796·625	725	1 166·774
396	637·300	446	717·767	496	798·235	730	1 174·821
397	638·910	447	719·377	497	799·844	735	1 182·868
398	640·519	448	720·986	498	801·453	740	1 190·915
399	642·128	449	722·595	499	803·063	745	1 198·961
400	643·738	450	724·205	500	804·672	750	1 207·008
401	645·347	451	725·814	505	812·719	755	1 215·055
402	646·956	452	727·423	510	820·765	760	1 223·101
403	648·566	453	729·033	515	828·812	765	1 231·148
404	650·175	454	730·642	520	836·859	770	1 239·195
405	651·784	455	732·252	525	844·906	775	1 247·242
406	653·394	456	733·861	530	852·952	780	1 255·288
407	655·003	457	735·470	535	860·999	785	1 263·335
408	656·612	458	737·080	540	869·046	790	1 271·382
409	658·222	459	738·689	545	877·092	795	1 279·428
410	659·831	460	740·298	550	885·139	800	1 287·475

miles	km	miles	km	miles	km	miles	km
805	1 295·522	1 550	2 494·48	4 050	6 517·84	6 600	10 621·7
810	1 303·569	1 600	2 574·95	4 100	6 598·31	6 700	10 782·6
815	1 311·615	1 650	2 655·42	4 150	6 678·78	6 800	10 943·5
820	1 319·662	1 700	2 735·88	4 200	6 759·24	6 900	11 104·5
825	1 327·709	1 750	2 816·35	4 250	6 839·71	7 000	11 265·4
830	1 335·756	1 800	2 896·82	4 300	6 920·18	7 100	11 426·3
835	1 343·802	1 850	2 977·29	4 350	7 000·65	7 200	11 587·3
840	1 351·849	1 900	3 057·75	4 400	7 081·11	7 300	11 748·2
845	1 359·896	1 950	3 138·22	4 450	7 161·58	7 400	11 909·1
850	1 367·942	2 000	3 218·69	4 500	7 242·05	7 500	12 070·1
855	1 375·989	2 050	3 299·16	4 550	7 322·52	7 600	12 231·0
860	1 384·036	2 100	3 379·62	4 600	7 402·98	7 700	12 391·9
865	1 392·083	2 150	3 460·09	4 650	7 483·45	7 800	12 552·9
870	1 400·129	2 200	3 540·56	4 700	7 563·92	7 900	12 713·8
875	1 408·176	2 250	3 621·02	4 750	7 644·38	8 000	12 874·8
880	1 416·223	2 300	3 701·49	4 800	7 724·85	8 100	13 035·7
885	1 424·269	2 350	3 781·96	4 850	7 805·32	8 200	13 196·6
890	1 432·316	2 400	3 862·43	4 900	7 885·79	8 300	13 357·6
895	1 440·363	2 450	3 942·89	4 950	7 966·25	8 400	13 518·5
900	1 448·410	2 500	4 023·36	5 000	8 046·72	8 500	13 679·4
905	1 456·456	2 550	4 103·83	5 050	8 127·19	8 600	13 840·4
910	1 464·503	2 600	4 184·29	5 100	8 207·65	8 700	14 001·3
915	1 472·550	2 650	4 264·76	5 150	8 288·12	8 800	14 162·2
920	1 480·596	2 700	4 345·23	5 200	8 368·59	8 900	14 323·2
925	1 488·643	2 750	4 425·70	5 250	8 449·06	9 000	14 484·1
930	1 496·690	2 800	4 506·16	5 300	8 529·52	9 100	14 645·0
935	1 504·737	2 850	4 586·63	5 350	8 609·99	9 200	14 806·0
940	1 512·783	2 900	4 667·10	5 400	8 690·46	9 300	14 966·9
945	1 520·830	2 950	4 747·56	5 450	8 770·92	9 400	15 127·8
950	1 528·877	3 000	4 828·03	5 500	8 851·39	9 500	15 288·8
955	1 536·924	3 050	4 908·50	5 550	8 931·86	9 600	15 449·7
960	1 544·970	3 100	4 988·97	5 600	9 012·33	9 700	15 610·6
965	1 553·017	3 150	5 069·43	5 650	9 092·79	9 800	15 771·6
970	1 561·064	3 200	5 149·90	5 700	9 173·26	9 900	15 932·5
975	1 569·110	3 250	5 230·37	5 750	9 253·73	10 000	16 093·4
980	1 577·157	3 300	5 310·84	5 800	9 334·20	11 000	17 702·8
985	1 585·204	3 350	5 391·30	5 850	9 414·66	12 000	19 312·1
990	1 593·251	3 400	5 471·77	5 900	9 495·13	13 000	20 921·5
995	1 601·297	3 450	5 552·24	5 950	9 575·60	14 000	22 530·8
1 000	1 609·344	3 500	5 632·70	6 000	9 656·06	15 000	24 140·2
1 050	1 689·811	3 550	5 713·17	6 050	9 736·53	16 000	25 749·5
1 100	1 770·278	3 600	5 793·64	6 100	9 817·00	17 000	27 358·8
1 150	1 850·746	3 650	5 874·11	6 150	9 897·47	18 000	28 968·2
1 200	1 931·213	3 700	5 954·57	6 200	9 977·93	19 000	30 577·5
1 250	2 011·680	3 750	6 035·04	6 250	10 058·40	20 000	32 186·9
1 300	2 092·147	3 800	6 115·51	6 300	10 138·87	21 000	33 796·2
1 350	2 172·614	3 850	6 195·97	6 350	10 219·33	22 000	35 405·6
1 400	2 253·082	3 900	6 276·44	6 400	10 299·80	23 000	37 014·9
1 450	2 333·549	3 950	6 356·91	6 450	10 380·27	24 000	38 624·3
1 500	2 414·016	4 000	6 437·38	6 500	10 460·74	25 000	40 233·6 ·

6 LENGTH

millimetres (mm) to inches (in)

[centimetres (cm), metres (m) to inches]

mm	in	mm	in	mm	in	mm	in
1	0·039 4	51	2·007 9	101	3·976 4	151	5·944 9
2	0·078 7	52	2·047 2	102	4·015 8	152	5·984 3
3	0·118 1	53	2·086 6	103	4·055 1	153	6·023 6
4	0·157 5	54	2·126 0	104	4·094 5	154	6·063 0
5	0·196 9	55	2·165 4	105	4·133 9	155	6·102 4
6	0·236 2	56	2·204 7	106	4·173 2	156	6·141 7
7	0·275 6	57	2·244 1	107	4·212 6	157	6·181 1
8	0·315 0	58	2·283 5	108	4·252 0	158	6·220 5
9	0·354 3	59	2·322 8	109	4·291 3	159	6·259 8
10	0·393 7	60	2·362 2	110	4·330 7	160	6·299 2
11	0·433 1	61	2·401 6	111	4·370 1	161	6·338 6
12	0·472 4	62	2·440 9	112	4·409 5	162	6·378 0
13	0·511 8	63	2·480 3	113	4·448 8	163	6·417 3
14	0·551 2	64	2·519 7	114	4·488 2	164	6·456 7
15	0·590 6	65	2·559 1	115	4·527 6	165	6·496 1
16	0·629 9	66	2·598 4	116	4·566 9	166	6·535 4
17	0·669 3	67	2·637 8	117	4·606 3	167	6·574 8
18	0·708 7	68	2·677 2	118	4·645 7	168	6·614 2
19	0·748 0	69	2·716 5	119	4·685 0	169	6·653 5
20	0·787 4	70	2·755 9	120	4·724 4	170	6·692 9
21	0·826 8	71	2·795 3	121	4·763 8	171	6·732 3
22	0·866 1	72	2·834 6	122	4·803 2	172	6·771 7
23	0·905 5	73	2·874 0	123	4·842 5	173	6·811 0
24	0·944 9	74	2·913 4	124	4·881 9	174	6·850 4
25	0·984 3	75	2·952 8	125	4·921 3	175	6·889 8
26	1·023 6	76	2·992 1	126	4·960 6	176	6·929 1
27	1·063 0	77	3·031 5	127	5·000 0	177	6·968 5
28	1·102 4	78	3·070 9	128	5·039 4	178	7·007 9
29	1·141 7	79	3·110 2	129	5·078 7	179	7·047 2
30	1·181 1	80	3·149 6	130	5·118 1	180	7·086 6
31	1·220 5	81	3·189 0	131	5·157 5	181	7·126 0
32	1·259 8	82	3·228 3	132	5·196 9	182	7·165 4
33	1·299 2	83	3·267 7	133	5·236 2	183	7·204 7
34	1·338 6	84	3·307 1	134	5·275 6	184	7·244 1
35	1·378 0	85	3·346 5	135	5·315 0	185	7·283 5
36	1·417 3	86	3·385 8	136	5·354 3	186	7·322 8
37	1·456 7	87	3·425 2	137	5·393 7	187	7·362 2
38	1·496 1	88	3·464 6	138	5·433 1	188	7·401 6
39	1·535 4	89	3·503 9	139	5·472 4	189	7·440 9
40	1·574 8	90	3·543 3	140	5·511 8	190	7·480 3
41	1·614 2	91	3·582 7	141	5·551 2	191	7·519 7
42	1·653 5	92	3·622 0	142	5·590 6	192	7·555 9
43	1·692 9	93	3·661 4	143	5·629 9	193	7·598 4
44	1·732 3	94	3·700 8	144	5·669 3	194	7·637 8
45	1·771 7	95	3·740 2	145	5·708 7	195	7·677 2
46	1·811 0	96	3·779 5	146	5·748 0	196	7·716 5
47	1·850 4	97	3·818 9	147	5·787 4	197	7·755 9
48	1·889 8	98	3·858 3	148	5·826 8	198	7·795 3
49	1·929 1	99	3·897 6	149	5·866 1	199	7·834 6
50	1·968 5	100	3·937 0	150	5·905 5	200	7·874 0

Note: 1 mm = 0·1 cm = 0·001 m
100 mm = 10 cm = 0·1 m etc.

millimetres (mm) to inches (in)

[centimetres (cm), metres (m) to inches]

mm	in	mm	in	mm	in	mm	in
201	7·9134	251	9·8819	301	11·8504	351	13·8189
202	7·9528	252	9·9213	302	11·8898	352	13·8583
203	7·9921	253	9·9606	303	11·9291	353	13·8976
204	8·0315	254	10·0000	304	11·9685	354	13·9370
205	8·0709	255	10·0394	305	12·0079	355	13·9764
206	8·1102	256	10·0787	306	12·0473	356	14·0158
207	8·1496	257	10·1181	307	12·0866	357	14·0551
208	8·1890	258	10·1575	308	12·1260	358	14·0945
209	8·2284	259	10·1969	309	12·1654	359	14·1339
210	8·2677	260	10·2362	310	12·2047	360	14·1732
211	8·3071	261	10·2756	311	12·2441	361	14·2126
212	8·3465	262	10·3150	312	12·2835	362	14·2520
213	8·3858	263	10·3543	313	12·3228	363	14·2913
214	8·4252	264	10·3937	314	12·3622	364	14·3307
215	8·4646	265	10·4331	315	12·4016	365	14·3701
216	8·5039	266	10·4724	316	12·4410	366	14·4095
217	8·5433	267	10·5118	317	12·4803	367	14·4488
218	8·5827	268	10·5512	318	12·5197	368	14·4882
219	8·6221	269	10·5906	319	12·5591	369	14·5276
220	8·6614	270	10·6299	320	12·5984	370	14·5669
221	8·7008	271	10·6693	321	12·6378	371	14·6063
222	8·7402	272	10·7087	322	12·6772	372	14·6457
223	8·7795	273	10·7480	323	12·7165	373	14·6850
224	8·8189	274	10·7874	324	12·7559	374	14·7244
225	8·8583	275	10·8268	325	12·7953	375	14·7638
226	8·8976	276	10·8661	326	12·8347	376	14·8032
227	8·9370	277	10·9055	327	12·8740	377	14·8425
228	8·9764	278	10·9449	328	12·9134	378	14·8819
229	9·0158	279	10·9843	329	12·9528	379	14·9213
230	9·0551	280	11·0236	330	12·9921	380	14·9606
231	9·0945	281	11·0630	331	13·0315	381	15·0000
232	9·1339	282	11·1024	332	13·0709	382	15·0394
233	9·1732	283	11·1417	333	13·1102	383	15·0787
234	9·2126	284	11·1811	334	13·1496	384	15·1181
235	9·2520	285	11·2205	335	13·1890	385	15·1575
236	9·2913	286	11·2598	336	13·2284	386	15·1969
237	9·3307	287	11·2992	337	13·2677	387	15·2362
238	9·3701	288	11·3386	338	13·3071	388	15·2756
239	9·4095	289	11·3780	339	13·3465	389	15·3150
240	9·4488	290	11·4173	340	13·3858	390	15·3543
241	9·4882	291	11·4567	341	13·4252	391	15·3937
242	9·5276	292	11·4961	342	13·4646	392	15·4331
243	9·5669	293	11·5354	343	13·5039	393	15·4724
244	9·6063	294	11·5748	344	13·5433	394	15·5118
245	9·6457	295	11·6142	345	13·5827	395	15·5512
246	9·6850	296	11·6535	346	13·6221	396	15·5906
247	9·7244	297	11·6929	347	13·6614	397	15·6299
248	9·7638	298	11·7323	348	13·7008	398	15·6693
249	9·8032	299	11·7717	349	13·7402	399	15·7087
250	9·8425	300	11·8110	350	13·7795	400	15·7480

mm	in	mm	in	mm	in	mm	in
401	15·7874	451	17·7559	501	19·7244	551	21·6929
402	15·8268	452	17·7953	502	19·7638	552	21·7323
403	15·8662	453	17·8347	503	19·8032	553	21·7717
404	15·9055	454	17·8740	504	19·8425	554	21·8110
405	15·9449	455	17·9134	505	19·8819	555	21·8504
406	15·9843	456	17·9528	506	19·9213	556	21·8898
407	16·0236	457	17·9921	507	19·9606	557	21·9291
408	16·0630	458	18·0315	508	20·0000	558	21·9685
409	16·1024	459	18·0709	509	20·0394	559	22·0079
410	16·1417	460	18·1102	510	20·0788	560	22·0473
411	16·1811	461	18·1496	511	20·1181	561	22·0866
412	16·2205	462	18·1890	512	20·1575	562	22·1260
413	16·2599	463	18·2284	513	20·1969	563	22·1654
414	16·2992	464	18·2677	514	20·2362	564	22·2047
415	16·3386	465	18·3071	515	20·2756	565	22·2441
416	16·3780	466	18·3465	516	20·3150	566	22·2835
417	16·4173	467	18·3858	517	20·3543	567	22·3228
418	16·4567	468	18·4252	518	20·3937	568	22·3622
419	16·4961	469	18·4646	519	20·4331	569	22·4016
420	16·5354	470	18·5039	520	20·4725	570	22·4410
421	16·5748	471	18·5433	521	20·5118	571	22·4803
422	16·6142	472	18·5827	522	20·5512	572	22·5197
423	16·6536	473	18·6221	523	20·5906	573	22·5591
424	16·6929	474	18·6614	524	20·6299	574	22·5984
425	16·7323	475	18·7008	525	20·6693	575	22·6378
426	16·7717	476	18·7402	526	20·7087	576	22·6772
427	16·8110	477	18·7795	527	20·7480	577	22·7165
428	16·8504	478	18·8189	528	20·7874	578	22·7559
429	16·8898	479	18·8583	529	20·8268	579	22·7953
430	16·9291	480	18·8976	530	20·8662	580	22·8347
431	16·9685	481	18·9370	531	20·9055	581	22·8740
432	17·0079	482	18·9764	532	20·9449	582	22·9134
433	17·0473	483	19·0158	533	20·9843	583	22·9528
434	17·0866	484	19·0551	534	21·0236	584	22·9921
435	17·1260	485	19·0945	535	21·0630	585	23·0315
436	17·1654	486	19·1339	536	21·1024	586	23·0709
437	17·2047	487	19·1732	537	21·1417	587	23·1102
438	17·2441	488	19·2126	538	21·1811	588	23·1496
439	17·2835	489	19·2520	539	21·2205	589	23·1890
440	17·3228	490	19·2913	540	21·2599	590	23·2284
441	17·3622	491	19·3307	541	21·2992	591	23·2677
442	17·4016	492	19·3701	542	21·3386	592	23·3071
443	17·4410	493	19·4095	543	21·3780	593	23·3465
444	17·4803	494	19·4488	544	21·4173	594	23·3858
445	17·5197	495	19·4882	545	21·4567	595	23·4252
446	17·5591	496	19·5276	546	21·4961	596	23·4646
447	17·5984	497	19·5669	547	21·5354	597	23·5039
448	17·6378	498	19·6063	548	21·5748	598	23·5433
449	17·6772	499	19·6457	549	21·6142	599	23·5827
450	17·7165	500	19·6851	550	21·6536	600	23·6221

mm	in	mm	in	mm	in	mm	in
601	23·6614	651	25·6299	701	27·5984	751	29·5669
602	23·7008	652	25·6693	702	27·6378	752	29·6063
603	23·7402	653	25·7087	703	27·6772	753	29·6457
604	23·7795	654	25·7480	704	27·7166	754	29·6851
605	23·8189	655	25·7874	705	27·7559	755	29·7244
606	23·8583	656	25·8268	706	27·7953	756	29·7638
607	23·8977	657	25·8662	707	27·8347	757	29·8032
608	23·9370	658	25·9055	708	27·8740	758	29·8425
609	23·9764	659	25·9449	709	27·9134	759	29·8819
610	24·0158	660	25·9843	710	27·9528	760	29·9213
611	24·0551	661	26·0236	711	27·9921	761	29·9606
612	24·0945	662	26·0630	712	28·0315	762	30·0000
613	24·1339	663	26·1024	713	28·0709	763	30·0394
614	24·1732	664	26·1417	714	28·1103	764	30·0788
615	24·2126	665	26·1811	715	28·1496	765	30·1181
616	24·2520	666	26·2205	716	28·1890	766	30·1575
617	24·2914	667	26·2599	717	28·2284	767	30·1969
618	24·3307	668	26·2992	718	28·2677	768	30·2362
619	24·3701	669	26·3386	719	28·3071	769	30·2756
620	24·4095	670	26·3780	720	28·3465	770	30·3150
621	24·4488	671	26·4173	721	28·3858	771	30·3543
622	24·4882	672	26·4567	722	28·4252	772	30·3937
623	24·5276	673	26·4961	723	28·4646	773	30·4331
624	24·5669	674	26·5354	724	28·5040	774	30·4725
625	24·6063	675	26·5748	725	28·5433	775	30·5118
626	24·6457	676	26·6142	726	28·5827	776	30·5512
627	24·6851	677	26·6536	727	28·6221	777	30·5906
628	24·7244	678	26·6929	728	28·6614	778	30·6299
629	24·7638	679	26·7323	729	28·7008	779	30·6693
630	24·8032	680	26·7717	730	28·7402	780	30·7087
631	24·8425	681	26·8110	731	28·7795	781	30·7480
632	24·8819	682	26·8504	732	28·8189	782	30·7874
633	24·9213	683	26·8898	733	28·8583	783	30·8268
634	24·9606	684	26·9291	734	28·8977	784	30·8662
635	25·0000	685	26·9685	735	28·9370	785	30·9055
636	25·0394	686	27·0079	736	28·9764	786	30·9449
637	25·0788	687	27·0473	737	29·0158	787	30·9843
638	25·1181	688	27·0866	738	29·0551	788	31·0236
639	25·1575	689	27·1260	739	29·0945	789	31·0630
640	25·1969	690	27·1654	740	29·1339	790	31·1024
641	25·2362	691	27·2047	741	29·1732	791	31·1417
642	25·2756	692	27·2441	742	29·2126	792	31·1811
643	25·3150	693	27·2835	743	29·2520	793	31·2205
644	25·3543	694	27·3228	744	29·2914	794	31·2599
645	25·3937	695	27·3622	745	29·3307	795	31·2992
646	25·4331	696	27·4016	746	29·3701	796	31·3386
647	25·4725	697	27·4410	747	29·4095	797	31·3780
648	25·5118	698	27·4803	748	29·4488	798	31·4173
649	25·5512	699	27·5197	749	29·4882	799	31·4567
650	25·5906	700	27·5591	750	29·5276	800	31·4961

mm	in	mm	in	mm	in	mm	in
801	31·535 5	851	33·504 0	901	35·472 5	951	37·441 0
802	31·574 8	852	33·543 3	902	35·511 8	952	37·480 3
803	31·614 2	853	33·582 7	903	35·551 2	953	37·519 7
804	31·653 6	854	33·622 1	904	35·590 6	954	37·559 1
805	31·692 9	855	33·661 4	905	35·629 9	955	37·598 4
806	31·732 3	856	33·700 8	906	35·669 3	956	37·637 8
807	31·771 7	857	33·740 2	907	35·708 7	957	37·677 2
808	31·811 0	858	33·779 5	908	35·748 1	958	37·716 6
809	31·850 4	859	33·818 9	909	35·787 4	959	37·755 9
810	31·889 8	860	33·858 3	910	35·826 8	960	37·795 3
811	31·929 2	861	33·897 7	911	35·866 2	961	37·834 7
812	31·968 5	862	33·937 0	912	35·905 5	962	37·874 0
813	32·007 9	863	33·976 4	913	35·944 9	963	37·913 4
814	32·047 3	864	34·015 8	914	35·984 3	964	37·952 8
815	32·086 6	865	34·055 1	915	36·023 6	965	37·992 1
816	32·126 0	866	34·094 5	916	36·063 0	966	38·031 5
817	32·165 4	867	34·133 9	917	36·102 4	967	38·070 9
818	32·204 7	868	34·173 2	918	36·141 8	968	38·110 3
819	32·244 1	869	34·212 6	919	36·181 1	969	38·149 6
820	32·283 5	870	34·252 0	920	36·220 5	970	38·189 0
821	32·322 9	871	34·291 4	921	36·259 9	971	38·228 4
822	32·362 2	872	34·330 7	922	36·299 2	972	38·267 7
823	32·401 6	873	34·370 1	923	36·338 6	973	38·307 1
824	32·441 0	874	34·409 5	924	36·378 0	974	38·346 5
825	32·480 3	875	34·448 8	925	36·417 3	975	38·385 8
826	32·519 7	876	34·488 2	926	36·456 7	976	38·425 2
827	32·559 1	877	34·527 6	927	36·496 1	977	38·464 6
828	32·598 4	878	34·566 9	928	36·535 5	978	38·504 0
829	32·637 8	879	34·606 3	929	36·574 8	979	38·543 3
830	32·677 2	880	34·645 7	930	36·614 2	980	38·582 7
831	32·716 6	881	34·685 1	931	36·653 6	981	38·622 1
832	32·755 9	882	34·724 4	932	36·692 9	982	38·661 4
833	32·795 3	883	34·763 8	933	36·732 3	983	38·700 8
834	32·834 7	884	34·803 2	934	36·771 7	984	38·740 2
835	32·874 0	885	34·842 5	935	36·811 0	985	38·779 5
836	32·913 4	886	34·881 9	936	36·850 4	986	38·818 9
837	32·952 8	887	34·921 3	937	36·889 8	987	38·858 3
838	32·992 1	888	34·960 6	938	36·929 2	988	38·897 7
839	33·031 5	889	35·000 0	939	36·968 5	989	38·937 0
840	33·070 9	890	35·039 4	940	37·007 9	990	38·976 4
841	33·110 3	891	35·078 8	941	37·047 3	991	39·015 8
842	33·149 6	892	35·118 1	942	37·086 6	992	39·055 1
843	33·189 0	893	35·157 5	943	37·126 0	993	39·094 5
844	33·228 4	894	35·196 9	944	37·165 4	994	39·133 9
845	33·267 7	895	35·236 2	945	37·204 7	995	39·173 2
846	33·307 1	896	35·275 6	946	37·244 1	996	39·212 6
847	33·346 5	897	35·315 0	947	37·283 5	997	39·252 0
848	33·385 8	898	35·354 3	948	37·322 9	998	39·291 4
849	33·425 2	899	35·393 7	949	37·362 2	999	39·330 7
850	33·464 6	900	35·433 1	950	37·401 6	1 000	39·370 1

cm	ft	in	cm	ft	in	m	ft	in
1		0·3937	51	1	8·0788	1·1	3	7·3071
2		0·7874	52	1	8·4725	1·2	3	11·2441
3		1·1811	53	1	8·8662	1·3	4	3·1811
4		1·5748	54	1	9·2599	1·4	4	7·1181
5		1·9685	55	1	9·6536	1·5	4	11·0552
6		2·3622	56	1	10·0473	1·6	5	2·9922
7		2·7559	57	1	10·4410	1·7	5	6·9292
8		3·1496	58	1	10·8347	1·8	5	10·8662
9		3·5433	59	1	11·2284	1·9	6	2·8032
10		3·9370	60	1	11·6221	2·0	6	6·7402
11		4·3307	61	2	0·0158	2·1	6	10·6772
12		4·7244	62	2	0·4095	2·2	7	2·6142
13		5·1181	63	2	0·8032	2·3	7	6·5512
14		5·5118	64	2	1·1969	2·4	7	10·4882
15		5·9055	65	2	1·5906	2·5	8	2·4253
16		6·2992	66	2	1·9843	2·6	8	6·3623
17		6·6929	67	2	2·3780	2·7	8	10·2993
18		7·0866	68	2	2·7717	2·8	9	2·2363
19		7·4803	69	2	3·1654	2·9	9	6·1733
20		7·8740	70	2	3·5591	3·0	9	10·1103
21		8·2677	71	2	3·9528	3·1	10	2·0473
22		8·6614	72	2	4·3465	3·2	10	5·9843
23		9·0551	73	2	4·7402	3·3	10	9·9213
24		9·4488	74	2	5·1339	3·4	11	1·8583
25		9·8425	75	2	5·5276	3·5	11	5·7954
26		10·2362	76	2	5·9213	3·6	11	9·7324
27		10·6299	77	2	6·3150	3·7	12	1·6694
28		11·0236	78	2	6·7087	3·8	12	5·6064
29		11·4173	79	2	7·1024	3·9	12	9·5434
30		11·8110	80	2	7·4961	4·0	13	1·4804
31	1	0·2047	81	2	7·8898	4·1	13	5·4174
32	1	0·5984	82	2	8·2835	4·2	13	9·3544
33	1	0·9921	83	2	8·6772	4·3	14	1·2914
34	1	1·3858	84	2	9·0709	4·4	14	5·2284
35	1	1·7795	85	2	9·4646	4·5	14	9·1655
36	1	2·1732	86	2	9·8583	4·6	15	1·1025
37	1	2·5669	87	2	10·2520	4·7	15	5·0395
38	1	2·9606	88	2	10·6457	4·8	15	8·9765
39	1	3·3543	89	2	11·0394	4·9	16	0·9135
40	1	3·7480	90	2	11·4331	5·0	16	4·8505
41	1	4·1417	91	2	11·8268	5·1	16	8·7875
42	1	4·5354	92	3	0·2205	5·2	17	0·7245
43	1	4·9291	93	3	0·6142	5·3	17	4·6615
44	1	5·3228	94	3	1·0079	5·4	17	8·5985
45	1	5·7165	95	3	1·4016	5·5	18	0·5356
46	1	6·1102	96	3	1·7953	5·6	18	4·4726
47	1	6·5039	97	3	2·1890	5·7	18	8·4096
48	1	6·8976	98	3	2·5827	5·8	19	0·3466
49	1	7·2913	99	3	2·9764	5·9	19	4·2836
50	1	7·6851	100	3	3·3701	6·0	19	8·2206

Note: 1·1 m = 110 cm

LENGTH

m	yd	ft	in	m	yd	ft	in
1	1	0	3·370 1	51	55	2	3·874 0
2	2	0	6·740 2	52	56	2	7·244 1
3	3	0	10·110 2	53	57	2	10·614 2
4	4	1	1·480 3	54	59	0	1·984 2
5	5	1	4·850 4	55	60	0	5·354 3
6	6	1	8·220 5	56	61	0	8·724 4
7	7	1	11·590 6	57	62	1	0·094 5
8	8	2	2·960 6	58	63	1	3·464 6
9	9	2	6·330 7	59	64	1	6·834 6
10	10	2	9·700 8	60	65	1	10·204 7
11	12	0	1·070 9	61	66	2	1·574 8
12	13	0	4·440 9	62	67	2	4·944 9
13	14	0	7·811 0	63	68	2	8·315 0
14	15	0	11·181 1	64	69	2	11·685 0
15	16	1	2·551 2	65	71	0	3·055 1
16	17	1	5·921 3	66	72	0	6·425 2
17	18	1	9·291 3	67	73	0	9·795 3
18	19	2	0·661 4	68	74	1	1·165 4
19	20	2	4·031 5	69	75	1	4·535 4
20	21	2	7·401 6	70	76	1	7·905 5
21	22	2	10·771 7	71	77	1	11·275 6
22	24	0	2·141 7	72	78	2	2·645 7
23	25	0	5·511 8	73	79	2	6·015 7
24	26	0	8·881 9	74	80	2	9·385 8
25	27	1	0·252 0	75	82	0	0·755 9
26	28	1	3·622 0	76	83	0	4·126 0
27	29	1	6·992 1	77	84	0	7·496 1
28	30	1	10·362 2	78	85	0	10·866 1
29	31	2	1·732 3	79	86	1	2·236 2
30	32	2	5·102 4	80	87	1	5·606 3
31	33	2	8·472 4	81	88	1	8·976 4
32	34	2	11·842 5	82	89	2	0·346 5
33	36	0	3·212 6	83	90	2	3·716 5
34	37	0	6·582 7	84	91	2	7·086 6
35	38	0	9·952 8	85	92	2	10·456 7
36	39	1	1·322 8	86	94	0	1·826 8
37	40	1	4·692 9	87	95	0	5·196 8
38	41	1	8·063 0	88	96	0	8·566 9
39	42	1	11·433 1	89	97	0	11·937 0
40	43	2	2·803 1	90	98	1	3·307 1
41	44	2	6·173 2	91	99	1	6·677 2
42	45	2	9·543 3	92	100	1	10·047 2
43	47	0	0·913 4	93	101	2	1·417 3
44	48	0	4·283 5	94	102	2	4·787 4
45	49	0	7·653 5	95	103	2	8·157 5
46	50	0	11·023 6	96	104	2	11·527 6
47	51	1	2·393 7	97	106	0	2·897 6
48	52	1	5·763 8	98	107	0	6·267 7
49	53	1	9·133 9	99	108	0	9·637 8
50	54	2	0·503 9	100	109	1	1·007 9

m	yd	m	yd	m	yd	m	yd
1	1·093 6	51	55·774 3	101	110·454 9	151	165·135 6
2	2·187 2	52	56·867 9	102	111·548 6	152	166·229 2
3	3·280 8	53	57·961 5	103	112·642 2	153	167·322 8
4	4·374 5	54	59·055 1	104	113·735 8	154	168·416 4
5	5·468 1	55	60·148 7	105	114·829 4	155	169·510 1
6	6·561 7	56	61·242 3	106	115·923 0	156	170·603 7
7	7·655 3	57	62·336 0	107	117·016 6	157	171·697 3
8	8·748 9	58	63·429 6	108	118·110 2	158	172·790 9
9	9·842 5	59	64·523 2	109	119·203 8	159	173·884 5
10	10·936 1	60	65·616 8	110	120·297 5	160	174·978 1
11	12·029 7	61	66·710 4	111	121·391 1	161	176·071 7
12	13·123 4	62	67·804 0	112	122·484 7	162	177·165 4
13	14·217 0	63	68·897 6	113	123·578 3	163	178·259 0
14	15·310 6	64	69·991 3	114	124·671 9	164	179·352 6
15	16·404 2	65	71·084 9	115	125·765 5	165	180·446 2
16	17·497 8	66	72·178 5	116	126·859 1	166	181·539 8
17	18·591 4	67	73·272 1	117	127·952 8	167	182·633 4
18	19·685 0	68	74·365 7	118	129·046 4	168	183·727 0
19	20·778 7	69	75·459 3	119	130·140 0	169	184·820 6
20	21·872 3	70	76·552 9	120	131·233 6	170	185·914 3
21	22·965 9	71	77·646 5	121	132·327 2	171	187·007 9
22	24·059 5	72	78·740 2	122	133·420 8	172	188·101 5
23	25·153 1	73	79·833 8	123	134·514 4	173	189·195 1
24	26·246 7	74	80·927 4	124	135·608 0	174	190·288 7
25	27·340 3	75	82·021 0	125	136·701 7	175	191·382 3
26	28·433 9	76	83·114 6	126	137·795 3	176	192·475 9
27	29·527 6	77	84·208 2	127	138·888 9	177	193·569 6
28	30·621 2	78	85·301 8	128	139·982 5	178	194·663 2
29	31·714 8	79	86·395 5	129	141·076 1	179	195·756 8
30	32·808 4	80	87·489 1	130	142·169 7	180	196·850 4
31	33·902 0	81	88·582 7	131	143·263 3	181	197·944 0
32	34·995 6	82	89·676 3	132	144·357 0	182	199·037 6
33	36·089 2	83	90·769 9	133	145·450 6	183	200·131 2
34	37·182 9	84	91·863 5	134	146·544 2	184	201·224 8
35	38·276 5	85	92·957 1	135	147·637 8	185	202·318 5
36	39·370 1	86	94·050 7	136	148·731 4	186	203·412 1
37	40·463 7	87	95·144 4	137	149·825 0	187	204·505 7
38	41·557 3	88	96·238 0	138	150·918 6	188	205·599 3
39	42·650 9	89	97·331 6	139	152·012 2	189	206·692 9
40	43·744 5	90	98·425 2	140	153·105 9	190	207·786 5
41	44·838 1	91	99·518 8	141	154·199 5	191	208·880 1
42	45·931 8	92	100·612 4	142	155·293 1	192	209·973 8
43	47·025 4	93	101·706 0	143	156·386 7	193	211·067 4
44	48·119 0	94	102·799 7	144	157·480 3	194	212·161 0
45	49·212 6	95	103·893 3	145	158·573 9	195	213·254 6
46	50·306 2	96	104·986 9	146	159·667 5	196	214·348 2
47	51·399 8	97	106·080 5	147	160·761 2	197	215·441 8
48	52·493 4	98	107·174 1	148	161·854 8	198	216·535 4
49	53·587 1	99	108·267 7	149	162·948 4	199	217·629 0
50	54·680 7	100	109·361 3	150	164·042 0	200	218·722 7

m	yd	m	yd	m	yd	m	yd
201	219·816	251	274·497	301	329·178	351	383·858
202	220·910	252	275·591	302	330·271	352	384·952
203	222·003	253	276·684	303	331·365	353	386·045
204	223·097	254	277·778	304	332·458	354	387·139
205	224·191	255	278·871	305	333·552	355	388·233
206	225·284	256	279·965	306	334·646	356	389·326
207	226·378	257	281·059	307	335·739	357	390·420
208	227·472	258	282·152	308	336·833	358	391·514
209	228·565	259	283·246	309	337·927	359	392·607
210	229·659	260	284·339	310	339·020	360	393·701
211	230·752	261	285·433	311	340·114	361	394·794
212	231·846	262	286·527	312	341·207	362	395·888
213	232·940	263	287·620	313	342·301	363	396·982
214	234·033	264	288·714	314	343·395	364	398·075
215	235·127	265	289·808	315	344·488	365	399·169
216	236·220	266	290·901	316	345·582	366	400·262
217	237·314	267	291·995	317	346·675	367	401·356
218	238·408	268	293·088	318	347·769	368	402·450
219	239·501	269	294·182	319	348·863	369	403·543
220	240·595	270	295·276	320	349·956	370	404·637
221	241·689	271	296·369	321	351·050	371	405·731
222	242·782	272	297·463	322	352·143	372	406·824
223	243·876	273	298·556	323	353·237	373	407·918
224	244·969	274	299·650	324	354·331	374	409·011
225	246·063	275	300·744	325	355·424	375	410·105
226	247·157	276	301·837	326	356·518	376	411·199
227	248·250	277	302·931	327	357·612	377	412·292
228	249·344	278	304·024	328	358·705	378	413·386
229	250·437	279	305·118	329	359·799	379	414·479
230	251·531	280	306·212	330	360·892	380	415·573
231	252·625	281	307·305	331	361·986	381	416·667
232	253·718	282	308·399	332	363·080	382	417·760
233	254·812	283	309·493	333	364·173	383	418·854
234	255·906	284	310·586	334	365·267	384	419·948
235	256·999	285	311·680	335	366·360	385	421·041
236	258·093	286	312·773	336	367·454	386	422·135
237	259·186	287	313·867	337	368·548	387	423·228
238	260·280	288	314·961	338	369·641	388	424·322
239	261·374	289	316·054	339	370·735	389	425·416
240	262·467	290	317·148	340	371·829	390	426·509
241	263·561	291	318·241	341	372·922	391	427·603
242	264·654	292	319·335	342	374·016	392	428·696
243	265·748	293	320·429	343	375·109	393	429·790
244	266·842	294	321·522	344	376·203	394	430·884
245	267·935	295	322·616	345	377·297	395	431·977
246	269·029	296	323·710	346	378·390	396	433·071
247	270·122	297	324·803	347	379·484	397	434·164
248	271·216	298	325·897	348	380·577	398	435·258
249	272·310	299	326·990	349	381·671	399	436·352
250	273·403	300	328·084	350	382·765	400	437·445

m	yd	m	yd	m	yd	m	yd
401	438·539	451	493·220	501	547·900	551	602·581
402	439·633	452	494·313	502	548·994	552	603·675
403	440·726	453	495·407	503	550·087	553	604·768
404	441·820	454	496·500	504	551·181	554	605·862
405	442·913	455	497·594	505	552·275	555	606·955
406	444·007	456	498·688	506	553·368	556	608·049
407	445·101	457	499·781	507	554·462	557	609·143
408	446·194	458	500·875	508	555·556	558	610·236
409	447·288	459	501·969	509	556·649	559	611·330
410	448·381	460	503·062	510	557·743	560	612·423
411	449·475	461	504·156	511	558·836	561	613·517
412	450·569	462	505·249	512	559·930	562	614·611
413	451·662	463	506·343	513	561·024	563	615·704
414	452·756	464	507·437	514	562·117	564	616·798
415	453·850	465	508·530	515	563·211	565	617·892
416	454·943	466	509·624	516	564·304	566	618·985
417	456·037	467	510·717	517	565·398	567	620·079
418	457·130	468	511·811	518	566·492	568	621·172
419	458·224	469	512·905	519	567·585	569	622·266
420	459·318	470	513·998	520	568·679	570	623·360
421	460·411	471	515·092	521	569·773	571	624·453
422	461·505	472	516·185	522	570·866	572	625·547
423	462·598	473	517·279	523	571·960	573	626·640
424	463·692	474	518·373	524	573·053	574	627·734
425	464·786	475	519·466	525	574·147	575	628·828
426	465·879	476	520·560	526	575·241	576	629·921
427	466·973	477	521·654	527	576·334	577	631·015
428	468·066	478	522·747	528	577·428	578	632·108
429	469·160	479	523·841	529	578·521	579	633·202
430	470·254	480	524·934	530	579·615	580	634·296
431	471·347	481	526·028	531	580·709	581	635·389
432	472·441	482	527·122	532	581·802	582	636·483
433	473·535	483	528·215	533	582·896	583	637·577
434	474·628	484	529·309	534	583·990	584	638·670
435	475·722	485	530·402	535	585·083	585	639·764
436	476·815	486	531·496	536	586·177	586	640·857
437	477·909	487	532·590	537	587·270	587	641·951
438	479·003	488	533·683	538	588·364	588	643·045
439	480·096	489	534·777	539	589·458	589	644·138
440	481·190	490	535·871	540	590·551	590	645·232
441	482·283	491	536·964	541	591·645	591	646·325
442	483·377	492	538·058	542	592·738	592	647·419
443	484·471	493	539·151	543	593·832	593	648·513
444	485·564	494	540·245	544	594·926	594	649·606
445	486·658	495	541·339	545	596·019	595	650·700
446	487·752	496	542·432	546	597·113	596	651·794
447	488·845	497	543·526	547	598·206	597	652·887
448	489·939	498	544·619	548	599·300	598	653·981
449	491·032	499	545·713	549	600·394	599	655·074
450	492·126	500	546·807	550	601·487	600	656·168

m	yd	m	yd	m	yd	m	yd
601	657·262	651	711·942	701	766·623	751	821·304
602	658·355	652	713·036	702	767·717	752	822·397
603	659·449	653	714·129	703	768·810	753	823·491
604	660·542	654	715·223	704	769·904	754	824·584
605	661·636	655	716·317	705	770·997	755	825·678
606	662·730	656	717·410	706	772·091	756	826·772
607	663·823	657	718·504	707	773·185	757	827·865
608	664·917	658	719·598	708	774·278	758	828·959
609	666·010	659	720·691	709	775·372	759	830·052
610	667·104	660	721·785	710	776·465	760	831·146
611	668·198	661	722·878	711	777·559	761	832·240
612	669·291	662	723·972	712	778·653	762	833·333
613	670·385	663	725·066	713	779·746	763	834·427
614	671·479	664	726·159	714	780·840	764	835·521
615	672·572	665	727·253	715	781·934	765	836·614
616	673·666	666	728·346	716	783·027	766	837·708
617	674·759	667	729·440	717	784·121	767	838·801
618	675·853	668	730·534	718	785·214	768	839·895
619	676·947	669	731·627	719	786·308	769	840·989
620	678·040	670	732·721	720	787·402	770	842·082
621	679·134	671	733·815	721	788·495	771	843·176
622	680·227	672	734·908	722	789·589	772	844·269
623	681·321	673	736·002	723	790·682	773	845·363
624	682·415	674	737·095	724	791·776	774	846·457
625	683·508	675	738·189	725	792·870	775	847·550
626	684·602	676	739·283	726	793·963	776	848·644
627	685·696	677	740·376	727	795·057	777	849·738
628	686·789	678	741·470	728	796·150	778	850·831
629	687·883	679	742·563	729	797·244	779	851·925
630	688·976	680	743·657	730	798·338	780	853·018
631	690·070	681	744·751	731	799·431	781	854·112
632	691·164	682	745·844	732	800·525	782	855·206
633	692·257	683	746·938	733	801·619	783	856·299
634	693·351	684	748·031	734	802·712	784	857·393
635	694·444	685	749·125	735	803·806	785	858·486
636	695·538	686	750·219	736	804·899	786	859·580
637	696·632	687	751·312	737	805·993	787	860·674
638	697·725	688	752·406	738	807·087	788	861·767
639	698·819	689	753·500	739	808·180	789	862·861
640	699·913	690	754·593	740	809·274	790	863·955
641	701·006	691	755·687	741	810·367	791	865·048
642	702·100	692	756·780	742	811·461	792	866·142
643	703·193	693	757·874	743	812·555	793	867·235
644	704·287	694	758·968	744	813·648	794	868·329
645	705·381	695	760·061	745	814·742	795	869·423
646	706·474	696	761·155	746	815·836	796	870·516
647	707·568	697	762·248	747	816·929	797	871·610
648	708·661	698	763·342	748	818·023	798	872·703
649	709·755	699	764·436	749	819·116	799	873·797
650	710·849	700	765·529	750	820·210	800	874·891

m	yd	m	yd	m	yd	m	yd
801	875·984	851	930·665	901	985·346	951	1 040·026
802	877·078	852	931·759	902	986·439	952	1 041·120
803	878·171	853	932·852	903	987·533	953	1 042·213
804	879·265	854	933·946	904	988·626	954	1 043·307
805	880·359	855	935·039	905	989·720	955	1 044·401
806	881·452	856	936·133	906	990·814	956	1 045·494
807	882·546	857	937·227	907	991·907	957	1 046·588
808	883·640	858	938·320	908	993·001	958	1 047·682
809	884·733	859	939·414	909	994·094	959	1 048·775
810	885·827	860	940·507	910	995·188	960	1 049·869
811	886·920	861	941·601	911	996·282	961	1 050·962
812	888·014	862	942·695	912	997·375	962	1 052·056
813	889·108	863	943·788	913	998·469	963	1 053·150
814	890·201	864	944·882	914	999·563	964	1 054·243
815	891·295	865	945·976	915	1 000·656	965	1 055·337
816	892·388	866	947·069	916	1 001·750	966	1 056·430
817	893·482	867	948·163	917	1 002·843	967	1 057·524
818	894·576	868	949·256	918	1 003·937	968	1 058·618
819	895·669	869	950·350	919	1 005·031	969	1 059·711
820	896·763	870	951·444	920	1 006·124	970	1 060·805
821	897·857	871	952·537	921	1 007·218	971	1 061·899
822	898·950	872	953·631	922	1 008·311	972	1 062·992
823	900·044	873	954·724	923	1 009·405	973	1 064·086
824	901·137	874	955·818	924	1 010·499	974	1 065·179
825	902·231	875	956·912	925	1 011·592	975	1 066·273
826	903·325	876	958·005	926	1 012·686	976	1 067·367
827	904·418	877	959·099	927	1 013·780	977	1 068·460
828	905·512	878	960·192	928	1 014·873	978	1 069·554
829	906·605	879	961·286	929	1 015·967	979	1 070·647
830	907·699	880	962·380	930	1 017·060	980	1 071·741
831	908·793	881	963·473	931	1 018·154	981	1 072·835
832	909·886	882	964·567	932	1 019·248	982	1 073·928
833	910·980	883	965·661	933	1 020·341	983	1 075·022
834	912·073	884	966·754	934	1 021·435	984	1 076·115
835	913·167	885	967·848	935	1 022·528	985	1 077·209
836	914·261	886	968·941	936	1 023·622	986	1 078·303
837	915·354	887	970·035	937	1 024·716	987	1 079·396
838	916·448	888	971·129	938	1 025·809	988	1 080·490
839	917·542	889	972·222	939	1 026·903	989	1 081·584
840	918·635	890	973·316	940	1 027·997	990	1 082·677
841	919·729	891	974·409	941	1 029·090	991	1 083·771
842	920·822	892	975·503	942	1 030·184	992	1 084·864
843	921·916	893	976·597	943	1 031·277	993	1 085·958
844	923·010	894	977·690	944	1 032·371	994	1 087·052
845	924·103	895	978·784	945	1 033·465	995	1 088·145
846	925·197	896	979·878	946	1 034·558	996	1 089·239
847	926·290	897	980·971	947	1 035·652	997	1 090·332
848	927·384	898	982·065	948	1 036·745	998	1 091·426
849	928·478	899	983·158	949	1 037·839	999	1 092·520
850	929·571	900	984·252	950	1 038·933	1 000	1 093·613

km	miles	yd	km	miles	yd
1		1 093·613	51	31	1 214·278
2	1	427·227	52	32	547·892
3	1	1 520·840	53	32	1 641·505
4	2	854·453	54	33	975·118
5	3	188·066	55	34	308·731
6	3	1 281·680	56	34	1 402·345
7	4	615·293	57	35	735·958
8	4	1 708·906	58	36	69·571
9	5	1 042·520	59	36	1 163·185
10	6	376·133	60	37	496·798
11	6	1 469·746	61	37	1 590·411
12	7	803·360	62	38	924·024
13	8	136·973	63	39	257·638
14	8	1 230·586	64	39	1 351·251
15	9	564·199	65	40	684·864
16	9	1 657·813	66	41	18·478
17	10	991·426	67	41	1 112·091
18	11	325·039	68	42	445·704
19	11	1 418·653	69	42	1 539·318
20	12	752·266	70	43	872·931
21	13	85·879	71	44	206·544
22	13	1 179·493	72	44	1 300·157
23	14	513·106	73	45	633·771
24	14	1 606·719	74	45	1 727·384
25	15	940·332	75	46	1 060·997
26	16	273·946	76	47	394·611
27	16	1 367·559	77	47	1 488·224
28	17	701·172	78	48	821·837
29	18	34·786	79	49	155·451
30	18	1 128·399	80	49	1 249·064
31	19	462·012	81	50	582·677
32	19	1 555·626	82	50	1 676·290
33	20	889·239	83	51	1 009·904
34	21	222·852	84	52	343·517
35	21	1 316·465	85	52	1 437·130
36	22	650·079	86	53	770·744
37	22	1 743·692	87	54	104·357
38	23	1 077·305	88	54	1 197·970
39	24	410·919	89	55	531·584
40	24	1 504·532	90	55	1 625·197
41	25	838·145	91	56	958·810
42	26	171·759	92	57	292·423
43	26	1 265·372	93	57	1 386·037
44	27	598·985	94	58	719·650
45	27	1 692·598	95	59	53·263
46	28	1 026·212	96	59	1 146·877
47	29	359·825	97	60	480·490
48	29	1 453·438	98	60	1 574·103
49	30	787·052	99	61	907·717
50	31	120·665	100	62	241·330

km	miles	km	miles	km	miles	km	miles
1	0·6214	51	31·6899	101	62·7585	151	93·8270
2	1·2427	52	32·3113	102	63·3798	152	94·4484
3	1·8641	53	32·9327	103	64·0012	153	95·0698
4	2·4855	54	33·5540	104	64·6226	154	95·6911
5	3·1069	55	34·1754	105	65·2440	155	96·3125
6	3·7282	56	34·7968	106	65·8653	156	96·9339
7	4·3496	57	35·4181	107	66·4867	157	97·5552
8	4·9710	58	36·0395	108	67·1081	158	98·1766
9	5·5923	59	36·6609	109	67·7294	159	98·7980
10	6·2137	60	37·2823	110	68·3508	160	99·4194
11	6·8351	61	37·9036	111	68·9722	161	100·0407
12	7·4565	62	38·5250	112	69·5936	162	100·6621
13	8·0778	63	39·1464	113	70·2149	163	101·2835
14	8·6992	64	39·7677	114	70·8363	164	101·9048
15	9·3206	65	40·3891	115	71·4577	165	102·5262
16	9·9419	66	41·0105	116	72·0790	166	103·1476
17	10·5633	67	41·6319	117	72·7004	167	103·7690
18	11·1847	68	42·2532	118	73·3218	168	104·3903
19	11·8060	69	42·8746	119	73·9431	169	105·0117
20	12·4274	70	43·4960	120	74·5645	170	105·6331
21	13·0488	71	44·1173	121	75·1859	171	106·2544
22	13·6702	72	44·7387	122	75·8073	172	106·8758
23	14·2915	73	45·3601	123	76·4286	173	107·4972
24	14·9129	74	45·9815	124	77·0500	174	108·1186
25	15·5343	75	46·6028	125	77·6714	175	108·7399
26	16·1556	76	47·2242	126	78·2927	176	109·3613
27	16·7770	77	47·8456	127	78·9141	177	109·9827
28	17·3984	78	48·4669	128	79·5355	178	110·6040
29	18·0198	79	49·0883	129	80·1569	179	111·2254
30	18·6411	80	49·7097	130	80·7782	180	111·8468
31	19·2625	81	50·3311	131	81·3996	181	112·4682
32	19·8839	82	50·9524	132	82·0210	182	113·0895
33	20·5052	83	51·5738	133	82·6423	183	113·7109
34	21·1266	84	52·1952	134	83·2637	184	114·3323
35	21·7480	85	52·8165	135	83·8851	185	114·9536
36	22·3694	86	53·4379	136	84·5065	186	115·5750
37	22·9907	87	54·0593	137	85·1278	187	116·1964
38	23·6121	88	54·6806	138	85·7492	188	116·8177
39	24·2335	89	55·3020	139	86·3706	189	117·4391
40	24·8548	90	55·9234	140	86·9919	190	118·0605
41	25·4762	91	56·5448	141	87·6133	191	118·6819
42	26·0976	92	57·1661	142	88·2347	192	119·3032
43	26·7190	93	57·7875	143	88·8561	193	119·9246
44	27·3403	94	58·4089	144	89·4774	194	120·5460
45	27·9617	95	59·0302	145	90·0988	195	121·1673
46	28·5831	96	59·6516	146	90·7202	196	121·7887
47	29·2044	97	60·2730	147	91·3415	197	122·4101
48	29·8258	98	60·8944	148	91·9629	198	123·0315
49	30·4472	99	61·5157	149	92·5843	199	123·6528
50	31·0686	100	62·1371	150	93·2057	200	124·2742

km	miles	km	miles	km	miles	km	miles
201	124·895 6	251	155·964 1	301	187·032 7	351	218·101 2
202	125·516 9	252	156·585 5	302	187·654 0	352	218·722 6
203	126·138 3	253	157·206 9	303	188·275 4	353	219·344 0
204	126·759 7	254	157·828 2	304	188·896 8	354	219·965 3
205	127·381 1	255	158·449 6	305	189·518 2	355	220·586 7
206	128·002 4	256	159·071 0	306	190·139 5	356	221·208 1
207	128·623 8	257	159·692 3	307	190·760 9	357	221·829 4
208	129·245 2	258	160·313 7	308	191·382 3	358	222·450 8
209	129·866 5	259	160·935 1	309	192·003 6	359	223·072 2
210	130·487 9	260	161·556 5	310	192·625 0	360	223·693 6
211	131·109 3	261	162·177 8	311	193·246 4	361	224·314 9
212	131·730 7	262	162·799 2	312	193·867 8	362	224·936 3
213	132·352 0	263	163·420 6	313	194·489 1	363	225·557 7
214	132·973 4	264	164·041 9	314	195·110 5	364	226·179 0
215	133·594 8	265	164·663 3	315	195·731 9	365	226·800 4
216	134·216 1	266	165·284 7	316	196·353 2	366	227·421 8
217	134·837 5	267	165·906 1	317	196·974 6	367	228·043 2
218	135·458 9	268	166·527 4	318	197·596 0	368	228·664 5
219	136·080 2	269	167·148 8	319	198·217 3	369	229·285 9
220	136·701 6	270	167·770 2	320	198·838 7	370	229·907 3
221	137·323 0	271	168·391 5	321	199·460 1	371	230·528 6
222	137·944 4	272	169·012 9	322	200·081 5	372	231·150 0
223	138·565 7	273	169·634 3	323	200·702 8	373	231·771 4
224	139·187 1	274	170·255 7	324	201·324 2	374	232·392 8
225	139·808 5	275	170·877 0	325	201·945 6	375	233·014 1
226	140·429 8	276	171·498 4	326	202·566 9	376	233·635 5
227	141·051 2	277	172·119 8	327	203·188 3	377	234·256 9
228	141·672 6	278	172·741 1	328	203·809 7	378	234·878 2
229	142·294 0	279	173·362 5	329	204·431 1	379	235·499 6
230	142·915 3	280	173·983 9	330	205·052 4	380	236·121 0
231	143·536 7	281	174·605 3	331	205·673 8	381	236·742 4
232	144·158 1	282	175·226 6	332	206·295 2	382	237·363 7
233	144·779 4	283	175·848 0	333	206·916 5	383	237·985 1
234	145·400 8	284	176·469 4	334	207·537 9	384	238·606 5
235	146·022 2	285	177·090 7	335	208·159 3	385	239·227 8
236	146·643 6	286	177·712 1	336	208·780 7	386	239·849 2
237	147·264 9	287	178·333 5	337	209·402 0	387	240·470 6
238	147·886 3	288	178·954 8	338	210·023 4	388	241·091 9
239	148·507 7	289	179·576 2	339	210·644 8	389	241·713 3
240	149·129 0	290	180·197 6	340	211·266 1	390	242·334 7
241	149·750 4	291	180·819 0	341	211·887 5	391	242·956 1
242	150·371 8	292	181·440 3	342	212·508 9	392	243·577 4
243	150·993 2	293	182·061 7	343	213·130 3	393	244·198 8
244	151·614 5	294	182·683 1	344	213·751 6	394	244·820 2
245	152·235 9	295	183·304 4	345	214·373 0	395	245·441 5
246	152·857 3	296	183·925 8	346	214·994 4	396	246·062 9
247	153·478 6	297	184·547 2	347	215·615 7	397	246·684 3
248	154·100 0	298	185·168 6	348	216·237 1	398	247·305 7
249	154·721 4	299	185·789 9	349	216·858 5	399	247·927 0
250	155·342 8	300	186·411 3	350	217·479 9	400	248·548 4

km	miles	km	miles	km	miles	km	miles
401	249·169 8	451	280·238 3	501	311·306 9	551	342·375 4
402	249·791 1	452	280·859 7	502	311·928 2	552	342·996 8
403	250·412 5	453	281·481 1	503	312·549 6	553	343·618 2
404	251·033 9	454	282·102 4	504	313·171 0	554	344·239 5
405	251·655 3	455	282·723 8	505	313·792 4	555	344·860 9
406	252·276 6	456	283·345 2	506	314·413 7	556	345·482 3
407	252·898 0	457	283·966 5	507	315·035 1	557	346·103 6
408	253·519 4	458	284·587 9	508	315·656 5	558	346·725 0
409	254·140 7	459	285·209 3	509	316·277 8	559	347·346 4
410	254·762 1	460	285·830 7	510	316·899 2	560	347·967 8
411	255·383 5	461	286·452 0	511	317·520 6	561	348·589 1
412	256·004 9	462	287·073 4	512	318·142 0	562	349·210 5
413	256·626 2	463	287·694 8	513	318·763 3	563	349·831 9
414	257·247 6	464	288·316 1	514	319·384 7	564	350·453 2
415	257·869 0	465	288·937 5	515	320·006 1	565	351·074 6
416	258·490 3	466	289·558 9	516	320·627 4	566	351·696 0
417	259·111 7	467	290·180 3	517	321·248 8	567	352·317 4
418	259·733 1	468	290·801 6	518	321·870 2	568	352·938 7
419	260·354 4	469	291·423 0	519	322·491 5	569	353·560 1
420	260·975 8	470	292·044 4	520	323·112 9	570	354·181 5
421	261·597 2	471	292·665 7	521	323·734 3	571	354·802 8
422	262·218 6	472	293·287 1	522	324·355 7	572	355·424 2
423	262·839 9	473	293·908 5	523	324·977 0	573	356·045 6
424	263·461 3	474	294·529 9	524	325·598 4	574	356·667 0
425	264·082 7	475	295·151 2	525	326·219 8	575	357·288 3
426	264·704 0	476	295·772 6	526	326·841 1	576	357·909 7
427	265·325 4	477	296·394 0	527	327·462 5	577	358·531 1
428	265·946 8	478	297·015 3	528	328·083 9	578	359·152 4
429	266·568 2	479	297·636 7	529	328·705 3	579	359·773 8
430	267·189 5	480	298·258 1	530	329·326 6	580	360·395 2
431	267·810 9	481	298·879 5	531	329·948 0	581	361·016 6
432	268·432 3	482	299·500 8	532	330·569 4	582	361·637 9
433	269·053 6	483	300·122 2	533	331·190 7	583	362·259 3
434	269·675 0	484	300·743 6	534	331·812 1	584	362·880 7
435	270·296 4	485	301·364 9	535	332·433 5	585	363·502 0
436	270·917 8	486	301·986 3	536	333·054 9	586	364·123 4
437	271·539 1	487	302·607 7	537	333·676 2	587	364·744 8
438	272·160 5	488	303·229 0	538	334·297 6	588	365·366 1
439	272·781 9	489	303·850 4	539	334·919 0	589	365·987 5
440	273·403 2	490	304·471 8	540	335·540 3	590	366·608 9
441	274·024 6	491	305·093 2	541	336·161 7	591	367·230 3
442	274·646 0	492	305·714 5	542	336·783 1	592	367·851 6
443	275·267 4	493	306·335 9	543	337·404 5	593	368·473 0
444	275·888 7	494	306·957 3	544	338·025 8	594	369·094 4
445	276·510 1	495	307·578 6	545	338·647 2	595	369·715 7
446	277·131 5	496	308·200 0	546	339·268 6	596	370·337 1
447	277·752 8	497	308·821 4	547	339·889 9	597	370·958 5
448	278·374 2	498	309·442 8	548	340·511 3	598	371·579 9
449	278·995 6	499	310·064 1	549	341·132 7	599	372·201 2
450	279·617 0	500	310·685 5	550	341·754 1	600	372·822 6

km	miles	km	miles	km	miles	km	miles
601	373·444	651	404·513	701	435·581	751	466·650
602	374·065	652	405·134	702	436·202	752	467·271
603	374·687	653	405·755	703	436·824	753	467·892
604	375·308	654	406·377	704	437·445	754	468·514
605	375·929	655	406·998	705	438·067	755	469·135
606	376·551	656	407·619	706	438·688	756	469·756
607	377·172	657	408·241	707	439·309	757	470·378
608	377·794	658	408·862	708	439·931	758	470·999
609	378·415	659	409·483	709	440·552	759	471·621
610	379·036	660	410·105	710	441·173	760	472·242
611	379·658	661	410·726	711	441·795	761	472·863
612	380·279	662	411·348	712	442·416	762	473·485
613	380·900	663	411·969	713	443·038	763	474·106
614	381·522	664	412·590	714	443·659	764	474·727
615	382·143	665	413·212	715	444·280	765	475·349
616	382·765	666	413·833	716	444·902	766	475·970
617	383·386	667	414·454	717	445·523	767	476·592
618	384·007	668	415·076	718	446·144	768	477·213
619	384·629	669	415·697	719	446·766	769	477·834
620	385·250	670	416·319	720	447·387	770	478·456
621	385·871	671	416·940	721	448·008	771	479·077
622	386·493	672	417·561	722	448·630	772	479·698
623	387·114	673	418·183	723	449·251	773	480·320
624	387·736	674	418·804	724	449·873	774	480·941
625	388·357	675	419·425	725	450·494	775	481·563
626	388·978	676	420·047	726	451·115	776	482·184
627	389·600	677	420·668	727	451·737	777	482·805
628	390·221	678	421·290	728	452·358	778	483·427
629	390·842	679	421·911	729	452·979	779	484·048
630	391·464	680	422·532	730	453·601	780	484·669
631	392·085	681	423·154	731	454·222	781	485·291
632	392·706	682	423·775	732	454·844	782	485·912
633	393·328	683	424·396	733	455·465	783	486·533
634	393·949	684	425·018	734	456·086	784	487·155
635	394·571	685	425·639	735	456·708	785	487·776
636	395·192	686	426·261	736	457·329	786	488·398
637	395·813	687	426·882	737	457·950	787	489·019
638	396·435	688	427·503	738	458·572	788	489·640
639	397·056	689	428·125	739	459·193	789	490·262
640	397·677	690	428·746	740	459·815	790	490·883
641	398·299	691	429·367	741	460·436	791	491·504
642	398·920	692	429·989	742	461·057	792	492·126
643	399·542	693	430·610	743	461·679	793	492·747
644	400·163	694	431·231	744	462·300	794	493·369
645	400·784	695	431·853	745	462·921	795	493·990
646	401·406	696	432·474	746	463·543	796	494·611
647	402·027	697	433·096	747	464·164	797	495·233
648	402·648	698	433·717	748	464·786	798	495·854
649	403·270	699	434·338	749	465·407	799	496·475
650	403·891	700	434·960	750	466·028	800	497·097

km	miles	km	miles	km	miles	km	miles
801	497·718	851	528·787	901	559·855	951	590·924
802	498·340	852	529·408	902	560·477	952	591·545
803	498·961	853	530·029	903	561·098	953	592·167
804	499·582	854	530·651	904	561·719	954	592·788
805	500·204	855	531·272	905	562·341	955	593·409
806	500·825	856	531·894	906	562·962	956	594·031
807	501·446	857	532·515	907	563·583	957	594·652
808	502·068	858	533·136	908	564·205	958	595·273
809	502·689	859	533·758	909	564·826	959	595·895
810	503·311	860	534·379	910	565·448	960	596·516
811	503·932	861	535·000	911	566·069	961	597·138
812	504·553	862	535·622	912	566·690	962	597·759
813	505·175	863	536·243	913	567·312	963	598·380
814	505·796	864	536·865	914	567·933	964	599·002
815	506·417	865	537·486	915	568·554	965	599·623
816	507·039	866	538·107	916	569·176	966	600·244
817	507·660	867	538·729	917	569·797	967	600·866
818	508·281	868	539·350	918	570·419	968	601·487
819	508·903	869	539·971	919	571·040	969	602·108
820	509·524	870	540·593	920	571·661	970	602·730
821	510·146	871	541·214	921	572·283	971	603·351
822	510·767	872	541·836	922	572·904	972	603·973
823	511·388	873	542·457	923	573·525	973	604·594
824	512·010	874	543·078	924	574·147	974	605·215
825	512·631	875	543·700	925	574·768	975	605·837
826	513·252	876	544·321	926	575·390	976	606·458
827	513·874	877	544·942	927	576·011	977	607·079
828	514·495	878	545·564	928	576·632	978	607·701
829	515·117	879	546·185	929	577·254	979	608·322
830	515·738	880	546·806	930	577·875	980	608·944
831	516·359	881	547·428	931	578·496	981	609·565
832	516·981	882	548·049	932	579·118	982	610·186
833	517·602	883	548·671	933	579·739	983	610·808
834	518·223	884	549·292	934	580·361	984	611·429
835	518·845	885	549·913	935	580·982	985	612·050
836	519·466	886	550·535	936	581·603	986	612·672
837	520·088	887	551·156	937	582·225	987	613·293
838	520·709	888	551·777	938	582·846	988	613·915
839	521·330	889	552·399	939	583·467	989	614·536
840	521·952	890	553·020	940	584·089	990	615·157
841	522·573	891	553·642	941	584·710	991	615·779
842	523·194	892	554·263	942	585·331	992	616·400
843	523·816	893	554·884	943	585·953	993	617·021
844	524·437	894	555·506	944	586·574	994	617·643
845	525·058	895	556·127	945	587·196	995	618·264
846	525·680	896	556·748	946	587·817	996	618·886
847	526·301	897	557·370	947	588·438	997	619·507
848	526·923	898	557·991	948	589·060	998	620·128
849	527·544	899	558·613	949	589·681	999	620·750
850	528·165	900	559·234	950	590·302	1 000	621·371

Area

SI derived unit: **square metre** (m²)

There are two special units which can be used:

$$\text{hectare (ha)} = 10\ 000\ \text{m}^2$$
$$\text{are (a)} = 100\ \text{m}^2$$

Imperial to SI

1 square inch (sq. in)		=	**645·16** mm²
1 square foot (sq. ft)	=144 sq. in	=	0·092 903 0 m²
1 square yard (sq. yd)	=9 sq. ft	=	0·836 127 m²
1 acre	=4 840 sq. yd	=$\begin{cases} \end{cases}$	4 046·86 m² 0·404 686 ha
1 square mile	=640 acres	=$\begin{cases} \end{cases}$	258·999 ha 2·589 99 km²

(Conversion factor in **bold type** indicates exact value.)

SI to Imperial

1 square centimetre (cm²)	=	0·155 000 sq. in
1 square metre (m²)	=	1·195 99 sq. yd
1 are (a)	=	119·599 sq. yd
1 hectare (ha)	=	2·471 05 acres
1 square kilometre (km²)	=$\begin{cases} \end{cases}$	247·105 acres 0·386 103 sq. mile

square inches (in²) to square centimetres (cm²)

[square inches to square millimetres (mm²)]

in²	cm²	in²	cm²	in²	cm²	in²	cm²
0·1	0·6452	26	167·7416	76	490·322	126	812·902
0·2	1·2903	27	174·1932	77	496·773	127	819·353
0·3	1·9355	28	180·6448	78	503·225	128	825·805
0·4	2·5806	29	187·0964	79	509·676	129	832·256
0·5	3·2258	30	193·5480	80	516·128	130	838·708
0·6	3·8710						
0·7	4·5161	31	199·9996	81	522·580	131	845·160
0·8	5·1613	32	206·4512	82	529·031	132	851·611
0·9	5·8064	33	212·9028	83	535·483	133	858·063
1·0	6·4516	34	219·3544	84	541·934	134	864·514
		35	225·8060	85	548·386	135	870·966
1·5	9·6774						
2·0	12·9032	36	232·2576	86	554·838	136	877·418
2·5	16·1290	37	238·7092	87	561·289	137	883·869
3·0	19·3548	38	245·1608	88	567·741	138	890·321
3·5	22·5806	39	251·6124	89	574·192	139	896·772
4·0	25·8064	40	258·0640	90	580·644	140	903·224
4·5	29·0322						
5·0	32·2580	41	264·5156	91	587·096	141	909·676
		42	270·9672	92	593·547	142	916·127
5·5	35·4838	43	277·4188	93	599·999	143	922·579
6·0	38·7096	44	283·8704	94	606·450	144	929·030
6·5	41·9354	45	290·3220	95	612·902	145	935·482
7·0	45·1612						
7·5	48·3870	46	296·7736	96	619·354	146	941·934
8·0	51·6128	47	303·2252	97	625·805	147	948·385
8·5	54·8386	48	309·6768	98	632·257	148	954·837
9·0	58·0644	49	316·1284	99	638·708	149	961·288
9·5	61·2902	50	322·5800	100	645·160	150	967·740
10·0	64·5160						
		51	329·0316	101	651·612	160	1 032·26
10·5	67·7418	52	335·4832	102	658·063	170	1 096·77
11·0	70·9676	53	341·9348	103	664·515	180	1 161·29
11·5	74·1934	54	348·3864	104	670·966	190	1 225·80
12·0	77·4192	55	354·8380	105	677·418	200	1 290·32
12·5	80·6450						
13·0	83·8708	56	361·2896	106	683·870	210	1 354·84
13·5	87·0966	57	367·7412	107	690·321	220	1 419·35
14·0	90·3224	58	374·1928	108	696·773	230	1 483·87
14·5	93·5482	59	380·6444	109	703·224	240	1 548·38
15·0	96·7740	60	387·0960	110	709·676	250	1 612·90
15·5	99·9998	61	393·5476	111	716·128	260	1 677·42
16·0	103·2256	62	399·9992	112	722·579	270	1 741·93
16·5	106·4514	63	406·4508	113	729·031	280	1 806·45
17·0	109·6772	64	412·9024	114	735·482	290	1 870·96
17·5	112·9030	65	419·3540	115	741·934	300	1 935·48
18·0	116·1288						
18·5	119·3546	66	425·8056	116	748·386	310	2 000·00
19·0	122·5804	67	432·2572	117	754·837	320	2 064·51
19·5	125·8062	68	438·7088	118	761·289	330	2 129·03
20·0	129·0320	69	445·1604	119	767·740	340	2 193·54
		70	451·6120	120	774·192	350	2 258·06
21	135·4836						
22	141·9352	71	458·0636	121	780·644	360	2 322·58
23	148·3868	72	464·5152	122	787·095	370	2 387·09
24	154·8384	73	470·9668	123	793·547	380	2 451·61
25	161·2900	74	477·4184	124	799·998	390	2 516·12
		75	483·8700	125	806·450	400	2 580·64

Note: 100 mm² = 1 cm². To obtain mm² from the given cm² value, move the decimal point two places to the right.

ft²	m²	ft²	m²	ft²	m²	ft²	m²
½	0·0465	26	2·4155	76	7·0606	126	11·7058
1	0·0929	27	2·5084	77	7·1535	127	11·7987
1½	0·1394	28	2·6013	78	7·2464	128	11·8916
2	0·1858	29	2·6942	79	7·3393	129	11·9845
2½	0·2323	30	2·7871	80	7·4322	130	12·0774
3	0·2787	31	2·8800	81	7·5251	131	12·1703
3½	0·3252	32	2·9729	82	7·6180	132	12·2632
4	0·3716	33	3·0658	83	7·7109	133	12·3561
4½	0·4181	34	3·1587	84	7·8039	134	12·4490
5	0·4645	35	3·2516	85	7·8968	135	12·5419
5½	0·5110	36	3·3445	86	7·9897	136	12·6348
6	0·5574	37	3·4374	87	8·0826	137	12·7277
6½	0·6039	38	3·5303	88	8·1755	138	12·8206
7	0·6503	39	3·6232	89	8·2684	139	12·9135
7½	0·6968	40	3·7161	90	8·3613	140	13·0064
8	0·7432	41	3·8090	91	8·4542	141	13·0993
8½	0·7897	42	3·9019	92	8·5471	142	13·1922
9	0·8361	43	3·9948	93	8·6400	143	13·2851
9½	0·8826	44	4·0877	94	8·7329	144	13·3780
10	0·9290	45	4·1806	95	8·8258	145	13·4709
10½	0·9755	46	4·2735	96	8·9187	146	13·5638
11	1·0219	47	4·3664	97	9·0116	147	13·6567
11½	1·0684	48	4·4593	98	9·1045	148	13·7496
12	1·1148	49	4·5522	99	9·1974	149	13·8425
12½	1·1613	50	4·6452	100	9·2903	150	13·9355
13	1·2077	51	4·7381	101	9·3832	151	14·0284
13½	1·2542	52	4·8310	102	9·4761	152	14·1213
14	1·3006	53	4·9239	103	9·5690	153	14·2142
14½	1·3471	54	5·0168	104	9·6619	154	14·3071
15	1·3935	55	5·1097	105	9·7548	155	14·4000
15½	1·4400	56	5·2026	106	9·8477	156	14·4929
16	1·4864	57	5·2955	107	9·9406	157	14·5858
16½	1·5329	58	5·3884	108	10·0335	158	14·6787
17	1·5794	59	5·4813	109	10·1264	159	14·7716
17½	1·6258	60	5·5742	110	10·2193	160	14·8645
18	1·6723	61	5·6671	111	10·3122	161	14·9574
18½	1·7187	62	5·7600	112	10·4051	162	15·0503
19	1·7652	63	5·8529	113	10·4980	163	15·1432
19½	1·8116	64	5·9458	114	10·5909	164	15·2361
20	1·8581	65	6·0387	115	10·6838	165	15·3290
20½	1·9045	66	6·1316	116	10·7767	166	15·4219
21	1·9510	67	6·2245	117	10·8697	167	15·5148
21½	1·9974	68	6·3174	118	10·9626	168	15·6077
22	2·0439	69	6·4103	119	11·0555	169	15·7006
22½	2·0903	70	6·5032	120	11·1484	170	15·7935
23	2·1368	71	6·5961	121	11·2413	171	15·8864
23½	2·1832	72	6·6890	122	11·3342	172	15·9793
24	2·2297	73	6·7819	123	11·4271	173	16·0722
24½	2·2761	74	6·8748	124	11·5200	174	16·1651
25	2·3226	75	6·9677	125	11·6129	175	16·2580

ft²	m²	ft²	m²	ft²	m²	ft²	m²
176	16·3509	330	30·6580	580	53·8837	830	77·1095
177	16·4438	335	31·1225	585	54·3483	835	77·5740
178	16·5367	340	31·5870	590	54·8128	840	78·0385
179	16·6296	345	32·0515	595	55·2773	845	78·5030
180	16·7225	350	32·5161	600	55·7418	850	78·9676
181	16·8154	355	32·9806	605	56·2063	855	79·4321
182	16·9083	360	33·4451	610	56·6708	860	79·8966
183	17·0012	365	33·9096	615	57·1353	865	80·3611
184	17·0942	370	34·3741	620	57·5999	870	80·8256
185	17·1871	375	34·8386	625	58·0644	875	81·2901
186	17·2800	380	35·3031	630	58·5289	880	81·7546
187	17·3729	385	35·7677	635	58·9934	885	82·2192
188	17·4658	390	36·2322	640	59·4579	890	82·6837
189	17·5587	395	36·6967	645	59·9224	895	83·1482
190	17·6516	400	37·1612	650	60·3870	900	83·6127
191	17·7445	405	37·6257	655	60·8515	905	84·0772
192	17·8374	410	38·0902	660	61·3160	910	84·5417
193	17·9303	415	38·5547	665	61·7805	915	85·0062
194	18·0232	420	39·0193	670	62·2450	920	85·4708
195	18·1161	425	39·4838	675	62·7095	925	85·9353
196	18·2090	430	39·9483	680	63·1740	930	86·3998
197	18·3019	435	40·4128	685	63·6386	935	86·8643
198	18·3948	440	40·8773	690	64·1031	940	87·3288
199	18·4877	445	41·3418	695	64·5676	945	87·7933
200	18·5806	450	41·8064	700	65·0321	950	88·2579
205	19·0451	455	42·2709	705	65·4966	955	88·7224
210	19·5096	460	42·7354	710	65·9611	960	89·1869
215	19·9741	465	43·1999	715	66·4256	965	89·6514
220	20·4387	470	43·6644	720	66·8902	970	90·1159
225	20·9032	475	44·1289	725	67·3547	975	90·5804
230	21·3677	480	44·5934	730	67·8192	980	91·0449
235	21·8322	485	45·0580	735	68·2837	985	91·5095
240	22·2967	490	45·5225	740	68·7482	990	91·9740
245	22·7612	495	45·9870	745	69·2127	995	92·4385
250	23·2258	500	46·4515	750	69·6773	1 000	92·9030
255	23·6903	505	46·9160	755	70·1418	2 000	185·806
260	24·1548	510	47·3805	760	70·6063	3 000	278·709
265	24·6193	515	47·8450	765	71·0708	4 000	371·612
270	25·0838	520	48·3096	770	71·5353	5 000	464·515
275	25·5483	525	48·7741	775	71·9998	6 000	557·418
						7 000	650·321
280	26·0128	530	49·2386	780	72·4643	8 000	743·224
285	26·4774	535	49·7031	785	72·9289	9 000	836·127
290	26·9419	540	50·1676	790	73·3934		
295	27·4064	545	50·6321	795	73·8579	10 000	929·030
300	27·8709	550	51·0967	800	74·3224	15 000	1 393·545
						20 000	1 858·060
						25 000	2 322·575
305	28·3354	555	51·5612	805	74·7869	30 000	2 787·090
310	28·7999	560	52·0257	810	75·2514	35 000	3 251·605
315	29·2644	565	52·4902	815	75·7159	40 000	3 716·120
320	29·7290	570	52·9547	820	76·1805	45 000	4 180·635
325	30·1935	575	53·4192	825	76·6450	50 000	4 645·150

yd²	m²	yd²	m²	yd²	m²	yd²	m²
½	0·4181	26	21·7393	76	63·5457	126	105·3520
1	0·8361	27	22·5754	77	64·3818	127	106·1881
1½	1·2542	28	23·4116	78	65·2179	128	107·0243
2	1·6723	29	24·2477	79	66·0540	129	107·8604
2½	2·0903	30	25·0838	80	66·8902	130	108·6965
3	2·5084						
3½	2·9264	31	25·9199	81	67·7263	131	109·5326
4	3·3445	32	26·7561	82	68·5624	132	110·3688
4½	3·7626	33	27·5922	83	69·3985	133	111·2049
5	4·1806	34	28·4283	84	70·2347	134	112·0410
		35	29·2644	85	71·0708	135	112·8771
5½	4·5987						
6	5·0168	36	30·1006	86	71·9069	136	113·7133
6½	5·4348	37	30·9367	87	72·7430	137	114·5494
7	5·8529	38	31·7728	88	73·5792	138	115·3855
7½	6·2710	39	32·6090	89	74·4153	139	116·2217
8	6·6890	40	33·4451	90	75·2514	140	117·0578
8½	7·1071						
9	7·5251	41	34·2812	91	76·0876	141	117·8939
9½	7·9432	42	35·1173	92	76·9237	142	118·7300
10	8·3613	43	35·9535	93	77·7598	143	119·5662
		44	36·7896	94	78·5959	144	120·4023
10½	8·7793	45	37·6257	95	79·4321	145	121·2384
11	9·1974						
11½	9·6155	46	38·4618	96	80·2682	146	122·0745
12	10·0335	47	39·2980	97	81·1043	147	122·9107
12½	10·4516	48	40·1341	98	81·9404	148	123·7468
13	10·8697	49	40·9702	99	82·7766	149	124·5829
13½	11·2877	50	41·8064	100	83·6127	150	125·4191
14	11·7058						
14½	12·1238	51	42·6425	101	84·4488	151	126·2552
15	12·5419	52	43·4786	102	85·2850	152	127·0913
		53	44·3147	103	86·1211	153	127·9274
15½	12·9600	54	45·1509	104	86·9572	154	128·7636
16	13·3780	55	45·9870	105	87·7933	155	129·5997
16½	13·7961						
17	14·2142	56	46·8231	106	88·6295	156	130·4358
17½	14·6322	57	47·6592	107	89·4656	157	131·2719
18	15·0503	58	48·4954	108	90·3017	158	132·1081
18½	15·4683	59	49·3315	109	91·1378	159	132·9442
19	15·8864	60	50·1676	110	91·9740	160	133·7803
19½	16·3045						
20	16·7225	61	51·0037	111	92·8101	161	134·6164
		62	51·8399	112	93·6462	162	135·4526
20½	17·1406	63	52·6760	113	94·4824	163	136·2887
21	17·5587	64	53·5121	114	95·3185	164	137·1248
21½	17·9767	65	54·3483	115	96·1546	165	137·9610
22	18·3948						
22½	18·8129	66	55·1844	116	96·9907	166	138·7971
23	19·2309	67	56·0205	117	97·8269	167	139·6332
23½	19·6490	68	56·8566	118	98·6630	168	140·4693
24	20·0670	69	57·6928	119	99·4991	169	141·3055
24½	20·4851	70	58·5289	120	100·3352	170	142·1416
25	20·9032						
		71	59·3650	121	101·1714	171	142·9777
		72	60·2011	122	102·0075	172	143·8138
		73	61·0373	123	102·8436	173	144·6500
		74	61·8734	124	103·6797	174	145·4861
		75	62·7095	125	104·5159	175	146·3222

yd²	m²	yd²	m²	yd²	m²	yd²	m²
176	147·1584	330	275·9219	580	484·954	830	693·985
177	147·9945	335	280·1025	585	489·134	835	698·166
178	148·8306	340	284·2832	590	493·315	840	702·347
179	149·6667	345	288·4638	595	497·496	845	706·527
180	150·5029	350	292·6445	600	501·676	850	710·708
181	151·3390	355	296·8251	605	505·857	855	714·889
182	152·1751	360	301·0057	610	510·037	860	719·069
183	153·0112	365	305·1864	615	514·218	865	723·250
184	153·8474	370	309·3670	620	518·399	870	727·430
185	154·6835	375	313·5476	625	522·579	875	731·611
186	155·5196	380	317·7283	630	526·760	880	735·792
187	156·3557	385	321·9089	635	530·941	885	739·972
188	157·1919	390	326·0895	640	535·121	890	744·153
189	158·0280	395	330·2702	645	539·302	895	748·334
190	158·8641	400	334·4508	650	543·483	900	752·514
191	159·7003	405	338·6314	655	547·663	905	756·695
192	160·5364	410	342·8121	660	551·844	910	760·876
193	161·3725	415	346·9927	665	556·024	915	765·056
194	162·2086	420	351·1733	670	560·205	920	769·237
195	163·0448	425	355·3540	675	564·386	925	773·417
196	163·8809	430	359·5346	680	568·566	930	777·598
197	164·7170	435	363·7152	685	572·747	935	781·779
198	165·5531	440	367·8959	690	576·928	940	785·959
199	166·3893	445	372·0765	695	581·108	945	790·140
200	167·2254	450	376·2572	700	585·289	950	794·321
205	171·4060	455	380·4378	705	589·470	955	798·501
210	175·5867	460	384·6184	710	593·650	960	802·682
215	179·7673	465	388·7991	715	597·831	965	806·863
220	183·9479	470	392·9797	720	602·011	970	811·043
225	188·1286	475	397·1603	725	606·192	975	815·224
230	192·3092	480	401·3410	730	610·373	980	819·404
235	196·4898	485	405·5216	735	614·553	985	823·585
240	200·6705	490	409·7022	740	618·734	990	827·766
245	204·8511	495	413·8829	745	622·915	995	831·946
250	209·0318	500	418·0635	750	627·095	1 000	836·127
255	213·2124	505	422·2441	755	631·276	2 000	1 672·25
260	217·3930	510	426·4248	760	635·457	3 000	2 508·38
265	221·5737	515	430·6054	765	639·637	4 000	3 344·51
270	225·7543	520	434·7860	770	643·818	5 000	4 180·64
275	229·9349	525	438·9667	775	647·998	6 000	5 016·76
						7 000	5 852·89
280	234·1156	530	443·1473	780	652·179	8 000	6 689·02
285	238·2962	535	447·3279	785	656·360	9 000	7 525·14
290	242·4768	540	451·5086	790	660·540		
295	246·6575	545	455·6892	795	664·721	10 000	8 361·27
300	250·8381	550	459·8699	800	668·902	15 000	12 541·91
						20 000	16 722·54
						25 000	20 903·18
305	255·0187	555	464·0505	805	673·082	30 000	25 083·81
310	259·1994	560	468·2311	810	677·263	35 000	29 264·45
315	263·3800	565	472·4118	815	681·444	40 000	33 445·08
320	267·5606	570	476·5924	820	685·624	45 000	37 625·72
325	271·7413	575	480·7730	825	689·805	50 000	41 806·35

acres	ha	acres	ha	acres	ha	acres	ha
½	0·202 3	26	10·521 8	76	30·756 1	126	50·990 4
1	0·404 7	27	10·926 5	77	31·160 8	127	51·395 1
1½	0·607 0	28	11·331 2	78	31·565 5	128	51·799 8
2	0·809 4	29	11·735 9	79	31·970 2	129	52·204 5
2½	1·011 7	30	12·140 6	80	32·374 9	130	52·609 2
3	1·214 1						
3½	1·416 4	31	12·545 3	81	32·779 6	131	53·013 9
4	1·618 7	32	12·950 0	82	33·184 3	132	53·418 6
4½	1·821 1	33	13·354 6	83	33·588 9	133	53·823 2
5	2·023 4	34	13·759 3	84	33·993 6	134	54·227 9
		35	14·164 0	85	34·398 3	135	54·632 6
5½	2·225 8						
6	2·428 1	36	14·568 7	86	34·803 0	136	55·037 3
6½	2·630 5	37	14·973 4	87	35·207 7	137	55·442 0
7	2·832 8	38	15·378 1	88	35·612 4	138	55·846 7
7½	3·035 1	39	15·782 8	89	36·017 1	139	56·251 4
8	3·237 5	40	16·187 4	90	36·421 7	140	56·656 0
8½	3·439 8						
9	3·642 2	41	16·592 1	91	36·826 4	141	57·060 7
9½	3·844 5	42	16·996 8	92	37·231 1	142	57·465 4
10	4·046 9	43	17·401 5	93	37·635 8	143	57·870 1
		44	17·806 2	94	38·040 5	144	58·274 8
10½	4·249 2	45	18·210 9	95	38·445 2	145	58·679 5
11	4·451 5						
11½	4·653 9	46	18·615 6	96	38·849 9	146	59·084 2
12	4·856 2	47	19·020 2	97	39·254 5	147	59·488 8
12½	5·058 6	48	19·424 9	98	39·659 2	148	59·893 5
13	5·260 9	49	19·829 6	99	40·063 9	149	60·298 2
13½	5·463 3	50	20·234 3	100	40·468 6	150	60·702 9
14	5·665 6						
14½	5·867 9	51	20·639 0	101	40·873 3	151	61·107 6
15	6·070 3	52	21·043 7	102	41·278 0	152	61·512 3
		53	21·448 4	103	41·682 7	153	61·917 0
15½	6·272 6	54	21·853 0	104	42·087 3	154	62·321 6
16	6·475 0	55	22·257 7	105	42·492 0	155	62·726 3
16½	6·677 3						
17	6·879 7	56	22·662 4	106	42·896 7	156	63·131 0
17½	7·082 0	57	23·067 1	107	43·301 4	157	63·535 7
18	7·284 3	58	23·471 8	108	43·706 1	158	63·940 4
18½	7·486 7	59	23·876 5	109	44·110 8	159	64·345 1
19	7·689 0	60	24·281 2	110	44·515 5	160	64·749 8
19½	7·891 4						
20	8·093 7	61	24·685 8	111	44·920 1	161	65·154 4
		62	25·090 5	112	45·324 8	162	65·559 1
20½	8·296 1	63	25·495 2	113	45·729 5	163	65·963 8
21	8·498 4	64	25·899 9	114	46·134 2	164	66·368 5
21½	8·700 7	65	26·304 6	115	46·538 9	165	66·773 2
22	8·903 1						
22½	9·105 4	66	26·709 3	116	46·943 6	166	67·177 9
23	9·307 8	67	27·114 0	117	47·348 3	167	67·582 6
23½	9·510 1	68	27·518 6	118	47·752 9	168	67·987 2
24	9·712 5	69	27·923 3	119	48·157 6	169	68·391 9
24½	9·914 8	70	28·328 0	120	48·562 3	170	68·796 6
25	10·117 2						
		71	28·732 7	121	48·967 0	171	69·201 3
		72	29·137 4	122	49·371 7	172	69·606 0
		73	29·542 1	123	49·776 4	173	70·010 7
		74	29·946 8	124	50·181 1	174	70·415 4
		75	30·351 5	125	50·585 8	175	70·820 1

acres to hectares (ha)

acres	ha	acres	ha	acres	ha	acres	ha
176	71·224 7	330	133·546 4	580	234·717 9	830	335·889 4
177	71·629 4	335	135·569 8	585	236·741 3	835	337·912 8
178	72·034 1	340	137·593 2	590	238·764 7	840	339·936 2
179	72·438 8	345	139·616 7	595	240·788 2	845	341·959 7
180	72·843 5	350	141·640 1	600	242·811 6	850	343·983 1
181	73·248 2	355	143·663 5	605	244·835 0	855	346·006 5
182	73·652 9	360	145·687 0	610	246·858 5	860	348·030 0
183	74·057 5	365	147·710 4	615	248·881 9	865	350·053 4
184	74·462 2	370	149·733 8	620	250·905 3	870	352·076 8
185	74·866 9	375	151·757 3	625	252·928 8	875	354·100 3
186	75·271 6	380	153·780 7	630	254·952 2	880	356·123 7
187	75·676 3	385	155·804 1	635	256·975 6	885	358·147 1
188	76·081 0	390	157·827 5	640	258·999 0	890	360·170 5
189	76·485 7	395	159·851 0	645	261·022 5	895	362·194 0
190	76·890 3	400	161·874 4	650	263·045 9	900	364·217 4
191	77·295 0	405	163·897 8	655	265·069 3	905	366·240 8
192	77·699 7	410	165·921 3	660	267·092 8	910	368·264 3
193	78·104 4	415	167·944 7	665	269·116 2	915	370·287 7
194	78·509 1	420	169·968 1	670	271·139 6	920	372·311 1
195	78·913 8	425	171·991 6	675	273·163 1	925	374·334 6
196	79·318 5	430	174·015 0	680	275·186 5	930	376·358 0
197	79·723 1	435	176·038 4	685	277·209 9	935	378·381 4
198	80·127 8	440	178·061 8	690	279·233 3	940	380·404 8
199	80·532 5	445	180·085 3	695	281·256 8	945	382·428 3
200	80·937 2	450	182·108 7	700	283·280 2	950	384·451 7
205	82·960 6	455	184·132 1	705	285·303 6	955	386·475 1
210	84·984 1	460	186·155 6	710	287·327 1	960	388·498 6
215	87·007 5	465	188·179 0	715	289·350 5	965	390·522 0
220	89·030 9	470	190·202 4	720	291·373 9	970	392·545 4
225	91·054 4	475	192·225 9	725	293·397 4	975	394·568 9
230	93·077 8	480	194·249 3	730	295·420 8	980	396·592 3
235	95·101 2	485	196·272 7	735	297·444 2	985	398·615 7
240	97·124 6	490	198·296 1	740	299·467 6	990	400·639 1
245	99·148 1	495	200·319 6	745	301·491 1	995	402·662 6
250	101·171 5	500	202·343 0	750	303·514 5	1 000	404·686 0
255	103·194 9	505	204·366 4	755	305·537 9	2 000	809·372
260	105·218 4	510	206·389 9	760	307·561 4	3 000	1 214·058
265	107·241 8	515	208·413 3	765	309·584 8	4 000	1 618·744
270	109·265 2	520	210·436 7	770	311·608 2	5 000	2 023·430
275	111·288 7	525	212·460 2	775	313·631 7	6 000	2 428·116
						7 000	2 832·802
280	113·312 1	530	214·483 6	780	315·655 1	8 000	3 237·488
285	115·335 5	535	216·507 0	785	317·678 5	9 000	3 642·174
290	117·358 9	540	218·530 4	790	319·701 9		
295	119·382 4	545	220·553 9	795	321·725 4	10 000	4 046·860
300	121·405 8	550	222·577 3	800	323·748 8	15 000	6 070·290
						20 000	8 093·720
						25 000	10 117·150
305	123·429 2	555	224·600 7	805	325·772 2	30 000	12 140·580
310	125·452 7	560	226·624 2	810	327·795 7	35 000	14 164·010
315	127·476 1	565	228·647 6	815	329·819 1	40 000	16 187·440
320	129·499 5	570	230·671 0	820	331·842 5	45 000	18 210·870
325	131·523 0	575	232·694 5	825	333·866 0	50 000	20 234·300

sq miles	km²	sq miles	km²	sq miles	km²	sq miles	km²
½	1·2950	26	67·3397	76	196·8391	126	326·3385
1	2·5900	27	69·9297	77	199·4291	127	328·9285
1½	3·8850	28	72·5197	78	202·0191	128	331·5185
2	5·1800	29	75·1097	79	204·6091	129	334·1085
2½	6·4750	30	77·6996	80	207·1990	130	336·6985
3	7·7700						
3½	9·0650	31	80·2896	81	209·7890	131	339·2884
4	10·3600	32	82·8796	82	212·3790	132	341·8784
4½	11·6549	33	85·4696	83	214·9690	133	344·4684
5	12·9499	34	88·0596	84	217·5590	134	347·0584
		35	90·6496	85	220·1490	135	349·6484
5½	14·2449						
6	15·5399	36	93·2396	86	222·7390	136	352·2384
6½	16·8349	37	95·8296	87	225·3290	137	354·8284
7	18·1299	38	98·4195	88	227·9190	138	357·4184
7½	19·4249	39	101·0095	89	230·5089	139	360·0083
8	20·7199	40	103·5995	90	233·0989	140	362·5983
8½	22·0149						
9	23·3099	41	106·1895	91	235·6889	141	365·1883
9½	24·6049	42	108·7795	92	238·2789	142	367·7783
10	25·8999	43	111·3695	93	240·8689	143	370·3683
		44	113·9595	94	243·4589	144	372·9583
10½	27·1949	45	116·5495	95	246·0489	145	375·5483
11	28·4899						
11½	29·7849	46	119·1395	96	248·6389	146	378·1383
12	31·0799	47	121·7294	97	251·2288	147	380·7283
12½	32·3749	48	124·3194	98	253·8188	148	383·3182
13	33·6698	49	126·9094	99	256·4088	149	385·9082
13½	34·9648	50	129·4994	100	258·9988	150	388·4982
14	36·2598						
14½	37·5548	51	132·0894	101	261·5888	151	391·0882
15	38·8498	52	134·6794	102	264·1788	152	393·6782
		53	137·2694	103	266·7688	153	396·2682
15½	40·1448	54	139·8594	104	269·3588	154	398·8582
16	41·4398	55	142·4493	105	271·9488	155	401·4482
16½	42·7348						
17	44·0298	56	145·0393	106	274·5387	156	404·0381
17½	45·3248	57	147·6293	107	277·1287	157	406·6281
18	46·6198	58	150·2193	108	279·7187	158	409·2181
18½	47·9148	59	152·8093	109	282·3087	159	411·8081
19	49·2098	60	155·3993	110	284·8987	160	414·3981
19½	50·5048						
20	51·7998	61	157·9893	111	287·4887	161	416·9881
		62	160·5793	112	290·0787	162	419·5781
20½	53·0948	63	163·1693	113	292·6687	163	422·1681
21	54·3898	64	165·7592	114	295·2586	164	424·7580
21½	55·6847	65	168·3492	115	297·8486	165	427·3480
22	56·9797						
22½	58·2747	66	170·9392	116	300·4386	166	429·9380
23	59·5697	67	173·5292	117	303·0286	167	432·5280
23½	60·8647	68	176·1192	118	305·6186	168	435·1180
24	62·1597	69	178·7092	119	308·2086	169	437·7080
24½	63·4547	70	181·2992	120	310·7986	170	440·2980
25	64·7497						
		71	183·8892	121	313·3886	171	442·8880
		72	186·4791	122	315·9785	172	445·4780
		73	189·0691	123	318·5685	173	448·0679
		74	191·6591	124	321·1585	174	450·6579
		75	194·2491	125	323·7485	175	453·2479

sq miles	km²	sq miles	km²	sq miles	km²	sq miles	km²
176	455·838	330	854·696	580	1 502·193	830	2 149·690
177	458·428	335	867·646	585	1 515·143	835	2 162·640
178	461·018	340	880·596	590	1 528·093	840	2 175·590
179	463·608	345	893·546	595	1 541·043	845	2 188·540
180	466·198	350	906·496	600	1 553·993	850	2 201·490
181	468·788	355	919·446	605	1 566·943	855	2 214·440
182	471·378	360	932·396	610	1 579·893	860	2 227·390
183	473·968	365	945·346	615	1 592·843	865	2 240·340
184	476·558	370	958·296	620	1 605·793	870	2 253·290
185	479·148	375	971·246	625	1 618·743	875	2 266·240
186	481·738	380	984·195	630	1 631·693	880	2 279·190
187	484·328	385	997·145	635	1 644·642	885	2 292·139
188	486·918	390	1 010·095	640	1 657·592	890	2 305·089
189	489·508	395	1 023·045	645	1 670·542	895	2 318·039
190	492·098	400	1 035·995	650	1 683·492	900	2 330·989
191	494·688	405	1 048·945	655	1 696·442	905	2 343·939
192	497·278	410	1 061·895	660	1 709·392	910	2 356·889
193	499·868	415	1 074·845	665	1 722·342	915	2 369·839
194	502·458	420	1 087·795	670	1 735·292	920	2 382·789
195	505·048	425	1 100·745	675	1 748·242	925	2 395·739
196	507·638	430	1 113·695	680	1 761·192	930	2 408·689
197	510·228	435	1 126·645	685	1 774·142	935	2 421·639
198	512·818	440	1 139·595	690	1 787·092	940	2 434·589
199	515·408	445	1 152·545	695	1 800·042	945	2 447·539
200	517·998	450	1 165·495	700	1 812·992	950	2 460·489
205	530·948	455	1 178·445	705	1 825·942	955	2 473·439
210	543·898	460	1 191·395	710	1 838·892	960	2 486·389
215	556·847	465	1 204·344	715	1 851·841	965	2 499·339
220	569·797	470	1 217·294	720	1 864·791	970	2 512·288
225	582·747	475	1 230·244	725	1 877·741	975	2 525·238
230	595·697	480	1 243·194	730	1 890·691	980	2 538·188
235	608·647	485	1 256·144	735	1 903·641	985	2 551·138
240	621·597	490	1 269·094	740	1 916·591	990	2 564·088
245	634·547	495	1 282·044	745	1 929·541	995	2 577·038
250	647·497	500	1 294·994	750	1 942·491	1 000	2 589·988
255	660·447	505	1 307·944	755	1 955·441	2 000	5 179·98
260	673·397	510	1 320·894	760	1 968·391	3 000	7 769·96
265	686·347	515	1 333·844	765	1 981·341	4 000	10 359·95
270	699·297	520	1 346·794	770	1 994·291	5 000	12 949·94
275	712·247	525	1 359·744	775	2 007·241	6 000	15 539·93
						7 000	18 129·92
280	725·197	530	1 372·694	780	2 020·191	8 000	20 719·90
285	738·147	535	1 385·644	785	2 033·141	9 000	23 309·89
290	751·097	540	1 398·594	790	2 046·091		
295	764·046	545	1 411·544	795	2 059·041	10 000	25 899·88
300	776·996	550	1 424·493	800	2 071·990	15 000	38 849·82
						20 000	51 799·76
						25 000	64 749·70
305	789·946	555	1 437·443	805	2 084·940	30 000	77 699·64
310	802·896	560	1 450·393	810	2 097·890	35 000	90 649·58
315	815·846	565	1 463·343	815	2 110·840	40 000	103 599·52
320	828·796	570	1 476·293	820	2 123·790	45 000	116 549·46
325	841·746	575	1 489·243	825	2 136·740	50 000	129 499·41

cm²	in²	cm²	in²	cm²	in²	cm²	in²
1	0·1550	51	7·9050	110	17·0500	610	94·550
2	0·3100	52	8·0600	120	18·6000	620	96·100
3	0·4650	53	8·2150	130	20·1500	630	97·650
4	0·6200	54	8·3700	140	21·7000	640	99·200
5	0·7750	55	8·5250	150	23·2500	650	100·750
6	0·9300	56	8·6800	160	24·8000	660	102·300
7	1·0850	57	8·8350	170	26·3500	670	103·850
8	1·2400	58	8·9900	180	27·9000	680	105·400
9	1·3950	59	9·1450	190	29·4500	690	106·950
10	1·5500	60	9·3000	200	31·0000	700	108·500
11	1·7050	61	9·4550	210	32·5500	710	110·050
12	1·8600	62	9·6100	220	34·1000	720	111·600
13	2·0150	63	9·7650	230	35·6500	730	113·150
14	2·1700	64	9·9200	240	37·2000	740	114·700
15	2·3250	65	10·0750	250	38·7500	750	116·250
16	2·4800	66	10·2300	260	40·3000	760	117·800
17	2·6350	67	10·3850	270	41·8500	770	119·350
18	2·7900	68	10·5400	280	43·4000	780	120·900
19	2·9450	69	10·6950	290	44·9500	790	122·450
20	3·1000	70	10·8500	300	46·5000	800	124·000
21	3·2550	71	11·0050	310	48·0500	810	125·550
22	3·4100	72	11·1600	320	49·6000	820	127·100
23	3·5650	73	11·3150	330	51·1500	830	128·650
24	3·7200	74	11·4700	340	52·7000	840	130·200
25	3·8750	75	11·6250	350	54·2500	850	131·750
26	4·0300	76	11·7800	360	55·8000	860	133·300
27	4·1850	77	11·9350	370	57·3500	870	134·850
28	4·3400	78	12·0900	380	58·9000	880	136·400
29	4·4950	79	12·2450	390	60·4500	890	137·950
30	4·6500	80	12·4000	400	62·0000	900	139·500
31	4·8050	81	12·5550	410	63·5500	910	141·050
32	4·9600	82	12·7100	420	65·1000	920	142·600
33	5·1150	83	12·8650	430	66·6500	930	144·150
34	5·2700	84	13·0200	440	68·2000	940	145·700
35	5·4250	85	13·1750	450	69·7500	950	147·250
36	5·5800	86	13·3300	460	71·3000	960	148·800
37	5·7350	87	13·4850	470	72·8500	970	150·350
38	5·8900	88	13·6400	480	74·4000	980	151·900
39	6·0450	89	13·7950	490	75·9500	990	153·450
40	6·2000	90	13·9500	500	77·5000	1 000	155·000
41	6·3550	91	14·1050	510	79·0500	2 000	310·00
42	6·5100	92	14·2600	520	80·6000	3 000	465·00
43	6·6650	93	14·4150	530	82·1500	4 000	620·00
44	6·8200	94	14·5700	540	83·7000	5 000	775·00
45	6·9750	95	14·7250	550	85·2500		
						6 000	930·00
46	7·1300	96	14·8800	560	86·8000	7 000	1 085·00
47	7·2850	97	15·0350	570	88·3500	8 000	1 240·00
48	7·4400	98	15·1900	580	89·9000	9 000	1 395·00
49	7·5950	99	15·3450	590	91·4500	10 000	1 550·00
50	7·7500	100	15·5000	600	93·0000		

Note: 1 cm² = 100 mm²
51 cm² = 5100 mm² etc.

m²	ft²	m²	ft²	m²	ft²	m²	ft²
1	10·7639	51	548·959	110	1 184·030	610	6 565·99
2	21·5278	52	559·723	120	1 291·669	620	6 673·62
3	32·2917	53	570·487	130	1 399·308	630	6 781·26
4	43·0556	54	581·251	140	1 506·947	640	6 888·90
5	53·8196	55	592·015	150	1 614·587	650	6 996·54
6	64·5835	56	602·779	160	1 722·226	660	7 104·18
7	75·3474	57	613·543	170	1 829·865	670	7 211·82
8	86·1113	58	624·307	180	1 937·504	680	7 319·46
9	96·8752	59	635·071	190	2 045·143	690	7 427·10
10	107·6391	60	645·835	200	2 152·782	700	7 534·74
11	118·4030	61	656·599	210	2 260·421	710	7 642·38
12	129·1669	62	667·362	220	2 368·060	720	7 750·02
13	139·9308	63	678·126	230	2 475·699	730	7 857·65
14	150·6947	64	688·890	240	2 583·338	740	7 965·29
15	161·4587	65	699·654	250	2 690·978	750	8 072·93
16	172·2226	66	710·418	260	2 798·617	760	8 180·57
17	182·9865	67	721·182	270	2 906·256	770	8 288·21
18	193·7504	68	731·946	280	3 013·895	780	8 395·85
19	204·5143	69	742·710	290	3 121·534	790	8 503·49
20	215·2782	70	753·474	300	3 229·173	800	8 611·13
21	226·0421	71	764·238	310	3 336·812	810	8 718·77
22	236·8060	72	775·002	320	3 444·451	820	8 826·41
23	247·5699	73	785·765	330	3 552·090	830	8 934·05
24	258·3338	74	796·529	340	3 659·730	840	9 041·68
25	269·0978	75	807·293	350	3 767·369	850	9 149·32
26	279·8617	76	818·057	360	3 875·008	860	9 256·96
27	290·6256	77	828·821	370	3 982·647	870	9 364·60
28	301·3895	78	839·585	380	4 090·286	880	9 472·24
29	312·1534	79	850·349	390	4 197·925	890	9 579·88
30	322·9173	80	861·113	400	4 305·564	900	9 687·52
31	333·6812	81	871·877	410	4 413·203	910	9 795·16
32	344·4451	82	882·641	420	4 520·842	920	9 902·80
33	355·2090	83	893·405	430	4 628·481	930	10 010·44
34	365·9730	84	904·168	440	4 736·121	940	10 118·08
35	376·7369	85	914·932	450	4 843·760	950	10 225·71
36	387·5008	86	925·696	460	4 951·399	960	10 333·35
37	398·2647	87	936·460	470	5 059·038	970	10 440·99
38	409·0286	88	947·224	480	5 166·677	980	10 548·63
39	419·7925	89	957·988	490	5 274·316	990	10 656·27
40	430·5564	90	968·752	500	5 381·955	1 000	10 763·91
41	441·3203	91	979·516	510	5 489·594	2 000	21 527·82
42	452·0842	92	990·280	520	5 597·233	3 000	32 291·73
43	462·8481	93	1 001·044	530	5 704·873	4 000	43 055·64
44	473·6121	94	1 011·808	540	5 812·512	5 000	53 819·55
45	484·3760	95	1 022·571	550	5 920·151		
						6 000	64 583·46
46	495·1399	96	1 033·335	560	6 027·790	7 000	75 347·37
47	505·9038	97	1 044·099	570	6 135·429	8 000	86 111·28
48	516·6677	98	1 054·863	580	6 243·068	9 000	96 875·19
49	527·4316	99	1 065·627	590	6 350·707	10 000	107 639·10
50	538·1955	100	1 076·391	600	6 458·346		

m²	yd²	m²	yd²	m²	yd²	m²	yd²
1	1·196 0	51	60·995 5	110	131·558 9	610	729·554
2	2·392 0	52	62·191 5	120	143·518 8	620	741·514
3	3·588 0	53	63·387 5	130	155·478 7	630	753·474
4	4·784 0	54	64·583 4	140	167·438 6	640	765·433
5	5·979 9	55	65·779 4	150	179·398 5	650	777·393
6	7·175 9	56	66·975 4	160	191·358 4	660	789·353
7	8·371 9	57	68·171 4	170	203·318 3	670	801·313
8	9·567 9	58	69·367 4	180	215·278 2	680	813·273
9	10·763 9	59	70·563 4	190	227·238 1	690	825·233
10	11·959 9	60	71·759 4	200	239·198 0	700	837·193
11	13·155 9	61	72·955 4	210	251·157 9	710	849·153
12	14·351 9	62	74·151 4	220	263·117 8	720	861·113
13	15·547 9	63	75·347 4	230	275·077 7	730	873·073
14	16·743 9	64	76·543 3	240	287·037 6	740	885·032
15	17·939 8	65	77·739 3	250	298·997 5	750	896·992
16	19·135 8	66	78·935 3	260	310·957 3	760	908·952
17	20·331 8	67	80·131 3	270	322·917 2	770	920·912
18	21·527 8	68	81·327 3	280	334·877 1	780	932·872
19	22·723 8	69	82·523 3	290	346·837 0	790	944·832
20	23·919 8	70	83·719 3	300	358·796 9	800	956·792
21	25·115 8	71	84·915 3	310	370·756 8	810	968·752
22	26·311 8	72	86·111 3	320	382·716 7	820	980·712
23	27·507 8	73	87·307 3	330	394·676 6	830	992·672
24	28·703 8	74	88·503 2	340	406·636 5	840	1 004·631
25	29·899 7	75	89·699 2	350	418·596 4	850	1 016·591
26	31·095 7	76	90·895 2	360	430·556 3	860	1 028·551
27	32·291 7	77	92·091 2	370	442·516 2	870	1 040·511
28	33·487 7	78	93·287 2	380	454·476 1	880	1 052·471
29	34·683 7	79	94·483 2	390	466·436 0	890	1 064·431
30	35·879 7	80	95·679 2	400	478·395 9	900	1 076·391
31	37·075 7	81	96·875 2	410	490·355 8	910	1 088·351
32	38·271 7	82	98·071 2	420	502·315 7	920	1 100·311
33	39·467 7	83	99·267 2	430	514·275 6	930	1 112·271
34	40·663 7	84	100·463 1	440	526·235 5	940	1 124·230
35	41·859 6	85	101·659 1	450	538·195 4	950	1 136·190
36	43·055 6	86	102·855 1	460	550·155 3	960	1 148·150
37	44·251 6	87	104·051 1	470	562·115 2	970	1 160·110
38	45·447 6	88	105·247 1	480	574·075 1	980	1 172·070
39	46·643 6	89	106·443 1	490	586·035 0	990	1 184·030
40	47·839 6	90	107·639 1	500	597·994 9	1 000	1 195·990
41	49·035 6	91	108·835 1	510	609·954 8	2 000	2 391·98
42	50·231 6	92	110·031 1	520	621·914 7	3 000	3 587·97
43	51·427 6	93	111·227 1	530	633·874 6	4 000	4 783·96
44	52·623 6	94	112·423 0	540	645·834 5	5 000	5 979·95
45	53·819 5	95	113·619 0	550	657·794 4		
						6 000	7 175·94
46	55·015 5	96	114·815 0	560	669·754 3	7 000	8 371·93
47	56·211 5	97	116·011 0	570	681·714 2	8 000	9 567·92
48	57·407 5	98	117·207 0	580	693·674 1	9 000	10 763·91
49	58·603 5	99	118·403 0	590	705·634 0	10 000	11 959·90
50	59·799 5	100	119·599 0	600	717·593 9		

ha	acres	ha	acres	ha	acres	ha	acres
1	2·4711	51	126·0236	110	271·816	610	1507·341
2	4·9421	52	128·4946	120	296·526	620	1532·051
3	7·4132	53	130·9657	130	321·237	630	1556·762
4	9·8842	54	133·4367	140	345·947	640	1581·472
5	12·3553	55	135·9078	150	370·658	650	1606·183
6	14·8263	56	138·3788	160	395·368	660	1630·893
7	17·2974	57	140·8499	170	420·079	670	1655·604
8	19·7684	58	143·3209	180	444·789	680	1680·314
9	22·2395	59	145·7920	190	469·500	690	1705·025
10	24·7105	60	148·2630	200	494·210	700	1729·735
11	27·1816	61	150·7341	210	518·921	710	1754·446
12	29·6526	62	153·2051	220	543·631	720	1779·156
13	32·1237	63	155·6762	230	568·342	730	1803·867
14	34·5947	64	158·1472	240	593·052	740	1828·577
15	37·0658	65	160·6183	250	617·763	750	1853·288
16	39·5368	66	163·0893	260	642·473	760	1877·998
17	42·0079	67	165·5604	270	667·184	770	1902·709
18	44·4789	68	168·0314	280	691·894	780	1927·419
19	46·9500	69	170·5025	290	716·605	790	1952·130
20	49·4210	70	172·9735	300	741·315	800	1976·840
21	51·8921	71	175·4446	310	766·026	810	2001·551
22	54·3631	72	177·9156	320	790·736	820	2026·261
23	56·8342	73	180·3867	330	815·447	830	2050·972
24	59·3052	74	182·8577	340	840·157	840	2075·682
25	61·7763	75	185·3288	350	864·868	850	2100·393
26	64·2473	76	187·7998	360	889·578	860	2125·103
27	66·7184	77	190·2709	370	914·289	870	2149·814
28	69·1894	78	192·7419	380	938·999	880	2174·524
29	71·6605	79	195·2130	390	963·710	890	2199·235
30	74·1315	80	197·6840	400	988·420	900	2223·945
31	76·6026	81	200·1551	410	1013·131	910	2248·656
32	79·0736	82	202·6261	420	1037·841	920	2273·366
33	81·5447	83	205·0972	430	1062·552	930	2298·077
34	84·0157	84	207·5682	440	1087·262	940	2322·787
35	86·4868	85	210·0393	450	1111·973	950	2347·498
36	88·9578	86	212·5103	460	1136·683	960	2372·208
37	91·4289	87	214·9814	470	1161·394	970	2396·919
38	93·8999	88	217·4524	480	1186·104	980	2421·629
39	96·3710	89	219·9235	490	1210·815	990	2446·340
40	98·8420	90	222·3945	500	1235·525	1000	2471·050
41	101·3131	91	224·8656	510	1260·236	2000	4942·10
42	103·7841	92	227·3366	520	1284·946	3000	7413·15
43	106·2552	93	229·8077	530	1309·657	4000	9884·20
44	108·7262	94	232·2787	540	1334·367	5000	12355·25
45	111·1973	95	234·7498	550	1359·078		
						6000	14826·30
46	113·6683	96	237·2208	560	1383·788	7000	17297·35
47	116·1394	97	239·6919	570	1408·499	8000	19768·40
48	118·6104	98	242·1629	580	1433·209	9000	22239·45
49	121·0815	99	244·6340	590	1457·920	10000	24710·50
50	123·5525	100	247·1050	600	1482·630		

km²	sq miles	km²	sq miles	km²	sq miles	km²	sq miles
1	0·386 1	51	19·691 2	110	42·471 2	610	235·522
2	0·772 2	52	20·077 3	120	46·332 2	620	239·383
3	1·158 3	53	20·463 4	130	50·193 3	630	243·244
4	1·544 4	54	20·849 5	140	54·054 3	640	247·105
5	1·930 5	55	21·235 6	150	57·915 3	650	250·966
6	2·316 6	56	21·621 7	160	61·776 3	660	254·827
7	2·702 7	57	22·007 8	170	65·637 3	670	258·688
8	3·088 8	58	22·393 9	180	69·498 4	680	262·549
9	3·474 9	59	22·780 0	190	73·359 4	690	266·410
10	3·861 0	60	23·166 1	200	77·220 4	700	270·271
11	4·247 1	61	23·552 2	210	81·081 4	710	274·132
12	4·633 2	62	23·938 3	220	84·942 4	720	277·993
13	5·019 3	63	24·324 4	230	88·803 5	730	281·854
14	5·405 4	64	24·710 5	240	92·664 5	740	285·715
15	5·791 5	65	25·096 6	250	96·525 5	750	289·577
16	6·177 6	66	25·482 7	260	100·386 5	760	293·438
17	6·563 7	67	25·868 8	270	104·247 5	770	297·299
18	6·949 8	68	26·254 9	280	108·108 6	780	301·160
19	7·335 9	69	26·641 0	290	111·969 6	790	305·021
20	7·722 0	70	27·027 1	300	115·830 6	800	308·882
21	8·108 1	71	27·413 2	310	119·691 6	810	312·743
22	8·494 2	72	27·799 3	320	123·552 6	820	316·604
23	8·880 3	73	28·185 4	330	127·413 7	830	320·465
24	9·266 4	74	28·571 5	340	131·274 7	840	324·326
25	9·652 6	75	28·957 7	350	135·135 7	850	328·187
26	10·038 7	76	29·343 8	360	138·996 7	860	332·048
27	10·424 8	77	29·729 9	370	142·857 7	870	335·909
28	10·810 9	78	30·116 0	380	146·718 8	880	339·770
29	11·197 0	79	30·502 1	390	150·579 8	890	343·631
30	11·583 1	80	30·888 2	400	154·440 8	900	347·492
31	11·969 2	81	31·274 3	410	158·301 8	910	351·353
32	12·355 3	82	31·660 4	420	162·162 8	920	355·214
33	12·741 4	83	32·046 5	430	166·023 9	930	359·075
34	13·127 5	84	32·432 6	440	169·884 9	940	362·936
35	13·513 6	85	32·818 7	450	173·745 9	950	366·797
36	13·899 7	86	33·204 8	460	177·606 9	960	370·658
37	14·285 8	87	33·590 9	470	181·467 9	970	374·519
38	14·671 9	88	33·977 0	480	185·329 0	980	378·380
39	15·058 0	89	34·363 1	490	189·190 0	990	382·241
40	15·444 1	90	34·749 2	500	193·051 0	1 000	386·102
41	15·830 2	91	35·135 3	510	196·912 0	2 000	772·204
42	16·216 3	92	35·521 4	520	200·773 0	3 000	1 158·306
43	16·602 4	93	35·907 5	530	204·634 1	4 000	1 544·408
44	16·988 5	94	36·293 6	540	208·495 1	5 000	1 930·510
45	17·374 6	95	36·679 7	550	212·356 1		
						6 000	2 316·612
46	17·760 7	96	37·065 8	560	216·217 1	7 000	2 702·714
47	18·146 8	97	37·451 9	570	220·078 1	8 000	3 088·816
48	18·532 9	98	37·838 0	580	223·939 2	9 000	3 474·918
49	18·919 0	99	38·224 1	590	227·800 2	10 000	3 861·020
50	19·305 1	100	38·610 2	600	231·661 2		

Volume

SI derived unit: **cubic metre** (m³)

Imperial to SI
1 cubic inch (cu. in)   =16·387 1 cm³
1 cubic foot (cu. ft) =1 728 cu. in=0·028 316 8 m³
1 cubic yard (cu. yd)=27 cu. ft   =0·764 555 m³

SI to Imperial
1 cubic centimetre (cm³)=0·061 023 7 cu. in
1 cubic metre (m³)   =1·307 95 cu. yd

VOLUME   cubic inches (in³) to cubic centimetres (cm³)
[in³ to millilitres (ml)]

in³	cm³	in³	cm³	in³	cm³	in³	cm³
1	16·387 1	51	835·740	110	1 802·577	610	9 996·11
2	32·774 1	52	852·127	120	1 966·448	620	10 159·98
3	49·161 2	53	868·514	130	2 130·318	630	10 323·85
4	65·548 3	54	884·901	140	2 294·189	640	10 487·72
5	81·935 3	55	901·289	150	2 458·060	650	10 651·59
6	98·322 4	56	917·676	160	2 621·930	660	10 815·46
7	114·709 4	57	934·063	170	2 785·801	670	10 979·33
8	131·096 5	58	950·450	180	2 949·672	680	11 143·20
9	147·483 6	59	966·837	190	3 113·542	690	11 307·07
10	163·870 6	60	983·224	200	3 277·413	700	11 470·94
11	180·257 7	61	999·611	210	3 441·283	710	11 634·82
12	196·644 8	62	1 015·998	220	3 605·154	720	11 798·69
13	213·031 8	63	1 032·385	230	3 769·025	730	11 962·56
14	229·418 9	64	1 048·772	240	3 932·895	740	12 126·43
15	245·806 0	65	1 065·159	250	4 096·766	750	12 290·30
16	262·193 0	66	1 081·546	260	4 260·637	760	12 454·17
17	278·580 1	67	1 097·933	270	4 424·507	770	12 618·04
18	294·967 2	68	1 114·320	280	4 588·378	780	12 781·91
19	311·354 2	69	1 130·707	290	4 752·249	790	12 945·78
20	327·741 3	70	1 147·094	300	4 916·119	800	13 109·65
21	344·128 3	71	1 163·482	310	5 079·990	810	13 273·52
22	360·515 4	72	1 179·869	320	5 243·860	820	13 437·39
23	376·902 5	73	1 196·256	330	5 407·731	830	13 601·26
24	393·289 5	74	1 212·643	340	5 571·602	840	13 765·13
25	409·676 6	75	1 229·030	350	5 735·472	850	13 929·00
26	426·063 7	76	1 245·417	360	5 899·343	860	14 092·88
27	442·450 7	77	1 261·804	370	6 063·214	870	14 256·75
28	458·837 8	78	1 278·191	380	6 227·084	880	14 420·62
29	475·224 9	79	1 294·578	390	6 390·955	890	14 584·49
30	491·611 9	80	1 310·965	400	6 554·826	900	14 748·36
31	507·999 0	81	1 327·352	410	6 718·696	910	14 912·23
32	524·386 0	82	1 343·739	420	6 882·567	920	15 076·10
33	540·773 1	83	1 360·126	430	7 046·438	930	15 239·97
34	557·160 2	84	1 376·513	440	7 210·308	940	15 403·84
35	573·547 2	85	1 392·900	450	7 374·179	950	15 567·71
36	589·934 3	86	1 409·288	460	7 538·049	960	15 731·58
37	606·321 4	87	1 425·675	470	7 701·920	970	15 895·45
38	622·708 4	88	1 442·062	480	7 865·791	980	16 059·32
39	639·095 5	89	1 458·449	490	8 029·661	990	16 223·19
40	655·482 6	90	1 474·836	500	8 193·532	1 000	16 387·06
41	671·869 6	91	1 491·223	510	8 357·403	2 000	32 774·13
42	688·256 7	92	1 507·610	520	8 521·273	3 000	49 161·19
43	704·643 8	93	1 523·997	530	8 685·144	4 000	65 548·26
44	721·030 8	94	1 540·384	540	8 849·015	5 000	81 935·32
45	737·417 9	95	1 556·771	550	9 012·885		
						6 000	98 322·38
46	753·804 9	96	1 573·158	560	9 176·756	7 000	114 709·45
47	770·192 0	97	1 589·545	570	9 340·626	8 000	131 096·51
48	786·579 1	98	1 605·932	580	9 504·497	9 000	147 483·58
49	802·966 1	99	1 622·319	590	9 668·368	10 000	163 870·64
50	819·353 2	100	1 638·706	600	9 832·238		

Note: 1 cm³ = 1 ml

ft³	m³	ft³	m³	ft³	m³	ft³	m³
1	0·0283	51	1·4442	110	3·1148	610	17·273
2	0·0566	52	1·4725	120	3·3980	620	17·556
3	0·0850	53	1·5008	130	3·6812	630	17·840
4	0·1133	54	1·5291	140	3·9644	640	18·123
5	0·1416	55	1·5574	150	4·2475	650	18·406
6	0·1699	56	1·5857	160	4·5307	660	18·689
7	0·1982	57	1·6141	170	4·8139	670	18·972
8	0·2265	58	1·6424	180	5·0970	680	19·255
9	0·2549	59	1·6707	190	5·3802	690	19·539
10	0·2832	60	1·6990	200	5·6634	700	19·822
11	0·3115	61	1·7273	210	5·9465	710	20·105
12	0·3398	62	1·7556	220	6·2297	720	20·388
13	0·3681	63	1·7840	230	6·5129	730	20·671
14	0·3964	64	1·8123	240	6·7960	740	20·954
15	0·4248	65	1·8406	250	7·0792	750	21·238
16	0·4531	66	1·8689	260	7·3624	760	21·521
17	0·4814	67	1·8972	270	7·6455	770	21·804
18	0·5097	68	1·9255	280	7·9287	780	22·087
19	0·5380	69	1·9539	290	8·2119	790	22·370
20	0·5663	70	1·9822	300	8·4950	800	22·653
21	0·5947	71	2·0105	310	8·7782	810	22·937
22	0·6230	72	2·0388	320	9·0614	820	23·220
23	0·6513	73	2·0671	330	9·3445	830	23·503
24	0·6796	74	2·0954	340	9·6277	840	23·786
25	0·7079	75	2·1238	350	9·9109	850	24·069
26	0·7362	76	2·1521	360	10·1940	860	24·352
27	0·7646	77	2·1804	370	10·4772	870	24·636
28	0·7929	78	2·2087	380	10·7604	880	24·919
29	0·8212	79	2·2370	390	11·0436	890	25·202
30	0·8495	80	2·2653	400	11·3267	900	25·485
31	0·8778	81	2·2937	410	11·6099	910	25·768
32	0·9061	82	2·3220	420	11·8931	920	26·051
33	0·9345	83	2·3503	430	12·1762	930	26·335
34	0·9628	84	2·3786	440	12·4594	940	26·618
35	0·9911	85	2·4069	450	12·7426	950	26·901
36	1·0194	86	2·4352	460	13·0257	960	27·184
37	1·0477	87	2·4636	470	13·3089	970	27·467
38	1·0760	88	2·4919	480	13·5921	980	27·750
39	1·1044	89	2·5202	490	13·8752	990	28·034
40	1·1327	90	2·5485	500	14·1584	1000	28·317
41	1·1610	91	2·5768	510	14·4416	2000	56·634
42	1·1893	92	2·6051	520	14·7247	3000	84·950
43	1·2176	93	2·6335	530	15·0079	4000	113·267
44	1·2459	94	2·6618	540	15·2911	5000	141·584
45	1·2743	95	2·6901	550	15·5742		
						6000	169·901
46	1·3026	96	2·7184	560	15·8574	7000	198·218
47	1·3309	97	2·7467	570	16·1406	8000	226·534
48	1·3592	98	2·7750	580	16·4237	9000	254·851
49	1·3875	99	2·8034	590	16·7069	10000	283·168
50	1·4158	100	2·8317	600	16·9901		

24 VOLUME

cubic yards (yd³) to cubic metres (m³)

yd³	m³	yd³	m³	yd³	m³	yd³	m³
1	0·7646	51	38·9923	110	84·1011	610	466·379
2	1·5291	52	39·7569	120	91·7466	620	474·024
3	2·2937	53	40·5214	130	99·3922	630	481·670
4	3·0582	54	41·2860	140	107·0377	640	489·315
5	3·8228	55	42·0505	150	114·6833	650	496·961
6	4·5873	56	42·8151	160	122·3288	660	504·606
7	5·3519	57	43·5796	170	129·9744	670	512·252
8	6·1164	58	44·3442	180	137·6199	680	519·897
9	6·8810	59	45·1087	190	145·2655	690	527·543
10	7·6456	60	45·8733	200	152·9110	700	535·189
11	8·4101	61	46·6379	210	160·5566	710	542·834
12	9·1747	62	47·4024	220	168·2021	720	550·480
13	9·9392	63	48·1670	230	175·8477	730	558·125
14	10·7038	64	48·9315	240	183·4932	740	565·771
15	11·4683	65	49·6961	250	191·1388	750	573·416
16	12·2329	66	50·4606	260	198·7843	760	581·062
17	12·9974	67	51·2252	270	206·4299	770	588·707
18	13·7620	68	51·9897	280	214·0754	780	596·353
19	14·5265	69	52·7543	290	221·7210	790	603·998
20	15·2911	70	53·5189	300	229·3665	800	611·644
21	16·0557	71	54·2834	310	237·0121	810	619·290
22	16·8202	72	55·0480	320	244·6576	820	626·935
23	17·5848	73	55·8125	330	252·3032	830	634·581
24	18·3493	74	56·5771	340	259·9487	840	642·226
25	19·1139	75	57·3416	350	267·5943	850	649·872
26	19·8784	76	58·1062	360	275·2398	860	657·517
27	20·6430	77	58·8707	370	282·8854	870	665·163
28	21·4075	78	59·6353	380	290·5309	880	672·808
29	22·1721	79	60·3998	390	298·1765	890	680·454
30	22·9367	80	61·1644	400	305·8220	900	688·100
31	23·7012	81	61·9290	410	313·4676	910	695·745
32	24·4658	82	62·6935	420	321·1131	920	703·391
33	25·2303	83	63·4581	430	328·7587	930	711·036
34	25·9949	84	64·2226	440	336·4042	940	718·682
35	26·7594	85	64·9872	450	344·0498	950	726·327
36	27·5240	86	65·7517	460	351·6953	960	733·973
37	28·2885	87	66·5163	470	359·3409	970	741·618
38	29·0531	88	67·2808	480	366·9864	980	749·264
39	29·8176	89	68·0454	490	374·6320	990	756·909
40	30·5822	90	68·8100	500	382·2775	1 000	764·555
41	31·3468	91	69·5745	510	389·9231	2 000	1 529·110
42	32·1113	92	70·3391	520	397·5686	3 000	2 293·665
43	32·8759	93	71·1036	530	405·2142	4 000	3 058·220
44	33·6404	94	71·8682	540	412·8597	5 000	3 822·775
45	34·4050	95	72·6327	550	420·5053		
46	35·1695	96	73·3973	560	428·1508	6 000	4 587·330
47	35·9341	97	74·1618	570	435·7964	7 000	5 351·885
48	36·6986	98	74·9264	580	443·4419	8 000	6 116·440
49	37·4632	99	75·6909	590	451·0875	9 000	6 880·995
50	38·2278	100	76·4555	600	458·7330	10 000	7 645·550

cubic centimetres (cm³) to cubic inches (in³)

[millilitres (ml) to in³]

VOLUME 25

cm³	in³	cm³	in³	cm³	in³	cm³	in³
1	0·0610	51	3·1122	110	6·7126	610	37·2245
2	0·1220	52	3·1732	120	7·3228	620	37·8347
3	0·1831	53	3·2343	130	7·9331	630	38·4449
4	0·2441	54	3·2953	140	8·5433	640	39·0552
5	0·3051	55	3·3563	150	9·1536	650	39·6654
6	0·3661	56	3·4173	160	9·7638	660	40·2756
7	0·4272	57	3·4784	170	10·3740	670	40·8859
8	0·4882	58	3·5394	180	10·9843	680	41·4961
9	0·5492	59	3·6004	190	11·5945	690	42·1064
10	0·6102	60	3·6614	200	12·2047	700	42·7166
11	0·6713	61	3·7224	210	12·8150	710	43·3268
12	0·7323	62	3·7835	220	13·4252	720	43·9371
13	0·7933	63	3·8445	230	14·0355	730	44·5473
14	0·8543	64	3·9055	240	14·6457	740	45·1575
15	0·9154	65	3·9665	250	15·2559	750	45·7678
16	0·9764	66	4·0276	260	15·8662	760	46·3780
17	1·0374	67	4·0886	270	16·4764	770	46·9882
18	1·0984	68	4·1496	280	17·0866	780	47·5985
19	1·1595	69	4·2106	290	17·6969	790	48·2087
20	1·2205	70	4·2717	300	18·3071	800	48·8190
21	1·2815	71	4·3327	310	18·9173	810	49·4292
22	1·3425	72	4·3937	320	19·5276	820	50·0394
23	1·4035	73	4·4547	330	20·1378	830	50·6497
24	1·4646	74	4·5158	340	20·7481	840	51·2599
25	1·5256	75	4·5768	350	21·3583	850	51·8701
26	1·5866	76	4·6378	360	21·9685	860	52·4804
27	1·6476	77	4·6988	370	22·5788	870	53·0906
28	1·7087	78	4·7598	380	23·1890	880	53·7009
29	1·7697	79	4·8209	390	23·7992	890	54·3111
30	1·8307	80	4·8819	400	24·4095	900	54·9213
31	1·8917	81	4·9429	410	25·0197	910	55·5316
32	1·9528	82	5·0039	420	25·6300	920	56·1418
33	2·0138	83	5·0650	430	26·2402	930	56·7520
34	2·0748	84	5·1260	440	26·8504	940	57·3623
35	2·1358	85	5·1870	450	27·4607	950	57·9725
36	2·1969	86	5·2480	460	28·0709	960	58·5828
37	2·2579	87	5·3091	470	28·6811	970	59·1930
38	2·3189	88	5·3701	480	29·2914	980	59·8032
39	2·3799	89	5·4311	490	29·9016	990	60·4135
40	2·4409	90	5·4921	500	30·5119	1000	61·0237
41	2·5020	91	5·5532	510	31·1221	2000	122·0474
42	2·5630	92	5·6142	520	31·7323	3000	183·0711
43	2·6240	93	5·6752	530	32·3426	4000	244·0948
44	2·6850	94	5·7362	540	32·9528	5000	305·1185
45	2·7461	95	5·7973	550	33·5630		
						6000	366·1422
46	2·8071	96	5·8583	560	34·1733	7000	427·1659
47	2·8681	97	5·9193	570	34·7835	8000	488·1896
48	2·9291	98	5·9803	580	35·3937	9000	549·2133
49	2·9902	99	6·0413	590	36·0040	10000	610·2370
50	3·0512	100	6·1024	600	36·6142		

Note: 1 cm³ = 1 ml

page 59

m³	ft³	m³	ft³	m³	ft³	m³	ft³
1	35·314 7	51	1 801·048	110	3 884·613	610	21 541·95
2	70·629 3	52	1 836·363	120	4 237·760	620	21 895·09
3	105·944 0	53	1 871·677	130	4 590·907	630	22 248·24
4	141·258 7	54	1 906·992	140	4 944·053	640	22 601·39
5	176·573 3	55	1 942·307	150	5 297·200	650	22 954·53
6	211·888 0	56	1 977·621	160	5 650·347	660	23 307·68
7	247·202 7	57	2 012·936	170	6 003·493	670	23 660·83
8	282·517 3	58	2 048·251	180	6 356·640	680	24 013·97
9	317·832 0	59	2 083·565	190	6 709·787	690	24 367·12
10	353·146 7	60	2 118·880	200	7 062·933	700	24 720·27
11	388·461 3	61	2 154·195	210	7 416·080	710	25 073·41
12	423·776 0	62	2 189·509	220	7 769·227	720	25 426·56
13	459·090 7	63	2 224·824	230	8 122·373	730	25 779·71
14	494·405 3	64	2 260·139	240	8 475·520	740	26 132·85
15	529·720 0	65	2 295·453	250	8 828·667	750	26 486·00
16	565·034 7	66	2 330·768	260	9 181·813	760	26 839·15
17	600·349 3	67	2 366·083	270	9 534·960	770	27 192·29
18	635·664 0	68	2 401·397	280	9 888·107	780	27 545·44
19	670·978 7	69	2 436·712	290	10 241·253	790	27 898·59
20	706·293 3	70	2 472·027	300	10 594·400	800	28 251·73
21	741·608 0	71	2 507·341	310	10 947·547	810	28 604·88
22	776·922 7	72	2 542·656	320	11 300·693	820	28 958·03
23	812·237 3	73	2 577·971	330	11 653·840	830	29 311·17
24	847·552 0	74	2 613·285	340	12 006·987	840	29 664·32
25	882·866 7	75	2 648·600	350	12 360·133	850	30 017·47
26	918·181 3	76	2 683·915	360	12 713·280	860	30 370·61
27	953·496 0	77	2 719·229	370	13 066·427	870	30 723·76
28	988·810 7	78	2 754·544	380	13 419·573	880	31 076·91
29	1 024·125 3	79	2 789·859	390	13 772·720	890	31 430·05
30	1 059·440 0	80	2 825·173	400	14 125·867	900	31 783·20
31	1 094·754 7	81	2 860·488	410	14 479·013	910	32 136·35
32	1 130·069 3	82	2 895·803	420	14 832·160	920	32 489·49
33	1 165·384 0	83	2 931·117	430	15 185·307	930	32 842·64
34	1 200·698 7	84	2 966·432	440	15 538·453	940	33 195·79
35	1 236·013 3	85	3 001·747	450	15 891·600	950	33 548·93
36	1 271·328 0	86	3 037·061	460	16 244·747	960	33 902·08
37	1 306·642 7	87	3 072·376	470	16 597·893	970	34 255·23
38	1 341·957 3	88	3 107·691	480	16 951·040	980	34 608·37
39	1 377·272 0	89	3 143·005	490	17 304·187	990	34 961·52
40	1 412·586 7	90	3 178·320	500	17 657·333	1 000	35 314·67
41	1 447·901 3	91	3 213·635	510	18 010·480	2 000	70 629·33
42	1 483·216 0	92	3 248·949	520	18 363·627	3 000	105 944·00
43	1 518·530 7	93	3 284·264	530	18 716·773	4 000	141 258·67
44	1 553·845 3	94	3 319·579	540	19 069·920	5 000	176 573·33
45	1 589·160 0	95	3 354·893	550	19 423·067		
						6 000	211 888·00
46	1 624·474 7	96	3 390·208	560	19 776·213	7 000	247 202·67
47	1 659·789 3	97	3 425·523	570	20 129·360	8 000	282 517·33
48	1 695·104 0	98	3 460·837	580	20 482·507	9 000	317 832·00
49	1 730·418 7	99	3 496·152	590	20 835·653	10 000	353 146·67
50	1 765·733 3	100	3 531·467	600	21 188·800		

m³	yd³	m³	yd³	m³	yd³	m³	yd³
1	1·308 0	51	66·705 5	110	143·875	610	797·850
2	2·615 9	52	68·013 4	120	156·954	620	810·929
3	3·923 9	53	69·321 4	130	170·034	630	824·009
4	5·231 8	54	70·629 3	140	183·113	640	837·088
5	6·539 8	55	71·937 3	150	196·193	650	850·168
6	7·847 7	56	73·245 2	160	209·272	660	863·247
7	9·155 7	57	74·553 2	170	222·352	670	876·327
8	10·463 6	58	75·861 1	180	235·431	680	889·406
9	11·771 6	59	77·169 1	190	248·511	690	902·486
10	13·079 5	60	78·477 0	200	261·590	700	915·565
11	14·387 5	61	79·785 0	210	274·670	710	928·645
12	15·695 4	62	81·092 9	220	287·749	720	941·724
13	17·003 4	63	82·400 9	230	300·829	730	954·804
14	18·311 3	64	83·708 8	240	313·908	740	967·883
15	19·619 3	65	85·016 8	250	326·988	750	980·963
16	20·927 2	66	86·324 7	260	340·067	760	994·042
17	22·235 2	67	87·632 7	270	353·147	770	1 007·122
18	23·543 1	68	88·940 6	280	366·226	780	1 020·201
19	24·851 1	69	90·248 6	290	379·306	790	1 033·281
20	26·159 0	70	91·556 5	300	392·385	800	1 046·360
21	27·467 0	71	92·864 5	310	405·465	810	1 059·440
22	28·774 9	72	94·172 4	320	418·544	820	1 072·519
23	30·082 9	73	95·480 4	330	431·624	830	1 085·599
24	31·390 8	74	96·788 3	340	444·703	840	1 098·678
25	32·698 8	75	98·096 3	350	457·783	850	1 111·758
26	34·006 7	76	99·404 2	360	470·862	860	1 124·837
27	35·314 7	77	100·712 2	370	483·942	870	1 137·917
28	36·622 6	78	102·020 1	380	497·021	880	1 150·996
29	37·930 6	79	103·328 1	390	510·101	890	1 164·076
30	39·238 5	80	104·636 0	400	523·180	900	1 177·155
31	40·546 5	81	105·944 0	410	536·260	910	1 190·235
32	41·854 4	82	107·251 9	420	549·339	920	1 203·314
33	43·162 4	83	108·559 9	430	562·419	930	1 216·394
34	44·470 3	84	109·867 8	440	575·498	940	1 229·473
35	45·778 3	85	111·175 8	450	588·578	950	1 242·553
36	47·086 2	86	112·483 7	460	601·657	960	1 255·632
37	48·394 2	87	113·791 7	470	614·737	970	1 268·712
38	49·702 1	88	115·099 6	480	627·816	980	1 281·791
39	51·010 1	89	116·407 6	490	640·896	990	1 294·871
40	52·318 0	90	117·715 5	500	653·975	1 000	1 307·950
41	53·626 0	91	119·023 5	510	667·055	2 000	2 615·900
42	54·933 9	92	120·331 4	520	680·134	3 000	3 923·851
43	56·241 9	93	121·639 4	530	693·214	4 000	5 231·801
44	57·549 8	94	122·947 3	540	706·293	5 000	6 539·751
45	58·857 8	95	124·255 3	550	719·373		
						6 000	7 847·701
46	60·165 7	96	125·563 2	560	732·452	7 000	9 155·651
47	61·473 7	97	126·871 2	570	745·532	8 000	10 463·602
48	62·781 6	98	128·179 1	580	758·611	9 000	11 771·552
49	64·089 6	99	129·487 1	590	771·691	10 000	13 079·502
50	65·397 5	100	130·795 0	600	784·770		

Capacity

Unit: **litre** (l)

The **litre** is used for general measures of capacity, not for scientific measurements, when the cubic metre, etc. are used.

$$1 \text{ litre (l)} = 1 \text{ cubic decimetre}$$
$$1 \text{ millilitre (ml)} = 1 \text{ cubic centimetre}$$

(Between 1901 and 1964 the '1901' litre was used, equal to $1 \cdot 000\ 028$ dm³)

SI to Imperial

1 fluid ounce (fl. oz)		$=28 \cdot 4$ ml
1 gill	$=\ 5$ fl. oz	$=142$ ml
1 pint (pt)	$=\left\{\begin{array}{l} 20 \text{ fl. oz} \\ 4 \text{ gills} \end{array}\right.$	$=0 \cdot 568$ l
1 quart (qt)	$=\ 2$ pt	$=1 \cdot 137$ l
1 gallon (gal)	$=\left\{\begin{array}{l} 8 \text{ pt} \\ 4 \text{ qt} \end{array}\right.$	$=4 \cdot 546$ l
1 bushel	$=\ 8$ gal	$=36 \cdot 369$ l
1 quarter	$=\ 8$ bushels	$=290 \cdot 95$ l

Imperial to SI

1 millilitre (ml) $=\left\{\begin{array}{l} 0 \cdot 061\ 02 \text{ cu. in} \\ 0 \cdot 007\ 04 \text{ gill} \end{array}\right.$	
1 litre (l) $=\left\{\begin{array}{l} 0 \cdot 220\ 0 \text{ gal} \\ 1 \cdot 760 \text{ pt} \\ 61 \cdot 024 \text{ cu. in} \end{array}\right.$	

US Units

1 US pint	$=\left\{\begin{array}{l} \frac{4}{5} \text{ Imperial pint} \\ 16 \text{ fl. oz} \end{array}\right.$	$=0 \cdot 473\ 2$ l
1 US gallon	$=\left\{\begin{array}{l} \frac{4}{5} \text{ Imperial gallon} \\ 8 \text{ US pints} \end{array}\right.$	$=3 \cdot 785$ l

fluid ounces (fl. oz)
to millilitres (ml)

gills to litres (l)

fl. oz	ml
$\frac{1}{2}$	14·207
1	28·413
$1\frac{1}{2}$	42·620
2	56·826
$2\frac{1}{2}$	71·033
3	85·239
$3\frac{1}{2}$	99·446
4	113·652
$4\frac{1}{2}$	127·859
5	142·066
$5\frac{1}{2}$	156·272
6	170·479
$6\frac{1}{2}$	184·685
7	198·892
$7\frac{1}{2}$	213·098
8	227·305
$8\frac{1}{2}$	241·511
9	255·718
$9\frac{1}{2}$	269·924
10	284·131
$10\frac{1}{2}$	298·338
11	312·544
$11\frac{1}{2}$	326·751
12	340·957
$12\frac{1}{2}$	355·164
13	369·370
$13\frac{1}{2}$	383·577
14	397·783
$14\frac{1}{2}$	411·990
15	426·197
$15\frac{1}{2}$	440·403
16	454·610
$16\frac{1}{2}$	468·816
17	483·023
$17\frac{1}{2}$	497·229
18	511·436
$18\frac{1}{2}$	525·642
19	539·849
$19\frac{1}{2}$	554·055
20	568·262

gills	l
$\frac{1}{2}$	0·0710
1	0·1421
$1\frac{1}{2}$	0·2131
2	0·2841
$2\frac{1}{2}$	0·3552
3	0·4262
$3\frac{1}{2}$	0·4972
4	0·5682
5	0·7103
6	0·8524
7	0·9944
8	1·1365
9	1·2786
10	1·4206
11	1·5627
12	1·7047
13	1·8468
14	1·9889
15	2·1309
16	2·2730
17	2·4150
18	2·5571
19	2·6992
20	2·8412
21	2·9833
22	3·1253
23	3·2674
24	3·4095
25	3·5515
26	3·6936
27	3·8357
28	3·9777
29	4·1198
30	4·2618
31	4·4039
32	4·5460

pt	l	pt	l	pt	l	pt	l
$\frac{1}{4}$	0·142 1	26	14·774 8	76	43·187 8	126	71·600 9
$\frac{1}{2}$	0·284 1	27	15·343 0	77	43·756 1	127	72·169 1
$\frac{3}{4}$	0·426 2	28	15·911 3	78	44·324 4	128	72·737 4
1	0·568 3	29	16·479 6	79	44·892 6	129	73·305 7
		30	17·047 8	80	45·460 9	130	73·873 9
$1\frac{1}{4}$	0·710 3						
$1\frac{1}{2}$	0·852 4	31	17·616 1	81	46·029 1	131	74·442 2
$1\frac{3}{4}$	0·994 5	32	18·184 4	82	46·597 4	132	75·010 5
2	1·136 5	33	18·752 6	83	47·165 7	133	75·578 7
		34	19·320 9	84	47·733 9	134	76·147 0
$2\frac{1}{4}$	1·278 6	35	19·889 1	85	48·302 2	135	76·715 2
$2\frac{1}{2}$	1·420 7						
$2\frac{3}{4}$	1·562 7	36	20·457 4	86	48·870 4	136	77·283 5
3	1·704 8	37	21·025 7	87	49·438 7	137	77·851 8
		38	21·593 9	88	50·007 0	138	78·420 0
$3\frac{1}{4}$	1·846 8	39	22·162 2	89	50·575 2	139	78·988 3
$3\frac{1}{2}$	1·988 9	40	22·730 4	90	51·143 5	140	79·556 5
$3\frac{3}{4}$	2·131 0						
4	2·273 0	41	23·298 7	91	51·711 8	141	80·124 8
		42	23·867 0	92	52·280 0	142	80·693 1
$4\frac{1}{4}$	2·415 1	43	24·435 2	93	52·848 3	143	81·261 3
$4\frac{1}{2}$	2·557 2	44	25·003 5	94	53·416 5	144	81·829 6
$4\frac{3}{4}$	2·699 2	45	25·571 7	95	53·984 8	145	82·397 8
5	2·841 3						
		46	26·140 0	96	54·553 1	146	82·966 1
$5\frac{1}{4}$	2·983 4	47	26·708 3	97	55·121 3	147	83·534 4
$5\frac{1}{2}$	3·125 4	48	27·276 5	98	55·689 6	148	84·102 6
$5\frac{3}{4}$	3·267 5	49	27·844 8	99	56·257 8	149	84·670 9
6	3·409 6	50	28·413 1	100	56·826 1	150	85·239 2
$6\frac{1}{4}$	3·551 6	51	28·981 3	101	57·394 4	160	90·921 8
$6\frac{1}{2}$	3·693 7	52	29·549 6	102	57·962 6	170	96·604 4
$6\frac{3}{4}$	3·835 8	53	30·117 8	103	58·530 9	180	102·287 0
7	3·977 8	54	30·686 1	104	59·099 1	190	107·969 6
		55	31·254 4	105	59·667 4	200	113·652 2
$7\frac{1}{4}$	4·119 9						
$7\frac{1}{2}$	4·262 0	56	31·822 6	106	60·235 7	210	119·334 8
$7\frac{3}{4}$	4·404 0	57	32·390 9	107	60·803 9	220	125·017 4
8	4·546 1	58	32·959 1	108	61·372 2	230	130·700 0
9	5·114 3	59	33·527 4	109	61·940 4	240	136·382 6
10	5·682 6	60	34·095 7	110	62·508 7	250	142·065 3
11	6·250 9	61	34·663 9	111	63·077 0	260	147·747 9
12	6·819 1	62	35·232 2	112	63·645 2	270	153·430 5
13	7·387 4	63	35·800 4	113	64·213 5	280	159·113 1
14	7·955 7	64	36·368 7	114	64·781 8	290	164·795 7
15	8·523 9	65	36·937 0	115	65·350 0	300	170·478 3
16	9·092 2	66	37·505 2	116	65·918 3	400	227·304 4
17	9·660 4	67	38·073 5	117	66·486 5	500	284·130 5
18	10·228 7	68	38·641 7	118	67·054 8		
19	10·797 0	69	39·210 0	119	67·623 1	600	340·956 6
20	11·365 2	70	39·778 3	120	68·191 3	700	397·782 7
						800	454·608 8
21	11·933 5	71	40·346 5	121	68·759 6	900	511·434 9
22	12·501 7	72	40·914 8	122	69·327 8	1 000	568·261 0
23	13·070 0	73	41·483 1	123	69·896 1		
24	13·638 3	74	42·051 3	124	70·464 4		
25	14·206 5	75	42·619 6	125	71·032 6		

gal	l	gal	l	gal	l	gal	l
1	4·546 1	51	231·850 5	101	459·154 9	151	686·459 3
2	9·092 2	52	236·396 6	102	463·701 0	152	691·005 4
3	13·638 3	53	240·942 7	103	468·247 1	153	695·551 5
4	18·184 4	54	245·488 8	104	472·793 2	154	700·097 6
5	22·730 4	55	250·034 8	105	477·339 2	155	704·643 6
6	27·276 5	56	254·580 9	106	481·885 3	156	709·189 7
7	31·822 6	57	259·127 0	107	486·431 4	157	713·735 8
8	36·368 7	58	263·673 1	108	490·977 5	158	718·281 9
9	40·914 8	59	268·219 2	109	495·523 6	159	722·828 0
10	45·460 9	·60	272·765 3	110	500·069 7	160	727·374 1
11	50·007 0	61	277·311 4	111	504·615 8	161	731·920 2
12	54·553 1	62	281·857 5	112	509·161 9	162	736·466 3
13	59·099 1	63	286·403 5	113	513·707 9	163	741·012 3
14	63·645 2	64	290·949 6	114	518·254 0	164	745·558 4
15	68·191 3	65	295·495 7	115	522·800 1	165	750·104 5
16	72·737 4	66	300·041 8	116	527·346 2	166	754·650 6
17	77·283 5	67	304·587 9	117	531·892 3	167	759·196 7
18	81·829 6	68	309·134 0	118	536·438 4	168	763·742 8
19	86·375 7	69	313·680 1	119	540·984 5	169	768·288 9
20	90·921 8	70	318·226 2	120	545·530 6	170	772·835 0
21	95·467 8	71	322·772 2	121	550·076 6	171	777·381 0
22	100·013 9	72	327·318 3	122	554·622 7	172	781·927 1
23	104·560 0	73	331·864 4	123	559·168 8	173	786·473 2
24	109·106 1	74	336·410 5	124	563·714 9	174	791·019 3
25	113·652 2	75	340·956 6	125	568·261 0	175	795·565 4
26	118·198 3	76	345·502 7	126	572·807 1	176	800·111 5
27	122·744 4	77	350·048 8	127	577·353 2	177	804·657 6
28	127·290 5	78	354·594 9	128	581·899 3	178	809·203 7
29	131·836 6	79	359·141 0	129	586·445 4	179	813·749 8
30	136·382 6	80	363·687 0	130	590·991 4	180	818·295 8
31	140·928 7	81	368·233 1	131	595·537 5	181	822·841 9
32	145·474 8	82	372·779 2	132	600·083 6	182	827·388 0
33	150·020 9	83	377·325 3	133	604·629 7	183	831·934 1
34	154·567 0	84	381·871 4	134	609·175 8	184	836·480 2
35	159·113 1	85	386·417 5	135	613·721 9	185	841·026 3
36	163·659 2	86	390·963 6	136	618·268 0	186	845·572 4
37	168·205 3	87	395·509 7	137	622·814 1	187	850·118 5
38	172·751 3	88	400·055 7	138	627·360 1	188	854·664 5
39	177·297 4	89	404·601 8	139	631·906 2	189	859·210 6
40	181·843 5	90	409·147 9	140	636·452 3	190	863·756 7
41	186·389 6	91	413·694 0	141	640·998 4	191	868·302 8
42	190·935 7	92	418·240 1	142	645·544 5	192	872·848 9
43	195·481 8	93	422·786 2	143	650·090 6	193	877·395 0
44	200·027 9	94	427·332 3	144	654·636 7	194	881·941 1
45	204·574 0	95	431·878 4	145	659·182 8	195	886·487 2
46	209·120 0	96	436·424 4	146	663·728 8	196	891·033 2
47	213·666 1	97	440·970 5	147	668·274 9	197	895·579 3
48	218·212 2	98	445·516 6	148	672·821 0	198	900·125 4
49	222·758 3	99	450·062 7	149	677·367 1	199	904·671 5
50	227·304 4	100	454·608 8	150	681·913 2	200	909·217 6

gal	l	gal	l	gal	l	gal	l
201	913·764	251	1 141·068	301	1 368·372	351	1 595·677
202	918·310	252	1 145·614	302	1 372·919	352	1 600·223
203	922·856	253	1 150·160	303	1 377·465	353	1 604·769
204	927·402	254	1 154·706	304	1 382·011	354	1 609·315
205	931·948	255	1 159·252	305	1 386·557	355	1 613·861
206	936·494	256	1 163·799	306	1 391·103	356	1 618·407
207	941·040	257	1 168·345	307	1 395·649	357	1 622·953
208	945·586	258	1 172·891	308	1 400·195	358	1 627·500
209	950·132	259	1 177·437	309	1 404·741	359	1 632·046
210	954·678	260	1 181·983	310	1 409·287	360	1 636·592
211	959·225	261	1 186·529	311	1 413·833	361	1 641·138
212	963·771	262	1 191·075	312	1 418·379	362	1 645·684
213	968·317	263	1 195·621	313	1 422·926	363	1 650·230
214	972·863	264	1 200·167	314	1 427·472	364	1 654·776
215	977·409	265	1 204·713	315	1 432·018	365	1 659·322
216	981·955	266	1 209·259	316	1 436·564	366	1 663·868
217	986·501	267	1 213·805	317	1 441·110	367	1 668·414
218	991·047	268	1 218·352	318	1 445·656	368	1 672·960
219	995·593	269	1 222·898	319	1 450·202	369	1 677·506
220	1 000·139	270	1 227·444	320	1 454·748	370	1 682·053
221	1 004·685	271	1 231·990	321	1 459·294	371	1 686·599
222	1 009·232	272	1 236·536	322	1 463·840	372	1 691·145
223	1 013·778	273	1 241·082	323	1 468·386	373	1 695·691
224	1 018·324	274	1 245·628	324	1 472·933	374	1 700·237
225	1 022·870	275	1 250·174	325	1 477·479	375	1 704·783
226	1 027·416	276	1 254·720	326	1 482·025	376	1 709·329
227	1 031·962	277	1 259·266	327	1 486·571	377	1 713·875
228	1 036·508	278	1 263·812	328	1 491·117	378	1 718·421
229	1 041·054	279	1 268·359	329	1 495·663	379	1 722·967
230	1 045·600	280	1 272·905	330	1 500·209	380	1 727·513
231	1 050·146	281	1 277·451	331	1 504·755	381	1 732·060
232	1 054·692	282	1 281·997	332	1 509·301	382	1 736·606
233	1 059·239	283	1 286·543	333	1 513·847	383	1 741·152
234	1 063·785	284	1 291·089	334	1 518·393	384	1 745·698
235	1 068·331	285	1 295·635	335	1 522·939	385	1 750·244
236	1 072·877	286	1 300·181	336	1 527·486	386	1 754·790
237	1 077·423	287	1 304·727	337	1 532·032	387	1 759·336
238	1 081·969	288	1 309·273	338	1 536·578	388	1 763·882
239	1 086·515	289	1 313·819	339	1 541·124	389	1 768·428
240	1 091·061	290	1 318·366	340	1 545·670	390	1 772·974
241	1 095·607	291	1 322·912	341	1 550·216	391	1 777·520
242	1 100·153	292	1 327·458	342	1 554·762	392	1 782·066
243	1 104·699	293	1 332·004	343	1 559·308	393	1 786·613
244	1 109·245	294	1 336·550	344	1 563·854	394	1 791·159
245	1 113·792	295	1 341·096	345	1 568·400	395	1 795·705
246	1 118·338	296	1 345·642	346	1 572·946	396	1 800·251
247	1 122·884	297	1 350·188	347	1 577·493	397	1 804·797
248	1 127·430	298	1 354·734	348	1 582·039	398	1 809·343
249	1 131·976	299	1 359·280	349	1 586·585	399	1 813·889
250	1 136·522	300	1 363·826	350	1 591·131	400	1 818·435

gal	l	gal	l	gal	l	gal	l
401	1 822·981	451	2 050·286	501	2 277·590	551	2 504·894
402	1 827·527	452	2 054·832	502	2 282·136	552	2 509·441
403	1 832·073	453	2 059·378	503	2 286·682	553	2 513·987
404	1 836·620	454	2 063·924	504	2 291·228	554	2 518·533
405	1 841·166	455	2 068·470	505	2 295·774	555	2 523·079
406	1 845·712	456	2 073·016	506	2 300·321	556	2 527·625
407	1 850·258	457	2 077·562	507	2 304·867	557	2 532·171
408	1 854·804	458	2 082·108	508	2 309·413	558	2 536·717
409	1 859·350	459	2 086·654	509	2 313·959	559	2 541·263
410	1 863·896	460	2 091·200	510	2 318·505	560	2 545·809
411	1 868·442	461	2 095·747	511	2 323·051	561	2 550·355
412	1 872·988	462	2 100·293	512	2 327·597	562	2 554·901
413	1 877·534	463	2 104·839	513	2 332·143	563	2 559·448
414	1 882·080	464	2 109·385	514	2 336·689	564	2 563·994
415	1 886·627	465	2 113·931	515	2 341·235	565	2 568·540
416	1 891·173	466	2 118·477	516	2 345·781	566	2 573·086
417	1 895·719	467	2 123·023	517	2 350·327	567	2 577·632
418	1 900·265	468	2 127·569	518	2 354·874	568	2 582·178
419	1 904·811	469	2 132·115	519	2 359·420	569	2 586·724
420	1 909·357	470	2 136·661	520	2 363·966	570	2 591·270
421	1 913·903	471	2 141·207	521	2 368·512	571	2 595·816
422	1 918·449	472	2 145·754	522	2 373·058	572	2 600·362
423	1 922·995	473	2 150·300	523	2 377·604	573	2 604·908
424	1 927·541	474	2 154·846	524	2 382·150	574	2 609·455
425	1 932·087	475	2 159·392	525	2 386·696	575	2 614·001
426	1 936·633	476	2 163·938	526	2 391·242	576	2 618·547
427	1 941·180	477	2 168·484	527	2 395·788	577	2 623·093
428	1 945·726	478	2 173·030	528	2 400·334	578	2 627·639
429	1 950·272	479	2 177·576	529	2 404·881	579	2 632·185
430	1 954·818	480	2 182·122	530	2 409·427	580	2 636·731
431	1 959·364	481	2 186·668	531	2 413·973	581	2 641·277
432	1 963·910	482	2 191·214	532	2 418·519	582	2 645·823
433	1 968·456	483	2 195·761	533	2 423·065	583	2 650·369
434	1 973·002	484	2 200·307	534	2 427·611	584	2 654·915
435	1 977·548	485	2 204·853	535	2 432·157	585	2 659·461
436	1 982·094	486	2 209·399	536	2 436·703	586	2 664·008
437	1 986·640	487	2 213·945	537	2 441·249	587	2 668·554
438	1 991·187	488	2 218·491	538	2 445·795	588	2 673·100
439	1 995·733	489	2 223·037	539	2 450·341	589	2 677·646
440	2 000·279	490	2 227·583	540	2 454·888	590	2 682·192
441	2 004·825	491	2 232·129	541	2 459·434	591	2 686·738
442	2 009·371	492	2 236·675	542	2 463·980	592	2 691·284
443	2 013·917	493	2 241·221	543	2 468·526	593	2 695·830
444	2 018·463	494	2 245·767	544	2 473·072	594	2 700·376
445	2 023·009	495	2 250·314	545	2 477·618	595	2 704·922
446	2 027·555	496	2 254·860	546	2 482·164	596	2 709·468
447	2 032·101	497	2 259·406	547	2 486·710	597	2 714·015
448	2 036·647	498	2 263·952	548	2 491·256	598	2 718·561
449	2 041·194	499	2 268·498	549	2 495·802	599	2 723·107
450	2 045·740	500	2 273·044	550	2 500·348	600	2 727·653

gal	l	gal	l	gal	l	gal	l
601	2 732·199	651	2 959·503	701	3 186·808	751	3 414·112
602	2 736·745	652	2 964·049	702	3 191·354	752	3 418·658
603	2 741·291	653	2 968·595	703	3 195·900	753	3 423·204
604	2 745·837	654	2 973·142	704	3 200·446	754	3 427·750
605	2 750·383	655	2 977·688	705	3 204·992	755	3 432·296
606	2 754·929	656	2 982·234	706	3 209·538	756	3 436·843
607	2 759·475	657	2 986·780	707	3 214·084	757	3 441·389
608	2 764·022	658	2 991·326	708	3 218·630	758	3 445·935
609	2 768·568	659	2 995·872	709	3 223·176	759	3 450·481
610	2 773·114	660	3 000·418	710	3 227·722	760	3 455·027
611	2 777·660	661	3 004·964	711	3 232·269	761	3 459·573
612	2 782·206	662	3 009·510	712	3 236·815	762	3 464·119
613	2 786·752	663	3 014·056	713	3 241·361	763	3 468·665
614	2 791·298	664	3 018·602	714	3 245·907	764	3 473·211
615	2 795·844	665	3 023·149	715	3 250·453	765	3 477·757
616	2 800·390	666	3 027·695	716	3 254·999	766	3 482·303
617	2 804·936	667	3 032·241	717	3 259·545	767	3 486·849
618	2 809·482	668	3 036·787	718	3 264·091	768	3 491·396
619	2 814·028	669	3 041·333	719	3 268·637	769	3 495·942
620	2 818·575	670	3 045·879	720	3 273·183	770	3 500·488
621	2 823·121	671	3 050·425	721	3 277·729	771	3 505·034
622	2 827·667	672	3 054·971	722	3 282·276	772	3 509·580
623	2 832·213	673	3 059·517	723	3 286·822	773	3 514·126
624	2 836·759	674	3 064·063	724	3 291·368	774	3 518·672
625	2 841·305	675	3 068·609	725	3 295·914	775	3 523·218
626	2 845·851	676	3 073·155	726	3 300·460	776	3 527·764
627	2 850·397	677	3 077·702	727	3 305·006	777	3 532·310
628	2 854·943	678	3 082·248	728	3 309·552	778	3 536·856
629	2 859·489	679	3 086·794	729	3 314·098	779	3 541·403
630	2 864·035	680	3 091·340	730	3 318·644	780	3 545·949
631	2 868·582	681	3 095·886	731	3 323·190	781	3 550·495
632	2 873·128	682	3 100·432	732	3 327·736	782	3 555·041
633	2 877·674	683	3 104·978	733	3 332·283	783	3 559·587
634	2 882·220	684	3 109·524	734	3 336·829	784	3 564·133
635	2 886·766	685	3 114·070	735	3 341·375	785	3 568·679
636	2 891·312	686	3 118·616	736	3 345·921	786	3 573·225
637	2 895·858	687	3 123·162	737	3 350·467	787	3 577·771
638	2 900·404	688	3 127·709	738	3 355·013	788	3 582·317
639	2 904·950	689	3 132·255	739	3 359·559	789	3 586·863
640	2 909·496	690	3 136·801	740	3 364·105	790	3 591·410
641	2 914·042	691	3 141·347	741	3 368·651	791	3 595·956
642	2 918·588	692	3 145·893	742	3 373·197	792	3 600·502
643	2 923·135	693	3 150·439	743	3 377·743	793	3 605·048
644	2 927·681	694	3 154·985	744	3 382·289	794	3 609·594
645	2 932·227	695	3 159·531	745	3 386·836	795	3 614·140
646	2 936·773	696	3 164·077	746	3 391·382	796	3 618·686
647	2 941·319	697	3 168·623	747	3 395·928	797	3 623·232
648	2 945·865	698	3 173·169	748	3 400·474	798	3 627·778
649	2 950·411	699	3 177·716	749	3 405·020	799	3 632·324
650	2 954·957	700	3 182·262	750	3 409·566	800	3 636·870

gal	l	gal	l	gal	l	gal	l
801	3 641·416	851	3 868·721	901	4 096·025	951	4 323·330
802	3 645·963	852	3 873·267	902	4 100·571	952	4 327·876
803	3 650·509	853	3 877·813	903	4 105·117	953	4 332·422
804	3 655·055	854	3 882·359	904	4 109·664	954	4 336·968
805	3 659·601	855	3 886·905	905	4 114·210	955	4 341·514
806	3 664·147	856	3 891·451	906	4 118·756	956	4 346·060
807	3 668·693	857	3 895·997	907	4 123·302	957	4 350·606
808	3 673·239	858	3 900·544	908	4 127·848	958	4 355·152
809	3 677·785	859	3 905·090	909	4 132·394	959	4 359·698
810	3 682·331	860	3 909·636	910	4 136·940	960	4 364·244
811	3 686·877	861	3 914·182	911	4 141·486	961	4 368·791
812	3 691·423	862	3 918·728	912	4 146·032	962	4 373·337
813	3 695·970	863	3 923·274	913	4 150·578	963	4 377·883
814	3 700·516	864	3 927·820	914	4 155·124	964	4 382·429
815	3 705·062	865	3 932·366	915	4 159·671	965	4 386·975
816	3 709·608	866	3 936·912	916	4 164·217	966	4 391·521
817	3 714·154	867	3 941·458	917	4 168·763	967	4 396·067
818	3 718·700	868	3 946·004	918	4 173·309	968	4 400·613
819	3 723·246	869	3 950·550	919	4 177·855	969	4 405·159
820	3 727·792	870	3 955·097	920	4 182·401	970	4 409·705
821	3 732·338	871	3 959·643	921	4 186·947	971	4 414·251
822	3 736·884	872	3 964·189	922	4 191·493	972	4 418·798
823	3 741·430	873	3 968·735	923	4 196·039	973	4 423·344
824	3 745·977	874	3 973·281	924	4 200·585	974	4 427·890
825	3 750·523	875	3 977·827	925	4 205·131	975	4 432·436
826	3 755·069	876	3 982·373	926	4 209·677	976	4 436·982
827	3 759·615	877	3 986·919	927	4 214·224	977	4 441·528
828	3 764·161	878	3 991·465	928	4 218·770	978	4 446·074
829	3 768·707	879	3 996·011	929	4 223·316	979	4 450·620
830	3 773·253	880	4 000·557	930	4 227·862	980	4 455·166
831	3 777·799	881	4 005·104	931	4 232·408	981	4 459·712
832	3 782·345	882	4 009·650	932	4 236·954	982	4 464·258
833	3 786·891	883	4 014·196	933	4 241·500	983	4 468·805
834	3 791·437	884	4 018·742	934	4 246·046	984	4 473·351
835	3 795·983	885	4 023·288	935	4 250·592	985	4 477·897
836	3 800·530	886	4 027·834	936	4 255·138	986	4 482·443
837	3 805·076	887	4 032·380	937	4 259·684	987	4 486·989
838	3 809·622	888	4 036·926	938	4 264·231	988	4 491·535
839	3 814·168	889	4 041·472	939	4 268·777	989	4 496·081
840	3 818·714	890	4 046·018	940	4 273·323	990	4 500·627
841	3 823·260	891	4 050·564	941	4 277·869	991	4 505·173
842	3 827·806	892	4 055·110	942	4 282·415	992	4 509·719
843	3 832·352	893	4 059·657	943	4 286·961	993	4 514·265
844	3 836·898	894	4 064·203	944	4 291·507	994	4 518·811
845	3 841·444	895	4 068·749	945	4 296·053	995	4 523·358
846	3 845·990	896	4 073·295	946	4 300·599	996	4 527·904
847	3 850·537	897	4 077·841	947	4 305·145	997	4 532·450
848	3 855·083	898	4 082·387	948	4 309·691	998	4 536·996
849	3 859·629	899	4 086·933	949	4 314·238	999	4 541·542
850	3 864·175	900	4 091·479	950	4 318·784	1 000	4 546·088

ml	fl. oz	gills	ml	fl. oz	gills
10	0·3520	0·0704	510	17·9500	3·5900
20	0·7039	0·1408	520	18·3020	3·6604
30	1·0559	0·2112	530	18·6539	3·7308
40	1·4078	0·2816	540	19·0059	3·8012
50	1·7598	0·3520	550	19·3579	3·8716
60	2·1118	0·4224	560	19·7098	3·9420
70	2·4637	0·4927	570	20·0618	4·0123
80	2·8157	0·5631	580	20·4137	4·0827
90	3·1676	0·6335	590	20·7657	4·1531
100	3·5196	0·7039	600	21·1177	4·2235
110	3·8716	0·7743	610	21·4696	4·2939
120	4·2235	0·8447	620	21·8216	4·3643
130	4·5755	0·9151	630	22·1735	4·4347
140	4·9275	0·9855	640	22·5255	4·5051
150	5·2794	1·0559	650	22·8775	4·5755
160	5·6314	1·1263	660	23·2294	4·6459
170	5·9833	1·1967	670	23·5814	4·7163
180	6·3353	1·2671	680	23·9333	4·7867
190	6·6873	1·3374	690	24·2853	4·8570
200	7·0392	1·4078	700	24·6373	4·9274
210	7·3912	1·4782	710	24·9892	4·9978
220	7·7431	1·5486	720	25·3412	5·0682
230	8·0951	1·6190	730	25·6932	5·1386
240	8·4471	1·6894	740	26·0451	5·2090
250	8·7990	1·7598	750	26·3971	5·2794
260	9·1510	1·8302	760	26·7490	5·3498
270	9·5029	1·9006	770	27·1010	5·4202
280	9·8549	1·9710	780	27·4530	5·4906
290	10·2069	2·0414	790	27·8049	5·5610
300	10·5588	2·1118	800	28·1569	5·6314
310	10·9108	2·1822	810	28·5088	5·7018
320	11·2628	2·2525	820	28·8608	5·7721
330	11·6147	2·3229	830	29·2128	5·8425
340	11·9667	2·3933	840	29·5647	5·9129
350	12·3186	2·4637	850	29·9167	5·9833
360	12·6706	2·5341	860	30·2686	6·0537
370	13·0226	2·6045	870	30·6206	6·1241
380	13·3745	2·6749	880	30·9726	6·1945
390	13·7265	2·7453	890	31·3245	6·2649
400	14·0784	2·8157	900	31·6765	6·3353
410	14·4304	2·8861	910	32·0285	6·4057
420	14·7824	2·9565	920	32·3804	6·4761
430	15·1343	3·0269	930	32·7324	6·5465
440	15·4863	3·0972	940	33·0843	6·6168
450	15·8382	3·1676	950	33·4363	6·6872
460	16·1902	3·2380	960	33·7883	6·7576
470	16·5422	3·3084	970	34·1402	6·8280
480	16·8941	3·3788	980	34·4922	6·8984
490	17·2461	3·4492	990	34·8441	6·9688
500	17·5981	3·5196	1 000	35·1961	7·0392

l	gal	pt	l	gal	pt	l	gal	pt
0·1		0·1760	6	1	2·5585	56	12	2·5463
0·2		0·3520	7	1	4·3183	57	12	4·3060
0·3		0·5279	8	1	6·0780	58	12	6·0658
0·4		0·7039	9	1	7·8378	59	12	7·8255
0·5		0·8799	10	2	1·5975	60	13	1·5853
0·6		1·0559	11	2	3·3573	61	13	3·3450
0·7		1·2318	12	2	5·1171	62	13	5·1048
0·8		1·4078	13	2	6·8768	63	13	6·8645
0·9		1·5838	14	3	0·6366	64	14	0·6243
1·0		1·7598	15	3	2·3963	65	14	2·3841
1·1		1·9357	16	3	4·1561	66	14	4·1438
1·2		2·1117	17	3	5·9158	67	14	5·9036
1·3		2·2877	18	3	7·6756	68	14	7·6633
1·4		2·4637	19	4	1·4353	69	15	1·4231
1·5		2·6396	20	4	3·1951	70	15	3·1828
1·6		2·8156	21	4	4·9548	71	15	4·9426
1·7		2·9916	22	4	6·7146	72	15	6·7023
1·8		3·1676	23	5	0·4744	73	16	0·4621
1·9		3·3435	24	5	2·2341	74	16	2·2218
2·0		3·5195	25	5	3·9939	75	16	3·9816
2·1		3·6955	26	5	5·7536	76	16	5·7414
2·2		3·8715	27	5	7·5134	77	16	7·5011
2·3		4·0474	28	6	1·2731	78	17	1·2609
2·4		4·2234	29	6	3·0329	79	17	3·0206
2·5		4·3994	30	6	4·7926	80	17	4·7804
2·6		4·5754	31	6	6·5524	81	17	6·5401
2·7		4·7513	32	7	0·3122	82	18	0·2999
2·8		4·9273	33	7	2·0719	83	18	2·0596
2·9		5·1033	34	7	3·8317	84	18	3·8194
3·0		5·2793	35	7	5·5914	85	18	5·5791
3·1		5·4552	36	7	7·3512	86	18	7·3389
3·2		5·6312	37	8	1·1109	87	19	1·0987
3·3		5·8072	38	8	2·8707	88	19	2·8584
3·4		5·9832	39	8	4·6304	89	19	4·6182
3·5		6·1591	40	8	6·3902	90	19	6·3779
3·6		6·3351	41	9	0·1499	91	20	0·1377
3·7		6·5111	42	9	1·9097	92	20	1·8974
3·8		6·6871	43	9	3·6695	93	20	3·6572
3·9		6·8630	44	9	5·4292	94	20	5·4169
4·0		7·0390	45	9	7·1890	95	20	7·1767
4·1		7·2150	46	10	0·9487	96	21	0·9365
4·2		7·3910	47	10	2·7085	97	21	2·6962
4·3		7·5669	48	10	4·4682	98	21	4·4560
4·4		7·7429	49	10	6·2280	99	21	6·2157
4·5		7·9189	50	10	7·9877	100	21	7·9755
4·6	1	0·0949	51	11	1·7475	200	43	7·9509
4·7	1	0·2708	52	11	3·5072	300	65	7·9264
4·8	1	0·4468	53	11	5·2670	400	87	7·9019
4·9	1	0·6228	54	11	7·0268	500	109	7·8774
5·0	1	0·7988	55	12	0·7865	1000	219	7·7547

l	gal	l	gal	l	gal	l	gal
1	0·220 0	51	11·218 4	101	22·216 9	151	33·215 4
2	0·439 9	52	11·438 4	102	22·436 9	152	33·435 3
3	0·659 9	53	11·658 4	103	22·656 8	153	33·655 3
4	0·879 9	54	11·878 3	104	22·876 8	154	33·875 3
5	1·099 8	55	12·098 3	105	23·096 8	155	34·095 2
6	1·319 8	56	12·318 3	106	23·316 7	156	34·315 2
7	1·539 8	57	12·538 3	107	23·536 7	157	34·535 2
8	1·759 8	58	12·758 2	108	23·756 7	158	34·755 1
9	1·979 7	59	12·978 2	109	23·976 7	159	34·975 1
10	2·199 7	60	13·198 2	110	24·196 6	160	35·195 1
11	2·419 7	61	13·418 1	111	24·416 6	161	35·415 1
12	2·639 6	62	13·638 1	112	24·636 6	162	35·635 0
13	2·859 6	63	13·858 1	113	24·856 5	163	35·855 0
14	3·079 6	64	14·078 0	114	25·076 5	164	36·075 0
15	3·299 5	65	14·298 0	115	25·296 5	165	36·294 9
16	3·519 5	66	14·518 0	116	25·516 4	166	36·514 9
17	3·739 5	67	14·737 9	117	25·736 4	167	36·734 9
18	3·959 4	68	14·957 9	118	25·956 4	168	36·954 8
19	4·179 4	69	15·177 9	119	26·176 3	169	37·174 8
20	4·399 4	70	15·397 9	120	26·396 3	170	37·394 8
21	4·619 4	71	15·617 8	121	26·616 3	171	37·614 8
22	4·839 3	72	15·837 8	122	26·836 3	172	37·834 7
23	5·059 3	73	16·057 8	123	27·056 2	173	38·054 7
24	5·279 3	74	16·277 7	124	27·276 2	174	38·274 7
25	5·499 2	75	16·497 7	125	27·496 2	175	38·494 6
26	5·719 2	76	16·717 7	126	27·716 1	176	38·714 6
27	5·939 2	77	16·937 6	127	27·936 1	177	38·934 6
28	6·159 1	78	17·157 6	128	28·156 1	178	39·154 5
29	6·379 1	79	17·377 6	129	28·376 0	179	39·374 5
30	6·599 1	80	17·597 5	130	28·596 0	180	39·594 5
31	6·819 0	81	17·817 5	131	28·816 0	181	39·814 4
32	7·039 0	82	18·037 5	132	29·035 9	182	40·034 4
33	7·259 0	83	18·257 5	133	29·255 9	183	40·254 4
34	7·479 0	84	18·477 4	134	29·475 9	184	40·474 4
35	7·698 9	85	18·697 4	135	29·695 9	185	40·694 3
36	7·918 9	86	18·917 4	136	29·915 8	186	40·914 3
37	8·138 9	87	19·137 3	137	30·135 8	187	41·134 3
38	8·358 8	88	19·357 3	138	30·355 8	188	41·354 2
39	8·578 8	89	19·577 3	139	30·575 7	189	41·574 2
40	8·798 8	90	19·797 2	140	30·795 7	190	41·794 2
41	9·018 7	91	20·017 2	141	31·015 7	191	42·014 1
42	9·238 7	92	20·237 2	142	31·235 6	192	42·234 1
43	9·458 7	93	20·457 1	143	31·455 6	193	42·454 1
44	9·678 6	94	20·677 1	144	31·675 6	194	42·674 0
45	9·898 6	95	20·897 1	145	31·895 5	195	42·894 0
46	10·118 6	96	21·117 1	146	32·115 5	196	43·114 0
47	10·338 6	97	21·337 0	147	32·335 5	197	43·334 0
48	10·558 5	98	21·557 0	148	32·555 5	198	43·553 9
49	10·778 5	99	21·777 0	149	32·775 4	199	43·773 9
50	10·998 5	100	21·996 9	150	32·995 4	200	43·993 9

l	gal	l	gal	l	gal	l	gal
201	44·213 8	251	55·212 3	301	66·210 8	351	77·209 2
202	44·433 8	252	55·432 3	302	66·430 7	352	77·429 2
203	44·653 8	253	55·652 2	303	66·650 7	353	77·649 2
204	44·873 7	254	55·872 2	304	66·870 7	354	77·869 1
205	45·093 7	255	56·092 2	305	67·090 6	355	78·089 1
206	45·313 7	256	56·312 1	306	67·310 6	356	78·309 1
207	45·533 6	257	56·532 1	307	67·530 6	357	78·529 0
208	45·753 6	258	56·752 1	308	67·750 5	358	78·749 0
209	45·973 6	259	56·972 0	309	67·970 5	359	78·969 0
210	46·193 6	260	57·192 0	310	68·190 5	360	79·188 9
211	46·413 5	261	57·412 0	311	68·410 5	361	79·408 9
212	46·633 5	262	57·632 0	312	68·630 4	362	79·628 9
213	46·853 5	263	57·851 9	313	68·850 4	363	79·848 9
214	47·073 4	264	58·071 9	314	69·070 4	364	80·068 8
215	47·293 4	265	58·291 9	315	69·290 3	365	80·288 8
216	47·513 4	266	58·511 8	316	69·510 3	366	80·508 8
217	47·733 3	267	58·731 8	317	69·730 3	367	80·728 7
218	47·953 3	268	58·951 8	318	69·950 2	368	80·948 7
219	48·173 3	269	59·171 7	319	70·170 2	369	81·168 7
220	48·393 2	270	59·391 7	320	70·390 2	370	81·388 6
221	48·613 2	271	59·611 7	321	70·610 1	371	81·608 6
222	48·833 2	272	59·831 6	322	70·830 1	372	81·828 6
223	49·053 2	273	60·051 6	323	71·050 1	373	82·048 5
224	49·273 1	274	60·271 6	324	71·270 1	374	82·268 5
225	49·493 1	275	60·491 6	325	71·490 0	375	82·488 5
226	49·713 1	276	60·711 5	326	71·710 0	376	82·708 5
227	49·933 0	277	60·931 5	327	71·930 0	377	82·928 4
228	50·153 0	278	61·151 5	328	72·149 9	378	83·148 4
229	50·373 0	279	61·371 4	329	72·369 9	379	83·368 4
230	50·592 9	280	61·591 4	330	72·589 9	380	83·588 3
231	50·812 9	281	61·811 4	331	72·809 8	381	83·808 3
232	51·032 9	282	62·031 3	332	73·029 8	382	84·028 3
233	51·252 8	283	62·251 3	333	73·249 8	383	84·248 2
234	51·472 8	284	62·471 3	334	73·469 7	384	84·468 2
235	51·692 8	285	62·691 3	335	73·689 7	385	84·688 2
236	51·912 8	286	62·911 2	336	73·909 7	386	84·908 1
237	52·132 7	287	63·131 2	337	74·129 7	387	85·128 1
238	52·352 7	288	63·351 2	338	74·349 6	388	85·348 1
239	52·572 7	289	63·571 1	339	74·569 6	389	85·568 1
240	52·792 6	290	63·791 1	340	74·789 6	390	85·788 0
241	53·012 6	291	64·011 1	341	75·009 5	391	86·008 0
242	53·232 6	292	64·231 0	342	75·229 5	392	86·228 0
243	53·452 5	293	64·451 0	343	75·449 5	393	86·447 9
244	53·672 5	294	64·671 0	344	75·669 4	394	86·667 9
245	53·892 5	295	64·890 9	345	75·889 4	395	86·887 9
246	54·112 4	296	65·110 9	346	76·109 4	396	87·107 8
247	54·332 4	297	65·330 9	347	76·329 3	397	87·327 8
248	54·552 4	298	65·550 9	348	76·549 3	398	87·547 8
249	54·772 4	299	65·770 8	349	76·769 3	399	87·767 8
250	54·992 3	300	65·990 8	350	76·989 3	400	87·987 7

l	gal	l	gal	l	gal	l	gal
401	88·2077	451	99·206	501	110·205	551	121·203
402	88·4277	452	99·426	502	110·425	552	121·423
403	88·6476	453	99·646	503	110·645	553	121·643
404	88·8676	454	99·866	504	110·865	554	121·863
405	89·0876	455	100·086	505	111·084	555	122·083
406	89·3075	456	100·306	506	111·304	556	122·303
407	89·5275	457	100·526	507	111·524	557	122·523
408	89·7475	458	100·746	508	111·744	558	122·743
409	89·9674	459	100·966	509	111·964	559	122·963
410	90·1874	460	101·186	510	112·184	560	123·183
411	90·4074	461	101·406	511	112·404	561	123·403
412	90·6274	462	101·626	512	112·624	562	123·623
413	90·8473	463	101·846	513	112·844	563	123·843
414	91·0673	464	102·066	514	113·064	564	124·063
415	91·2873	465	102·286	515	113·284	565	124·283
416	91·5072	466	102·506	516	113·504	566	124·503
417	91·7272	467	102·726	517	113·724	567	124·723
418	91·9472	468	102·946	518	113·944	568	124·943
419	92·1671	469	103·166	519	114·164	569	125·163
420	92·3871	470	103·386	520	114·384	570	125·383
421	92·6071	471	103·606	521	114·604	571	125·602
422	92·8270	472	103·826	522	114·824	572	125·822
423	93·0470	473	104·045	523	115·044	573	126·042
424	93·2670	474	104·265	524	115·264	574	126·262
425	93·4870	475	104·485	525	115·484	575	126·482
426	93·7069	476	104·705	526	115·704	576	126·702
427	93·9269	477	104·925	527	115·924	577	126·922
428	94·1469	478	105·145	528	116·144	578	127·142
429	94·3668	479	105·365	529	116·364	579	127·362
430	94·5868	480	105·585	530	116·584	580	127·582
431	94·8068	481	105·805	531	116·804	581	127·802
432	95·0267	482	106·025	532	117·024	582	128·022
433	95·2467	483	106·245	533	117·244	583	128·242
434	95·4667	484	106·465	534	117·464	584	128·462
435	95·6866	485	106·685	535	117·684	585	128·682
436	95·9066	486	106·905	536	117·904	586	128·902
437	96·1266	487	107·125	537	118·124	587	129·122
438	96·3466	488	107·345	538	118·343	588	129·342
439	96·5665	489	107·565	539	118·563	589	129·562
440	96·7865	490	107·785	540	118·783	590	129·782
441	97·0065	491	108·005	541	119·003	591	130·002
442	97·2264	492	108·225	542	119·223	592	130·222
443	97·4464	493	108·445	543	119·443	593	130·442
444	97·6664	494	108·665	544	119·663	594	130·662
445	97·8863	495	108·885	545	119·883	595	130·882
446	98·1063	496	109·105	546	120·103	596	131·102
447	98·3263	497	109·325	547	120·323	597	131·322
448	98·5462	498	109·545	548	120·543	598	131·542
449	98·7662	499	109·765	549	120·763	599	131·762
450	98·9862	500	109·985	550	120·983	600	131·982

l	gal	l	gal	l	gal	l	gal
601	132·202	651	143·200	701	154·198	751	165·197
602	132·422	652	143·420	702	154·418	752	165·417
603	132·641	653	143·640	703	154·638	753	165·637
604	132·861	654	143·860	704	154·858	754	165·857
605	133·081	655	144·080	705	155·078	755	166·077
606	133·301	656	144·300	706	155·298	756	166·297
607	133·521	657	144·520	707	155·518	757	166·517
608	133·741	658	144·740	708	155·738	758	166·737
609	133·961	659	144·960	709	155·958	759	166·957
610	134·181	660	145·180	710	156·178	760	167·177
611	134·401	661	145·400	711	156·398	761	167·397
612	134·621	662	145·620	712	156·618	762	167·617
613	134·841	663	145·840	713	156·838	763	167·837
614	135·061	664	146·060	714	157·058	764	168·057
615	135·281	665	146·280	715	157·278	765	168·277
616	135·501	666	146·500	716	157·498	766	168·496
617	135·721	667	146·720	717	157·718	767	168·716
618	135·941	668	146·939	718	157·938	768	168·936
619	136·161	669	147·159	719	158·158	769	169·156
620	136·381	670	147·379	720	158·378	770	169·376
621	136·601	671	147·599	721	158·598	771	169·596
622	136·821	672	147·819	722	158·818	772	169·816
623	137·041	673	148·039	723	159·038	773	170·036
624	137·261	674	148·259	724	159·258	774	170·256
625	137·481	675	148·479	725	159·478	775	170·476
626	137·701	676	148·699	726	159·698	776	170·696
627	137·921	677	148·919	727	159·918	777	170·916
628	138·141	678	149·139	728	160·138	778	171·136
629	138·361	679	149·359	729	160·358	779	171·356
630	138·581	680	149·579	730	160·578	780	171·576
631	138·801	681	149·799	731	160·798	781	171·796
632	139·021	682	150·019	732	161·018	782	172·016
633	139·241	683	150·239	733	161·237	783	172·236
634	139·461	684	150·459	734	161·457	784	172·456
635	139·681	685	150·679	735	161·677	785	172·676
636	139·900	686	150·899	736	161·897	786	172·896
637	140·120	687	151·119	737	162·117	787	173·116
638	140·340	688	151·339	738	162·337	788	173·336
639	140·560	689	151·559	739	162·557	789	173·556
640	140·780	690	151·779	740	162·777	790	173·776
641	141·000	691	151·999	741	162·997	791	173·996
642	141·220	692	152·219	742	163·217	792	174·216
643	141·440	693	152·439	743	163·437	793	174·436
644	141·660	694	152·659	744	163·657	794	174·656
645	141·880	695	152·879	745	163·877	795	174·876
646	142·100	696	153·099	746	164·097	796	175·096
647	142·320	697	153·319	747	164·317	797	175·316
648	142·540	698	153·539	748	164·537	798	175·536
649	142·760	699	153·759	749	164·757	799	175·755
650	142·980	700	153·979	750	164·977	800	175·975

l	gal	l	gal	l	gal	l	gal
801	176·195	851	187·194	901	198·192	951	209·191
802	176·415	852	187·414	902	198·412	952	209·411
803	176·635	853	187·634	903	198·632	953	209·631
804	176·855	854	187·854	904	198·852	954	209·851
805	177·075	855	188·074	905	199·072	955	210·071
806	177·295	856	188·294	906	199·292	956	210·291
807	177·515	857	188·514	907	199·512	957	210·511
808	177·735	858	188·734	908	199·732	958	210·731
809	177·955	859	188·954	909	199·952	959	210·951
810	178·175	860	189·174	910	200·172	960	211·171
811	178·395	861	189·394	911	200·392	961	211·390
812	178·615	862	189·614	912	200·612	962	211·610
813	178·835	863	189·834	913	200·832	963	211·830
814	179·055	864	190·053	914	201·052	964	212·050
815	179·275	865	190·273	915	201·272	965	212·270
816	179·495	866	190·493	916	201·492	966	212·490
817	179·715	867	190·713	917	201·712	967	212·710
818	179·935	868	190·933	918	201·932	968	212·930
819	180·155	869	191·153	919	202·152	969	213·150
820	180·375	870	191·373	920	202·372	970	213·370
821	180·595	871	191·593	921	202·592	971	213·590
822	180·815	872	191·813	922	202·812	972	213·810
823	181·035	873	192·033	923	203·032	973	214·030
824	181·255	874	192·253	924	203·252	974	214·250
825	181·475	875	192·473	925	203·472	975	214·470
826	181·695	876	192·693	926	203·692	976	214·690
827	181·915	877	192·913	927	203·912	977	214·910
828	182·135	878	193·133	928	204·132	978	215·130
829	182·355	879	193·353	929	204·351	979	215·350
830	182·575	880	193·573	930	204·571	980	215·570
831	182·794	881	193·793	931	204·791	981	215·790
832	183·014	882	194·013	932	205·011	982	216·010
833	183·234	883	194·233	933	205·231	983	216·230
834	183·454	884	194·453	934	205·451	984	216·450
835	183·674	885	194·673	935	205·671	985	216·670
836	183·894	886	194·893	936	205·891	986	216·890
837	184·114	887	195·113	937	206·111	987	217·110
838	184·334	888	195·333	938	206·331	988	217·330
839	184·554	889	195·553	939	206·551	989	217·550
840	184·774	890	195·773	940	206·771	990	217·770
841	184·994	891	195·993	941	206·991	991	217·990
842	185·214	892	196·213	942	207·211	992	218·210
843	185·434	893	196·433	943	207·431	993	218·430
844	185·654	894	196·653	944	207·651	994	218·649
845	185·874	895	196·873	945	207·871	995	218·869
846	186·094	896	197·092	946	208·091	996	219·089
847	186·314	897	197·312	947	208·311	997	219·309
848	186·534	898	197·532	948	208·531	998	219·529
849	186·754	899	197·752	949	208·751	999	219·749
850	186·974	900	197·972	950	208·971	1 000	219·969

pt	l	pt	l	gal	l	gal	l
1	0·4732	51	24·1320	1	3·7854	51	193·0559
2	0·9464	52	24·6052	2	7·5708	52	196·8413
3	1·4195	53	25·0783	3	11·3562	53	200·6267
4	1·8927	54	25·5515	4	15·1416	54	204·4121
5	2·3659	55	26·0247	5	18·9271	55	208·1976
6	2·8391	56	26·4979	6	22·7125	56	211·9830
7	3·3122	57	26·9710	7	26·4979	57	215·7684
8	3·7854	58	27·4442	8	30·2833	58	219·5538
9	4·2586	59	27·9174	9	34·0687	59	223·3392
10	4·7318	60	28·3906	10	37·8541	60	227·1246
11	5·2049	61	28·8637	11	41·6395	61	230·9100
12	5·6781	62	29·3369	12	45·4249	62	234·6954
13	6·1513	63	29·8101	13	49·2103	63	238·4808
14	6·6245	64	30·2833	14	52·9957	64	242·2662
15	7·0976	65	30·7564	15	56·7812	65	246·0517
16	7·5708	66	31·2296	16	60·5666	66	249·8371
17	8·0440	67	31·7028	17	64·3520	67	253·6225
18	8·5172	68	32·1760	18	68·1374	68	257·4079
19	8·9903	69	32·6491	19	71·9228	69	261·1933
20	9·4635	70	33·1223	20	75·7082	70	264·9787
21	9·9367	71	33·5955	21	79·4936	71	268·7641
22	10·4099	72	34·0687	22	83·2790	72	272·5495
23	10·8830	73	34·5418	23	87·0644	73	276·3349
24	11·3562	74	35·0150	24	90·8498	74	280·1203
25	11·8294	75	35·4882	25	94·6353	75	283·9058
26	12·3026	76	35·9614	26	98·4207	76	287·6912
27	12·7758	77	36·4346	27	102·2061	77	291·4766
28	13·2489	78	36·9077	28	105·9915	78	295·2620
29	13·7221	79	37·3809	29	109·7769	79	299·0474
30	14·1953	80	37·8541	30	113·5623	80	302·8328
31	14·6685	81	38·3273	31	117·3477	81	306·6182
32	15·1416	82	38·8004	32	121·1331	82	310·4036
33	15·6148	83	39·2736	33	124·9185	83	314·1890
34	16·0880	84	39·7468	34	128·7039	84	317·9744
35	16·5612	85	40·2200	35	132·4894	85	321·7599
36	17·0343	86	40·6931	36	136·2748	86	325·5453
37	17·5075	87	41·1663	37	140·0602	87	329·3307
38	17·9807	88	41·6395	38	143·8456	88	333·1161
39	18·4539	89	42·1127	39	147·6310	89	336·9015
40	18·9270	90	42·5858	40	151·4164	90	340·6869
41	19·4002	91	43·0590	41	155·2018	91	344·4723
42	19·8734	92	43·5322	42	158·9872	92	348·2577
43	20·3466	93	44·0054	43	162·7726	93	352·0431
44	20·8197	94	44·4785	44	166·5580	94	355·8285
45	21·2929	95	44·9517	45	170·3435	95	359·6140
46	21·7661	96	45·4249	46	174·1289	96	363·3994
47	22·2393	97	45·8981	47	177·9143	97	367·1848
48	22·7124	98	46·3712	48	181·6997	98	370·9702
49	23·1856	99	46·8444	49	185·4851	99	374·7556
50	23·6588	100	47·3176	50	189·2705	100	378·5410

l	gal	pt	l	gal	pt	l	gal	pt
0·1		0·2113	6	1	4·6803	56	14	6·3492
0·2		0·4227	7	1	6·7936	57	15	0·4626
0·3		0·6340	8	2	0·9070	58	15	2·5760
0·4		0·8454	9	2	3·0204	59	15	4·6893
0·5		1·0567	10	2	5·1338	60	15	6·8027
0·6		1·2680	11	2	7·2472	61	16	0·9161
0·7		1·4794	12	3	1·3605	62	16	3·0295
0·8		1·6907	13	3	3·4739	63	16	5·1428
0·9		1·9020	14	3	5·5873	64	16	7·2562
1·0		2·1134	15	3	7·7007	65	17	1·3696
1·1		2·3247	16	4	1·8141	66	17	3·4830
1·2		2·5361	17	4	3·9274	67	17	5·5964
1·3		2·7474	18	4	6·0408	68	17	7·7097
1·4		2·9587	19	5	0·1542	69	18	1·8231
1·5		3·1701	20	5	2·2676	70	18	3·9365
1·6		3·3814	21	5	4·3809	71	18	6·0499
1·7		3·5927	22	5	6·4943	72	19	0·1633
1·8		3·8041	23	6	0·6077	73	19	2·2766
1·9		4·0154	24	6	2·7211	74	19	4·3900
2·0		4·2268	25	6	4·8345	75	19	6·5034
2·1		4·4381	26	6	6·9478	76	20	0·6168
2·2		4·6494	27	7	1·0612	77	20	2·7301
2·3		4·8608	28	7	3·1746	78	20	4·8435
2·4		5·0721	29	7	5·2880	79	20	6·9569
2·5		5·2834	30	7	7·4014	80	21	1·0703
2·6		5·4948	31	8	1·5147	81	21	3·1837
2·7		5·7061	32	8	3·6281	82	21	5·2970
2·8		5·9175	33	8	5·7415	83	21	7·4104
2·9		6·1288	34	8	7·8549	84	22	1·5238
3·0		6·3401	35	9	1·9682	85	22	3·6372
3·1		6·5515	36	9	4·0816	86	22	5·7506
3·2		6·7628	37	9	6·1950	87	22	7·8639
3·3		6·9741	38	10	0·3084	88	23	1·9773
3·4		7·1855	39	10	2·4218	89	23	4·0907
3·5		7·3968	40	10	4·5351	90	23	6·2041
3·6		7·6082	41	10	6·6485	91	24	0·3174
3·7		7·8195	42	11	0·7619	92	24	2·4308
3·8	1	0·0308	43	11	2·8753	93	24	4·5442
3·9	1	0·2422	44	11	4·9887	94	24	6·6576
4·0	1	0·4535	45	11	7·1020	95	25	0·7710
4·1	1	0·6649	46	12	1·2154	96	25	2·8843
4·2	1	0·8762	47	12	3·3288	97	25	4·9977
4·3	1	1·0875	48	12	5·4422	98	25	7·1111
4·4	1	1·2989	49	12	7·5555	99	26	1·2245
4·5	1	1·5102	50	13	1·6689	100	26	3·3379
4·6	1	1·7215	51	13	3·7823	200	52	6·6757
4·7	1	1·9329	52	13	5·8957	300	79	2·0136
4·8	1	2·1442	53	14	0·0091	400	105	5·3514
4·9	1	2·3556	54	14	2·1224	500	132	0·6893
5·0	1	2·5669	55	14	4·2358	1 000	264	1·3785

Weight

The gramme was originally defined as the mass of one cubic centimetre of water at 0°C. The **kilogramme** is now defined in terms of an international prototype which is kept in France.

One special unit used is the tonne.

$$1 \text{ tonne (t)} = 1\ 000 \text{ kilogrammes}$$

The metric carat which is equal to 0·2 g is used for commercial transactions in diamonds, fine pearls and precious stones.

Imperial to SI

1 ounce (oz)			=28·349 5 g
1 pound (lb)	=	16 oz	=453·592 g
1 stone	=	14 lb	=6·350 29 kg
1 quarter	=	$\begin{cases} 28 \text{ lb} \\ 2 \text{ stones} \end{cases}$	=12·700 6 kg
1 hundredweight (cwt)	=	$\begin{cases} 112 \text{ lb} \\ 8 \text{ stones} \\ 4 \text{ quarters} \end{cases}$	=50·802 3 kg
1 ton	=	$\begin{cases} 2\ 240 \text{ lb} \\ 20 \text{ cwt} \end{cases}$	=1·016 05 t

SI to Imperial

1 gramme (g)	=0·035 274 0 oz
1 kilogramme (kg)	=2·204 62 lb
1 tonne (t)	=0·984 207 ton

US Units

1 US cwt (1 cental)	=	100 lb	=45·359 2 kg
1 US ton (1 short ton)	=	$\begin{cases} 2\ 000 \text{ lb} \\ 20 \text{ US cwt} \end{cases}$	=0·907 185 t

oz	g	oz	g	oz	g	oz	g
$\frac{1}{4}$	7·0874	$12\frac{1}{4}$	347·2817	$24\frac{1}{4}$	687·476	$36\frac{1}{4}$	1 027·670
$\frac{1}{2}$	14·1748	$12\frac{1}{2}$	354·3690	$24\frac{1}{2}$	694·563	$36\frac{1}{2}$	1 034·758
$\frac{3}{4}$	21·2621	$12\frac{3}{4}$	361·4564	$24\frac{3}{4}$	701·651	$36\frac{3}{4}$	1 041·845
1	28·3495	13	368·5438	25	708·738	37	1 048·932
$1\frac{1}{4}$	35·4369	$13\frac{1}{4}$	375·6312	$25\frac{1}{4}$	715·825	$37\frac{1}{4}$	1 056·020
$1\frac{1}{2}$	42·5243	$13\frac{1}{2}$	382·7186	$25\frac{1}{2}$	722·913	$37\frac{1}{2}$	1 063·107
$1\frac{3}{4}$	49·6117	$13\frac{3}{4}$	389·8059	$25\frac{3}{4}$	730·000	$37\frac{3}{4}$	1 070·194
2	56·6990	14	396·8933	26	737·088	38	1 077·282
$2\frac{1}{4}$	63·7864	$14\frac{1}{4}$	403·9807	$26\frac{1}{4}$	744·175	$38\frac{1}{4}$	1 084·369
$2\frac{1}{2}$	70·8738	$14\frac{1}{2}$	411·0681	$26\frac{1}{2}$	751·262	$38\frac{1}{2}$	1 091·457
$2\frac{3}{4}$	77·9612	$14\frac{3}{4}$	418·1555	$26\frac{3}{4}$	758·350	$38\frac{3}{4}$	1 098·544
3	85·0486	15	425·2428	27	765·437	39	1 105·631
$3\frac{1}{4}$	92·1360	$15\frac{1}{4}$	432·3302	$27\frac{1}{4}$	772·525	$39\frac{1}{4}$	1 112·719
$3\frac{1}{2}$	99·2233	$15\frac{1}{2}$	439·4176	$27\frac{1}{2}$	779·612	$39\frac{1}{2}$	1 119·806
$3\frac{3}{4}$	106·3107	$15\frac{3}{4}$	446·5050	$27\frac{3}{4}$	786·699	$39\frac{3}{4}$	1 126·894
4	113·3981	16	453·5924	28	793·787	40	1 133·981
$4\frac{1}{4}$	120·4855	$16\frac{1}{4}$	460·6798	$28\frac{1}{4}$	800·874	$40\frac{1}{4}$	1 141·068
$4\frac{1}{2}$	127·5729	$16\frac{1}{2}$	467·7671	$28\frac{1}{2}$	807·961	$40\frac{1}{2}$	1 148·156
$4\frac{3}{4}$	134·6602	$16\frac{3}{4}$	474·8545	$28\frac{3}{4}$	815·049	$40\frac{3}{4}$	1 155·243
5	141·7476	17	481·9419	29	822·136	41	1 162·330
$5\frac{1}{4}$	148·8350	$17\frac{1}{4}$	489·0293	$29\frac{1}{4}$	829·224	$41\frac{1}{4}$	1 169·418
$5\frac{1}{2}$	155·9224	$17\frac{1}{2}$	496·1167	$29\frac{1}{2}$	836·311	$41\frac{1}{2}$	1 176·505
$5\frac{3}{4}$	163·0098	$17\frac{3}{4}$	503·2040	$29\frac{3}{4}$	843·398	$41\frac{3}{4}$	1 183·593
6	170·0971	18	510·2914	30	850·486	42	1 190·680
$6\frac{1}{4}$	177·1845	$18\frac{1}{4}$	517·3788	$30\frac{1}{4}$	857·573	$42\frac{1}{4}$	1 197·767
$6\frac{1}{2}$	184·2719	$18\frac{1}{2}$	524·4662	$30\frac{1}{2}$	864·660	$42\frac{1}{2}$	1 204·855
$6\frac{3}{4}$	191·3593	$18\frac{3}{4}$	531·5536	$30\frac{3}{4}$	871·748	$42\frac{3}{4}$	1 211·942
7	198·4467	19	538·6409	31	878·835	43	1 219·029
$7\frac{1}{4}$	205·5340	$19\frac{1}{4}$	545·7283	$31\frac{1}{4}$	885·923	$43\frac{1}{4}$	1 226·117
$7\frac{1}{2}$	212·6214	$19\frac{1}{2}$	552·8157	$31\frac{1}{2}$	893·010	$43\frac{1}{2}$	1 233·204
$7\frac{3}{4}$	219·7088	$19\frac{3}{4}$	559·9031	$31\frac{3}{4}$	900·097	$43\frac{3}{4}$	1 240·292
8	226·7962	20	566·9905	32	907·185	44	1 247·379
$8\frac{1}{4}$	233·8836	$20\frac{1}{4}$	574·0778	$32\frac{1}{4}$	914·272	$44\frac{1}{4}$	1 254·466
$8\frac{1}{2}$	240·9709	$20\frac{1}{2}$	581·1652	$32\frac{1}{2}$	921·360	$44\frac{1}{2}$	1 261·554
$8\frac{3}{4}$	248·0583	$20\frac{3}{4}$	588·2526	$32\frac{3}{4}$	928·447	$44\frac{3}{4}$	1 268·641
9	255·1457	21	595·3400	33	935·534	45	1 275·729
$9\frac{1}{4}$	262·2331	$21\frac{1}{4}$	602·4274	$33\frac{1}{4}$	942·622	$45\frac{1}{4}$	1 282·816
$9\frac{1}{2}$	269·3205	$21\frac{1}{2}$	609·5147	$33\frac{1}{2}$	949·709	$45\frac{1}{2}$	1 289·903
$9\frac{3}{4}$	276·4079	$21\frac{3}{4}$	616·6021	$33\frac{3}{4}$	956·796	$45\frac{3}{4}$	1 296·991
10	283·4952	22	623·6895	34	963·884	46	1 304·078
$10\frac{1}{4}$	290·5826	$22\frac{1}{4}$	630·7769	$34\frac{1}{4}$	970·971	$46\frac{1}{4}$	1 311·165
$10\frac{1}{2}$	297·6700	$22\frac{1}{2}$	637·8643	$34\frac{1}{2}$	978·059	$46\frac{1}{2}$	1 318·253
$10\frac{3}{4}$	304·7574	$22\frac{3}{4}$	644·9517	$34\frac{3}{4}$	985·146	$46\frac{3}{4}$	1 325·340
11	311·8448	23	652·0390	35	992·233	47	1 332·428
$11\frac{1}{4}$	318·9321	$23\frac{1}{4}$	659·1264	$35\frac{1}{4}$	999·321	$47\frac{1}{4}$	1 339·515
$11\frac{1}{2}$	326·0195	$23\frac{1}{2}$	666·2138	$35\frac{1}{2}$	1 006·408	$47\frac{1}{2}$	1 346·602
$11\frac{3}{4}$	333·1069	$23\frac{3}{4}$	673·3012	$35\frac{3}{4}$	1 013·495	$47\frac{3}{4}$	1 353·690
12	340·1943	24	680·3886	36	1 020·583	48	1 360·777

lb	oz	kg	lb	oz	kg	lb	oz	kg
	1	0·0283	3	1	1·3891	6	1	2·7499
	2	0·0567	3	2	1·4175	6	2	2·7783
	3	0·0850	3	3	1·4458	6	3	2·8066
	4	0·1134	3	4	1·4742	6	4	2·8350
	5	0·1417	3	5	1·5025	6	5	2·8633
	6	0·1701	3	6	1·5309	6	6	2·8916
	7	0·1984	3	7	1·5592	6	7	2·9200
	8	0·2268	3	8	1·5876	6	8	2·9483
	9	0·2551	3	9	1·6159	6	9	2·9767
	10	0·2835	3	10	1·6443	6	10	3·0050
	11	0·3118	3	11	1·6726	6	11	3·0334
	12	0·3402	3	12	1·7010	6	12	3·0617
	13	0·3685	3	13	1·7293	6	13	3·0901
	14	0·3969	3	14	1·7577	6	14	3·1184
	15	0·4252	3	15	1·7860	6	15	3·1468
1	0	0·4536	4	0	1·8144	7	0	3·1751
1	1	0·4819	4	1	1·8427	7	1	3·2035
1	2	0·5103	4	2	1·8711	7	2	3·2318
1	3	0·5386	4	3	1·8994	7	3	3·2602
1	4	0·5670	4	4	1·9278	7	4	3·2885
1	5	0·5953	4	5	1·9561	7	5	3·3169
1	6	0·6237	4	6	1·9845	7	6	3·3452
1	7	0·6520	4	7	2·0128	7	7	3·3736
1	8	0·6804	4	8	2·0412	7	8	3·4019
1	9	0·7087	4	9	2·0695	7	9	3·4303
1	10	0·7371	4	10	2·0979	7	10	3·4586
1	11	0·7654	4	11	2·1262	7	11	3·4870
1	12	0·7938	4	12	2·1546	7	12	3·5153
1	13	0·8221	4	13	2·1829	7	13	3·5437
1	14	0·8505	4	14	2·2113	7	14	3·5720
1	15	0·8788	4	15	2·2396	7	15	3·6004
2	0	0·9072	5	0	2·2680	8	0	3·6287
2	1	0·9355	5	1	2·2963	8	1	3·6571
2	2	0·9639	5	2	2·3247	8	2	3·6854
2	3	0·9922	5	3	2·3530	8	3	3·7138
2	4	1·0206	5	4	2·3814	8	4	3·7421
2	5	1·0489	5	5	2·4097	8	5	3·7705
2	6	1·0773	5	6	2·4381	8	6	3·7988
2	7	1·1056	5	7	2·4664	8	7	3·8272
2	8	1·1340	5	8	2·4948	8	8	3·8555
2	9	1·1623	5	9	2·5231	8	9	3·8839
2	10	1·1907	5	10	2·5515	8	10	3·9122
2	11	1·2190	5	11	2·5798	8	11	3·9406
2	12	1·2474	5	12	2·6082	8	12	3·9689
2	13	1·2757	5	13	2·6365	8	13	3·9973
2	14	1·3041	5	14	2·6649	8	14	4·0256
2	15	1·3324	5	15	2·6932	8	15	4·0540
3	0	1·3608	6	0	2·7216	9	0	4·0823

lb	oz	kg	lb	oz	kg	lb	kg	lb	kg
9	1	4·1107	12	1	5·4715	31	14·0614	81	36·7410
9	2	4·1390	12	2	5·4998	32	14·5150	82	37·1946
9	3	4·1674	12	3	5·5282	33	14·9685	83	37·6482
9	4	4·1957	12	4	5·5565	34	15·4221	84	38·1018
						35	15·8757	85	38·5554
9	5	4·2241	12	5	5·5849				
9	6	4·2524	12	6	5·6132	36	16·3293	86	39·0089
9	7	4·2808	12	7	5·6416	37	16·7829	87	39·4625
9	8	4·3091	12	8	5·6699	38	17·2365	88	39·9161
						39	17·6901	89	40·3697
9	9	4·3375	12	9	5·6982	40	18·1437	90	40·8233
9	10	4·3658	12	10	5·7266				
9	11	4·3942	12	11	5·7549	41	18·5973	91	41·2769
9	12	4·4225	12	12	5·7833	42	19·0509	92	41·7305
						43	19·5045	93	42·1841
9	13	4·4509	12	13	5·8116	44	19·9581	94	42·6377
9	14	4·4792	12	14	5·8400	45	20·4117	95	43·0913
9	15	4·5076	12	15	5·8683				
10	0	4·5359	13	0	5·8967	46	20·8653	96	43·5449
						47	21·3188	97	43·9985
10	1	4·5643	13	1	5·9250	48	21·7724	98	44·4521
10	2	4·5926	13	2	5·9534	49	22·2260	99	44·9056
10	3	4·6210	13	3	5·9817	50	22·6796	100	45·3592
10	4	4·6493	13	4	6·0101				
						51	23·1332	101	45·8128
10	5	4·6777	13	5	6·0384	52	23·5868	102	46·2664
10	6	4·7060	13	6	6·0668	53	24·0404	103	46·7200
10	7	4·7344	13	7	6·0951	54	24·4940	104	47·1736
10	8	4·7627	13	8	6·1235	55	24·9476	105	47·6272
10	9	4·7911	13	9	6·1518	56	25·4012	106	48·0808
10	10	4·8194	13	10	6·1802	57	25·8548	107	48·5344
10	11	4·8478	13	11	6·2085	58	26·3084	108	48·9880
10	12	4·8761	13	12	6·2369	59	26·7620	109	49·4416
						60	27·2155	110	49·8952
10	13	4·9045	13	13	6·2652				
10	14	4·9328	13	14	6·2936	61	27·6691	111	50·3488
10	15	4·9612	13	15	6·3219	62	28·1227	112	50·8023
11	0	4·9895	14	0	6·3503	63	28·5763	113	51·2559
						64	29·0299	114	51·7095
11	1	5·0179	15		6·8039	65	29·4835	115	52·1631
11	2	5·0462							
11	3	5·0746	16		7·2575	66	29·9371	116	52·6167
11	4	5·1029	17		7·7111	67	30·3907	117	53·0703
			18		8·1647	68	30·8443	118	53·5239
11	5	5·1313	19		8·6183	69	31·2979	119	53·9775
11	6	5·1596	20		9·0718	70	31·7515	120	54·4311
11	7	5·1880							
11	8	5·2163	21		9·5254	71	32·2051	121	54·8847
			22		9·9790	72	32·6587	122	55·3383
11	9	5·2447	23		10·4326	73	33·1122	123	55·7919
11	10	5·2730	24		10·8862	74	33·5658	124	56·2455
11	11	5·3014	25		11·3398	75	34·0194	125	56·6991
11	12	5·3297							
			26		11·7934	76	34·4730	126	57·1526
11	13	5·3581	27		12·2470	77	34·9266	127	57·6062
11	14	5·3864	28		12·7006	78	35·3802	128	58·0598
11	15	5·4148	29		13·1542	79	35·8338	129	58·5134
12	0	5·4431	30		13·6078	80	36·2874	130	58·9670

lb	kg	lb	kg	lb	kg	lb	kg
131	59·420 6	181	82·100 2	231	104·780	560	254·012
132	59·874 2	182	82·553 8	232	105·233	570	258·548
133	60·327 8	183	83·007 4	233	105·687	580	263·084
134	60·781 4	184	83·461 0	234	106·141	590	267·620
135	61·235 0	185	83·914 6	235	106·594	600	272·155
136	61·688 6	186	84·368 2	236	107·048	610	276·691
137	62·142 2	187	84·821 8	237	107·501	620	281·227
138	62·595 8	188	85·275 4	238	107·955	630	285·763
139	63·049 3	189	85·729 0	239	108·409	640	290·299
140	63·502 9	190	86·182 6	240	108·862	650	294·835
141	63·956 5	191	86·636 1	241	109·316	660	299·371
142	64·410 1	192	87·089 7	242	109·769	670	303·907
143	64·863 7	193	87·543 3	243	110·223	680	308·443
144	65·317 3	194	87·999 9	244	110·677	690	312·979
145	65·770 9	195	88·450 5	245	111·130	700	317·515
146	66·224 5	196	88·904 1	246	111·584	710	322·051
147	66·678 1	197	89·357 7	247	112·037	720	326·587
148	67·131 7	198	89·811 3	248	112·491	730	331·122
149	67·585 3	199	90·264 9	249	112·945	740	335·658
150	68·038 9	200	90·718 5	250	113·398	750	340·194
151	68·492 5	201	91·172 1	260	117·934	760	344·730
152	68·946 0	202	91·625 7	270	122·470	770	349·266
153	69·399 6	203	92·079 3	280	127·006	780	353·802
154	69·853 2	204	92·532 8	290	131·542	790	358·338
155	70·306 8	205	92·986 4	300	136·078	800	362·874
156	70·760 4	206	93·440 0	310	140·614	810	367·410
157	71·214 0	207	93·893 6	320	145·150	820	371·946
158	71·667 6	208	94·347 2	330	149·685	830	376·482
159	72·121 2	209	94·800 8	340	154·221	840	381·018
160	72·574 8	210	95·254 4	350	158·757	850	385·554
161	73·028 4	211	95·708 0	360	163·293	860	390·089
162	73·482 0	212	96·161 6	370	167·829	870	394·625
163	73·935 6	213	96·615 2	380	172·365	880	399·161
164	74·389 2	214	97·068 8	390	176·901	890	403·697
165	74·842 7	215	97·522 4	400	181·437	900	408·233
166	75·296 3	216	97·976 0	410	185·973	910	412·769
167	75·749 9	217	98·429 6	420	190·509	920	417·305
168	76·203 5	218	98·883 1	430	195·045	930	421·841
169	76·657 1	219	99·336 7	440	199·581	940	426·377
170	77·110 7	220	99·790 3	450	204·117	950	430·913
171	77·564 3	221	100·243 9	460	208·653	960	435·449
172	78·017 9	222	100·697 5	470	213·188	970	439·985
173	78·471 5	223	101·151 1	480	217·724	980	444·521
174	78·925 1	224	101·604 7	490	222·260	990	449·056
175	79·378 7	225	102·058 3	500	226·796	1 000	453·592
176	79·832 3	226	102·511 9	510	231·332	2 000	907·185
177	80·285 9	227	102·965 5	520	235·868	3 000	1 360·777
178	80·739 4	228	103·419 1	530	240·404	4 000	1 814·370
179	81·193 0	229	103·872 7	540	244·940	5 000	2 267·962
180	81·646 6	230	104·326 3	550	249·476	10 000	4 535·924

stones	lb	kg	stones	lb	kg	stones	lb	kg
	1	0·453 6	3	8	22·679 6	7	1	44·905 6
	2	0·907 2	3	9	23·133 2	7	2	45·359 2
	3	1·360 8	3	10	23·586 8	7	3	45·812 8
	4	1·814 4	3	11	24·040 4	7	4	46·266 4
	5	2·268 0	3	12	24·494 0	7	5	46·720 0
	6	2·721 6	3	13	24·947 6	7	6	47·173 6
	7	3·175 1	4	0	25·401 2	7	7	47·627 2
	8	3·628 7	4	1	25·854 8	7	8	48·080 8
	9	4·082 3	4	2	26·308 4	7	9	48·534 4
	10	4·535 9	4	3	26·762 0	7	10	48·988 0
	11	4·989 5	4	4	27·215 5	7	11	49·441 6
	12	5·443 1	4	5	27·669 1	7	12	49·895 2
	13	5·896 7	4	6	28·122 7	7	13	50·348 8
1	0	6·350 3	4	7	28·576 3	8	0	50·802 3
1	1	6·803 9	4	8	29·029 9	8	1	51·255 9
1	2	7·257 5	4	9	29·483 5	8	2	51·709 5
1	3	7·711 1	4	10	29·937 1	8	3	52·163 1
1	4	8·164 7	4	11	30·390 7	8	4	52·616 7
1	5	8·618 3	4	12	30·844 3	8	5	53·070 3
1	6	9·071 8	4	13	31·297 9	8	6	53·523 9
1	7	9·525 4	5	0	31·751 5	8	7	53·977 5
1	8	9·979 0	5	1	32·205 1	8	8	54·431 1
1	9	10·432 6	5	2	32·658 7	8	9	54·884 7
1	10	10·886 2	5	3	33·112 2	8	10	55·338 3
1	11	11·339 8	5	4	33·565 8	8	11	55·791 9
1	12	11·793 4	5	5	34·019 4	8	12	56·245 5
1	13	12·247 0	5	6	34·473 0	8	13	56·699 1
2	0	12·700 6	5	7	34·926 6	9	0	57·152 6
2	1	13·154 2	5	8	35·380 2	9	1	57·606 2
2	2	13·607 8	5	9	35·833 8	9	2	58·059 8
2	3	14·061 4	5	10	36·287 4	9	3	58·513 4
2	4	14·515 0	5	11	36·741 0	9	4	58·967 0
2	5	14·968 5	5	12	37·194 6	9	5	59·420 6
2	6	15·422 1	5	13	37·648 2	9	6	59·874 2
2	7	15·875 7	6	0	38·101 8	9	7	60·327 8
2	8	16·329 3	6	1	38·555 4	9	8	60·781 4
2	9	16·782 9	6	2	39·008 9	9	9	61·235 0
2	10	17·236 5	6	3	39·462 5	9	10	61·688 6
2	11	17·690 1	6	4	39·916 1	9	11	62·142 2
2	12	18·143 7	6	5	40·369 7	9	12	62·595 8
2	13	18·597 3	6	6	40·823 3	9	13	63·049 3
3	0	19·050 9	6	7	41·276 9	10	0	63·502 9
3	1	19·504 5	6	8	41·730 5	10	1	63·956 5
3	2	19·958 1	6	9	42·184 1	10	2	64·410 1
3	3	20·411 7	6	10	42·637 7	10	3	64·863 7
3	4	20·865 3	6	11	43·091 3	10	4	65·317 3
3	5	21·318 8	6	12	43·544 9	10	5	65·770 9
3	6	21·772 4	6	13	43·998 5	10	6	66·224 5
3	7	22·226 0	7	0	44·452 1	10	7	66·678 1

stones	lb	kg	stones	lb	kg	stones	lb	kg
10	8	67·131 7	14	8	92·532 8	18	8	117·934
10	9	67·585 3	14	9	92·986 4	18	9	118·388
10	10	68·038 9	14	10	93·440 0	18	10	118·841
10	11	68·492 5	14	11	93·893 6	18	11	119·295
10	12	68·946 0	14	12	94·347 2	18	12	119·748
10	13	69·399 6	14	13	94·800 8	18	13	120·202
11	0	69·853 2	15	0	95·254 4	19	0	120·656
11	1	70·306 8	15	1	95·708 0			
11	2	70·760 4	15	2	96·161 6	19	1	121·109
11	3	71·214 0	15	3	96·615 2	19	2	121·563
11	4	71·667 6	15	4	97·068 8	19	3	122·016
11	5	72·121 2	15	5	97·522 4	19	4	122·470
11	6	72·574 8	15	6	97·976 0	19	5	122·924
11	7	73·028 4	15	7	98·429 6	19	6	123·377
						19	7	123·831
11	8	73·482 0	15	8	98·883 1			
11	9	73·935 6	15	9	99·336 7	19	8	124·284
11	10	74·389 2	15	10	99·790 3	19	9	124·738
11	11	74·842 7	15	11	100·243 9	19	10	125·192
11	12	75·296 3	15	12	100·697 5	19	11	125·645
11	13	75·749 9	15	13	101·151 1	19	12	126·099
12	0	76·203 5	16	0	101·604 7	19	13	126·552
12	1	76·657 1	16	1	102·058 3	20	0	127·006
12	2	77·110 7	16	2	102·511 9			
12	3	77·564 3	16	3	102·965 5	21		133·356
12	4	78·017 9	16	4	103·419 1	22		139·706
12	5	78·471 5	16	5	103·872 7	23		146·057
12	6	78·925 1	16	6	104·326 3	24		152·407
12	7	79·378 7	16	7	104·779 8	25		158·757
12	8	79·832 3	16	8	105·233 4	26		165·108
12	9	80·285 9	16	9	105·687 0	27		171·458
12	10	80·739 4	16	10	106·140 6	28		177·808
12	11	81·193 0	16	11	106·594 2	29		184·159
12	12	81·646 6	16	12	107·047 8	30		190·509
12	13	82·100 2	16	13	107·501 4			
13	0	82·553 8	17	0	107·955 0	31		196·859
13	1	83·007 4	17	1	108·408 6	32		203·209
13	2	83·461 0	17	2	108·862 2	33		209·560
13	3	83·914 6	17	3	109·315 8	34		215·910
13	4	84·368 2	17	4	109·769 4	35		222·260
13	5	84·821 8	17	5	110·223 0			
13	6	85·275 4	17	6	110·676 5	36		228·611
13	7	85·729 0	17	7	111·130 1	37		234·961
						38		241·311
13	8	86·182 6	17	8	111·583 7	39		247·661
13	9	86·636 1	17	9	112·037 3	40		254·012
13	10	87·089 7	17	10	112·490 9			
13	11	87·543 3	17	11	112·944 5	41		260·362
13	12	87·996 9	17	12	113·398 1	42		266·712
13	13	88·450 5	17	13	113·851 7	43		273·063
14	0	88·904 1	18	0	114·305 3	44		279·413
14	1	89·357 7	18	1	114·758 9	45		285·763
14	2	89·811 3	18	2	115·212 5			
14	3	90·264 9	18	3	115·666 1	46		292·114
14	4	90·718 5	18	4	116·119 7	47		298·464
14	5	91·172 1	18	5	116·573 2	48		304·814
14	6	91·625 7	18	6	117·026 8	49		311·164
14	7	92·079 3	18	7	117·480 4	50		317·515

tons	t	tons	t	tons	t	tons	t
½	0·5080	26	26·4172	76	77·2196	126	128·0219
1	1·0160	27	27·4333	77	78·2356	127	129·0380
1½	1·5241	28	28·4493	78	79·2517	128	130·0540
2	2·0321	29	29·4654	79	80·2677	129	131·0701
2½	2·5401	30	30·4814	80	81·2838	130	132·0861
3	3·0481						
3½	3·5562	31	31·4975	81	82·2998	131	133·1021
4	4·0642	32	32·5135	82	83·3158	132	134·1182
4½	4·5722	33	33·5295	83	84·3319	133	135·1342
5	5·0802	34	34·5456	84	85·3479	134	136·1503
		35	35·5616	85	86·3640	135	137·1663
5½	5·5883						
6	6·0963	36	36·5777	86	87·3800	136	138·1824
6½	6·6043	37	37·5937	87	88·3961	137	139·1984
7	7·1123	38	38·6098	88	89·4121	138	140·2145
7½	7·6204	39	39·6258	89	90·4282	139	141·2305
8	8·1284	40	40·6419	90	91·4442	140	142·2466
8½	8·6364						
9	9·1444	41	41·6579	91	92·4603	141	143·2626
9½	9·6524	42	42·6740	92	93·4763	142	144·2787
10	10·1605	43	43·6900	93	94·4924	143	145·2947
		44	44·7061	94	95·5084	144	146·3108
10½	10·6685	45	45·7221	95	96·5245	145	147·3268
11	11·1765						
11½	11·6845	46	46·7382	96	97·5405	146	148·3428
12	12·1926	47	47·7542	97	98·5565	147	149·3589
12½	12·7006	48	48·7703	98	99·5726	148	150·3749
13	13·2086	49	49·7863	99	100·5886	149	151·3910
13½	13·7166	50	50·8023	100	101·6047	150	152·4070
14	14·2247						
14½	14·7327	51	51·8184	101	102·6207	151	153·4231
15	15·2407	52	52·8344	102	103·6368	152	154·4391
		53	53·8505	103	104·6528	153	155·4552
15½	15·7487	54	54·8665	104	105·6689	154	156·4712
16	16·2568	55	55·8826	105	106·6849	155	157·4873
16½	16·7648						
17	17·2728	56	56·8986	106	107·7010	156	158·5033
17½	17·7808	57	57·9147	107	108·7170	157	159·5194
18	18·2888	58	58·9307	108	109·7331	158	160·5354
18½	18·7969	59	59·9468	109	110·7491	159	161·5515
19	19·3049	60	60·9628	110	111·7652	160	162·5675
19½	19·8129						
20	20·3209	61	61·9789	111	112·7812	161	163·5836
		62	62·9949	112	113·7973	162	164·5996
20½	20·8290	63	64·0110	113	114·8133	163	165·6156
21	21·3370	64	65·0270	114	115·8293	164	166·6317
21½	21·8450	65	66·0430	115	116·8454	165	167·6477
22	22·3530						
22½	22·8611	66	67·0591	116	117·8614	166	168·6638
23	23·3691	67	68·0751	117	118·8775	167	169·6798
23½	23·8771	68	69·0912	118	119·8935	168	170·6959
24	24·3851	69	70·1072	119	120·9096	169	171·7119
24½	24·8931	70	71·1233	120	121·9256	170	172·7280
25	25·4012						
		71	72·1393	121	122·9417	171	173·7440
		72	73·1554	122	123·9577	172	174·7601
		73	74·1714	123	124·9738	173	175·7761
		74	75·1875	124	125·9898	174	176·7922
		75	76·2035	125	127·0059	175	177·8082

tons	t	tons	t	tons	t	tons	t
176	178·824 3	330	335·295 5	580	589·307 2	830	843·318 9
177	179·840 3	335	340·375 7	585	594·387 4	835	848·399 2
178	180·856 3	340	345·455 9	590	599·467 7	840	853·479 4
179	181·872 4	345	350·536 2	595	604·547 9	845	858·559 6
180	182·888 4	350	355·616 4	600	609·628 1	850	863·639 9
181	183·904 5	355	360·696 6	605	614·708 4	855	868·720 1
182	184·920 5	360	365·776 9	610	619·788 6	860	873·800 3
183	185·936 6	365	370·857 1	615	624·868 8	865	878·880 6
184	186·952 6	370	375·937 4	620	629·949 1	870	883·960 8
185	187·968 7	375	381·017 6	625	635·029 3	875	889·041 0
186	188·984 7	380	386·097 8	630	640·109 5	880	894·121 3
187	190·000 8	385	391·178 1	635	645·189 8	885	899·201 5
188	191·016 8	390	396·258 3	640	650·270 0	890	904·281 7
189	192·032 9	395	401·338 5	645	655·350 3	895	909·362 0
190	193·048 9	400	406·418 8	650	660·430 5	900	914·442 2
191	194·065 0	405	411·499 0	655	665·510 7	905	919·522 4
192	195·081 0	410	416·579 2	660	670·591 0	910	924·602 7
193	196·097 1	415	421·659 5	665	675·671 2	915	929·682 9
194	197·113 1	420	426·739 7	670	680·751 4	920	934·763 1
195	198·129 1	425	431·819 9	675	685·831 7	925	939·843 4
196	199·145 2	430	436·900 2	680	690·911 9	930	944·923 6
197	200·161 2	435	441·980 4	685	695·992 1	935	950·003 9
198	201·177 3	440	447·060 6	690	701·072 4	940	955·084 1
199	202·193 3	445	452·140 9	695	706·152 6	945	960·164 3
200	203·209 4	450	457·221 1	700	711·232 8	950	965·244 6
205	208·289 6	455	462·301 3	705	716·313 1	955	970·324 8
210	213·369 8	460	467·381 6	710	721·393 3	960	975·405 0
215	218·450 1	465	472·461 8	715	726·473 5	965	980·485 3
220	223·530 3	470	477·542 0	720	731·553 8	970	985·565 5
225	228·610 6	475	482·622 3	725	736·634 0	975	990·645 7
230	233·690 8	480	487·702 5	730	741·714 2	980	995·726 0
235	238·771 0	485	492·782 7	735	746·794 5	985	1 000·806 2
240	243·851 3	490	497·863 0	740	751·874 7	990	1 005·886 4
245	248·931 5	495	502·943 2	745	756·954 9	995	1 010·966 7
250	254·011 7	500	508·023 5	750	762·035 2	1 000	1 016·046 9
255	259·092 0	505	513·103 7	755	767·115 4	2 000	2 032·093 8
260	264·172 2	510	518·183 9	760	772·195 6	3 000	3 048·140 7
265	269·252 4	515	523·264 2	765	777·275 9	4 000	4 064·187 6
270	274·332 7	520	528·344 4	770	782·356 1	5 000	5 080·234 5
275	279·412 9	525	533·424 6	775	787·436 3	6 000	6 096·281 4
						7 000	7 112·328 3
280	284·493 1	530	538·504 9	780	792·516 6	8 000	8 128·375 2
285	289·573 4	535	543·585 1	785	797·596 8	9 000	9 144·422 1
290	294·653 6	540	548·665 3	790	802·677 1		
295	299·733 8	545	553·745 6	795	807·757 3	10 000	10 160·469
300	304·814 1	550	558·825 8	800	812·837 5	15 000	15 240·704
						20 000	20 320·938
305	309·894 3	555	563·906 0	805	817·917 8	25 000	25 401·173
310	314·974 5	560	568·986 3	810	822·998 0	30 000	30 481·407
315	320·054 8	565	574·066 5	815	828·078 2	35 000	35 561·642
320	325·135 0	570	579·146 7	820	833·158 5	40 000	40 641·876
325	330·215 2	575	584·227 0	825	838·238 7	45 000	45 722·111
						50 000	50 802·345

g	oz	g	oz	g	oz	g	oz
1	0·035 3	51	1·799 0	110	3·880 1	610	21·517 1
2	0·070 5	52	1·834 2	120	4·232 9	620	21·869 9
3	0·105 8	53	1·869 5	130	4·585 6	630	22·222 6
4	0·141 1	54	1·904 8	140	4·938 4	640	22·575 4
5	0·176 4	55	1·940 1	150	5·291 1	650	22·928 1
6	0·211 6	56	1·975 3	160	5·643 8	660	23·280 8
7	0·246 9	57	2·010 6	170	5·996 6	670	23·633 6
8	0·282 2	58	2·045 9	180	6·349 3	680	23·986 3
9	0·317 5	59	2·081 2	190	6·702 1	690	24·339 1
10	0·352 7	60	2·116 4	200	7·054 8	700	24·691 8
11	0·388 0	61	2·151 7	210	7·407 5	710	25·044 5
12	0·423 3	62	2·187 0	220	7·760 3	720	25·397 3
13	0·458 6	63	2·222 3	230	8·113 0	730	25·750 0
14	0·493 8	64	2·257 5	240	8·465 8	740	26·102 8
15	0·529 1	65	2·292 8	250	8·818 5	750	26·455 5
16	0·564 4	66	2·328 1	260	9·171 2	760	26·808 2
17	0·599 7	67	2·363 4	270	9·524 0	770	27·161 0
18	0·634 9	68	2·398 6	280	9·876 7	780	27·513 7
19	0·670 2	69	2·433 9	290	10·229 5	790	27·866 5
20	0·705 5	70	2·469 2	300	10·582 2	800	28·219 2
21	0·740 8	71	2·504 5	310	10·934 9	810	28·571 9
22	0·776 0	72	2·539 7	320	11·287 7	820	28·924 7
23	0·811 3	73	2·575 0	330	11·640 4	830	29·277 4
24	0·846 6	74	2·610 3	340	11·993 2	840	29·630 2
25	0·881 9	75	2·645 6	350	12·345 9	850	29·982 9
26	0·917 1	76	2·680 8	360	12·698 6	860	30·335 6
27	0·952 4	77	2·716 1	370	13·051 4	870	30·688 4
28	0·987 7	78	2·751 4	380	13·404 1	880	31·041 1
29	1·022 9	79	2·786 6	390	13·756 9	890	31·393 9
30	1·058 2	80	2·821 9	400	14·109 6	900	31·746 6
31	1·093 5	81	2·857 2	410	14·462 3	910	32·099 3
32	1·128 8	82	2·892 5	420	14·815 1	920	32·452 1
33	1·164 0	83	2·927 7	430	15·167 8	930	32·804 8
34	1·199 3	84	2·963 0	440	15·520 6	940	33·157 6
35	1·234 6	85	2·998 3	450	15·873 3	950	33·510 3
36	1·269 9	86	3·033 6	460	16·226 0	960	33·863 0
37	1·305 1	87	3·068 8	470	16·578 8	970	34·215 8
38	1·340 4	88	3·104 1	480	16·931 5	980	34·568 5
39	1·375 7	89	3·139 4	490	17·284 3	990	34·921 3
40	1·411 0	90	3·174 7	500	17·637 0	1 000	35·274 0
41	1·446 2	91	3·209 9	510	17·989 7		
42	1·481 5	92	3·245 2	520	18·342 5		
43	1·516 8	93	3·280 5	530	18·695 2		
44	1·552 1	94	3·315 8	540	19·048 0		
45	1·587 3	95	3·351 0	550	19·400 7		
46	1·622 6	96	3·386 3	560	19·753 4		
47	1·657 9	97	3·421 6	570	20·106 2		
48	1·693 2	98	3·456 9	580	20·458 9		
49	1·728 4	99	3·492 1	590	20·811 7		
50	1·763 7	100	3·527 4	600	21·164 4		

kg	lb	kg	lb	kg	lb	kg	lb
1	2·2046	51	112·4358	101	222·6669	151	332·8980
2	4·4092	52	114·6404	102	224·8715	152	335·1026
3	6·6139	53	116·8450	103	227·0761	153	337·3073
4	8·8185	54	119·0496	104	229·2808	154	339·5119
5	11·0231	55	121·2542	105	231·4854	155	341·7165
6	13·2277	56	123·4589	106	233·6900	156	343·9211
7	15·4324	57	125·6635	107	235·8946	157	346·1257
8	17·6370	58	127·8681	108	238·0992	158	348·3304
9	19·8416	59	130·0727	109	240·3039	159	350·5350
10	22·0462	60	132·2774	110	242·5085	160	352·7396
11	24·2508	61	134·4820	111	244·7131	161	354·9442
12	26·4555	62	136·6866	112	246·9177	162	357·1489
13	28·6601	63	138·8912	113	249·1224	163	359·3535
14	30·8647	64	141·0958	114	251·3270	164	361·5581
15	33·0693	65	143·3005	115	253·5316	165	363·7627
16	35·2740	66	145·5051	116	255·7362	166	365·9674
17	37·4786	67	147·7097	117	257·9408	167	368·1720
18	39·6832	68	149·9143	118	260·1455	168	370·3766
19	41·8878	69	152·1190	119	262·3501	169	372·5812
20	44·0925	70	154·3236	120	264·5547	170	374·7858
21	46·2971	71	156·5282	121	266·7593	171	376·9905
22	48·5017	72	158·7328	122	268·9640	172	379·1951
23	50·7063	73	160·9374	123	271·1686	173	381·3997
24	52·9109	74	163·1421	124	273·3732	174	383·6043
25	55·1156	75	165·3467	125	275·5778	175	385·8090
26	57·3202	76	167·5513	126	277·7824	176	388·0136
27	59·5248	77	169·7559	127	279·9871	177	390·2182
28	61·7294	78	171·9606	128	282·1917	178	392·4228
29	63·9341	79	174·1652	129	284·3963	179	394·6274
30	66·1387	80	176·3698	130	286·6009	180	396·8321
31	68·3433	81	178·5744	131	288·8056	181	399·0367
32	70·5479	82	180·7791	132	291·0102	182	401·2413
33	72·7525	83	182·9837	133	293·2148	183	403·4459
34	74·9572	84	185·1883	134	295·4194	184	405·6506
35	77·1618	85	187·3929	135	297·6241	185	407·8552
36	79·3664	86	189·5975	136	299·8287	186	410·0598
37	81·5710	87	191·8022	137	302·0333	187	412·2644
38	83·7757	88	194·0068	138	304·2379	188	414·4690
39	85·9803	89	196·2114	139	306·4425	189	416·6737
40	88·1849	90	198·4160	140	308·6472	190	418·8783
41	90·3895	91	200·6207	141	310·8518	191	421·0829
42	92·5941	92	202·8253	142	313·0564	192	423·2875
43	94·7988	93	205·0299	143	315·2610	193	425·4922
44	97·0034	94	207·2345	144	317·4657	194	427·6968
45	99·2080	95	209·4391	145	319·6703	195	429·9014
46	101·4126	96	211·6438	146	321·8749	196	432·1060
47	103·6173	97	213·8484	147	324·0795	197	434·3107
48	105·8219	98	216·0530	148	326·2841	198	436·5153
49	108·0265	99	218·2576	149	328·4888	199	438·7199
50	110·2311	100	220·4623	150	330·6934	200	440·9245

kg	lb	kg	lb	kg	lb	kg	lb
201	443·129 1	251	553·360 3	301	663·591 4	351	773·822 5
202	445·333 8	252	555·564 9	302	665·796 0	352	776·027 2
203	447·538 4	253	557·769 5	303	668·000 6	353	778·231 8
204	449·743 0	254	559·974 1	304	670·205 3	354	780·436 4
205	451·947 6	255	562·178 8	305	672·409 9	355	782·641 0
206	454·152 3	256	564·383 4	306	674·614 5	356	784·845 6
207	456·356 9	257	566·588 0	307	676·819 1	357	787·050 3
208	458·561 5	258	568·792 6	308	679·023 8	358	789·254 9
209	460·766 1	259	570·997 3	309	681·228 4	359	791·459 5
210	462·970 7	260	573·201 9	310	683·433 0	360	793·664 1
211	465·175 4	261	575·406 5	311	685·637 6	361	795·868 8
212	467·380 0	262	577·611 1	312	687·842 3	362	798·073 4
213	469·584 6	263	579·815 7	313	690·046 9	363	800·278 0
214	471·789 2	264	582·020 4	314	692·251 5	364	802·482 6
215	473·993 9	265	584·225 0	315	694·456 1	365	804·687 2
216	476·198 5	266	586·429 6	316	696·660 7	366	806·891 9
217	478·403 1	267	588·634 2	317	698·865 4	367	809·096 5
218	480·607 7	268	590·838 9	318	701·070 0	368	811·301 1
219	482·812 3	269	593·043 5	319	703·274 6	369	813·505 7
220	485·017 0	270	595·248 1	320	705·479 2	370	815·710 4
221	487·221 6	271	597·452 7	321	707·683 9	371	817·915 0
222	489·426 2	272	599·657 3	322	709·888 5	372	820·119 6
223	491·630 8	273	601·862 0	323	712·093 1	373	822·324 2
224	493·835 5	274	604·066 6	324	714·297 7	374	824·528 9
225	496·040 1	275	606·271 2	325	716·502 3	375	826·733 5
226	498·244 7	276	608·475 8	326	718·707 0	376	828·938 1
227	500·449 3	277	610·680 5	327	720·911 6	377	831·142 7
228	502·654 0	278	612·885 1	328	723·116 2	378	833·347 3
229	504·858 6	279	615·089 7	329	725·320 8	379	835·552 0
230	507·063 2	280	617·294 3	330	727·525 5	380	837·756 6
231	509·267 8	281	619·499 0	331	729·730 1	381	839·961 2
232	511·472 4	282	621·703 6	332	731·934 7	382	842·165 8
233	513·677 1	283	623·908 2	333	734·139 3	383	844·370 5
234	515·881 7	284	626·112 8	334	736·343 9	384	846·575 1
235	518·086 3	285	628·317 4	335	738·548 6	385	848·779 7
236	520·290 9	286	630·522 1	336	740·753 2	386	850·984 3
237	522·495 6	287	632·726 7	337	742·957 8	387	853·188 9
238	524·700 2	288	634·931 3	338	745·162 4	388	855·393 6
239	526·904 8	289	637·135 9	339	747·367 1	389	857·598 2
240	529·109 4	290	639·340 6	340	749·571 7	390	859·802 8
241	531·314 0	291	641·545 2	341	751·776 3	391	862·007 4
242	533·518 7	292	643·749 8	342	753·980 9	392	864·212 1
243	535·723 3	293	645·954 4	343	756·185 6	393	866·416 7
244	537·927 9	294	648·159 0	344	758·390 2	394	868·621 3
245	540·132 5	295	650·363 7	345	760·594 8	395	870·825 9
246	542·337 2	296	652·568 3	346	762·799 4	396	873·030 5
247	544·541 8	297	654·772 9	347	765·004 0	397	875·235 2
248	546·746 4	298	656·977 5	348	767·208 7	398	877·439 8
249	548·951 0	299	659·182 2	349	769·413 3	399	879·644 4
250	551·155 7	300	661·386 8	350	771·617 9	400	881·849 0

kg	lb	kg	lb	kg	lb	kg	lb
401	884·054	451	994·285	501	1 104·516	551	1 214·747
402	886·258	452	996·489	502	1 106·721	552	1 216·952
403	888·463	453	998·694	503	1 108·925	553	1 219·156
404	890·668	454	1 000·899	504	1 111·130	554	1 221·361
405	892·872	455	1 003·103	505	1 113·334	555	1 223·566
406	895·077	456	1 005·308	506	1 115·539	556	1 225·770
407	897·281	457	1 007·513	507	1 117·744	557	1 227·975
408	899·486	458	1 009·717	508	1 119·948	558	1 230·179
409	901·691	459	1 011·922	509	1 122·153	559	1 232·384
410	903·895	460	1 014·126	510	1 124·358	560	1 234·589
411	906·100	461	1 016·331	511	1 126·562	561	1 236·793
412	908·305	462	1 018·536	512	1 128·767	562	1 238·998
413	910·509	463	1 020·740	513	1 130·971	563	1 241·203
414	912·714	464	1 022·945	514	1 133·176	564	1 243·407
415	914·918	465	1 025·150	515	1 135·381	565	1 245·612
416	917·123	466	1 027·354	516	1 137·585	566	1 247·816
417	919·328	467	1 029·559	517	1 139·790	567	1 250·021
418	921·532	468	1 031·763	518	1 141·995	568	1 252·226
419	923·737	469	1 033·968	519	1 144·199	569	1 254·430
420	925·941	470	1 036·173	520	1 146·404	570	1 256·635
421	928·146	471	1 038·377	521	1 148·608	571	1 258·840
422	930·351	472	1 040·582	522	1 150·813	572	1 261·044
423	932·555	473	1 042·786	523	1 153·018	573	1 263·249
424	934·760	474	1 044·991	524	1 155·222	574	1 265·453
425	936·965	475	1 047·196	525	1 157·427	575	1 267·658
426	939·169	476	1 049·400	526	1 159·631	576	1 269·863
427	941·374	477	1 051·605	527	1 161·836	577	1 272·067
428	943·578	478	1 053·810	528	1 164·041	578	1 274·272
429	945·783	479	1 056·014	529	1 166·245	579	1 276·476
430	947·988	480	1 058·219	530	1 168·450	580	1 278·681
431	950·192	481	1 060·423	531	1 170·655	581	1 280·886
432	952·397	482	1 062·628	532	1 172·859	582	1 283·090
433	954·602	483	1 064·833	533	1 175·064	583	1 285·295
434	956·806	484	1 067·037	534	1 177·268	584	1 287·500
435	959·011	485	1 069·242	535	1 179·473	585	1 289·704
436	961·215	486	1 071·447	536	1 181·678	586	1 291·909
437	963·420	487	1 073·651	537	1 183·882	587	1 294·113
438	965·625	488	1 075·856	538	1 186·087	588	1 296·318
439	967·829	489	1 078·060	539	1 188·292	589	1 298·523
440	970·034	490	1 080·265	540	1 190·496	590	1 300·727
441	972·239	491	1 082·470	541	1 192·701	591	1 302·932
442	974·443	492	1 084·674	542	1 194·905	592	1 305·137
443	976·648	493	1 086·879	543	1 197·110	593	1 307·341
444	978·852	494	1 089·084	544	1 199·315	594	1 309·546
445	981·057	495	1 091·288	545	1 201·519	595	1 311·750
446	983·262	496	1 093·493	546	1 203·724	596	1 313·955
447	985·466	497	1 095·697	547	1 205·929	597	1 316·160
448	987·671	498	1 097·902	548	1 208·133	598	1 318·364
449	989·876	499	1 100·107	549	1 210·338	599	1 320·569
450	992·080	500	1 102·311	550	1 212·542	600	1 322·774

kg	lb	kg	lb	kg	lb	kg	lb
601	1 324·978	651	1 435·209	701	1 545·440	751	1 655·672
602	1 327·183	652	1 437·414	702	1 547·645	752	1 657·876
603	1 329·387	653	1 439·619	703	1 549·850	753	1 660·081
604	1 331·592	654	1 441·823	704	1 552·054	754	1 662·285
605	1 333·797	655	1 444·028	705	1 554·259	755	1 664·490
606	1 336·001	656	1 446·232	706	1 556·464	756	1 666·695
607	1 338·206	657	1 448·437	707	1 558·668	757	1 668·899
608	1 340·411	658	1 450·642	708	1 560·873	758	1 671·104
609	1 342·615	659	1 452·846	709	1 563·077	759	1 673·309
610	1 344·820	660	1 455·051	710	1 565·282	760	1 675·513
611	1 347·024	661	1 457·256	711	1 567·487	761	1 677·718
612	1 349·229	662	1 459·460	712	1 569·691	762	1 679·922
613	1 351·434	663	1 461·665	713	1 571·896	763	1 682·127
614	1 353·638	664	1 463·869	714	1 574·101	764	1 684·332
615	1 355·843	665	1 466·074	715	1 576·305	765	1 686·536
616	1 358·048	666	1 468·279	716	1 578·510	766	1 688·741
617	1 360·252	667	1 470·483	717	1 580·714	767	1 690·946
618	1 362·457	668	1 472·688	718	1 582·919	768	1 693·150
619	1 364·661	669	1 474·893	719	1 585·124	769	1 695·355
620	1 366·866	670	1 477·097	720	1 587·328	770	1 697·559
621	1 369·071	671	1 479·302	721	1 589·533	771	1 699·764
622	1 371·275	672	1 481·506	722	1 591·738	772	1 701·969
623	1 373·480	673	1 483·711	723	1 593·942	773	1 704·173
624	1 375·685	674	1 485·916	724	1 596·147	774	1 706·378
625	1 377·889	675	1 488·120	725	1 598·351	775	1 708·583
626	1 380·094	676	1 490·325	726	1 600·556	776	1 710·787
627	1 382·298	677	1 492·530	727	1 602·761	777	1 712·992
628	1 384·503	678	1 494·734	728	1 604·965	778	1 715·196
629	1 386·708	679	1 496·939	729	1 607·170	779	1 717·401
630	1 388·912	680	1 499·143	730	1 609·374	780	1 719·606
631	1 391·117	681	1 501·348	731	1 611·579	781	1 721·810
632	1 393·321	682	1 503·553	732	1 613·784	782	1 724·015
633	1 395·526	683	1 505·757	733	1 615·988	783	1 726·219
634	1 397·731	684	1 507·962	734	1 618·193	784	1 728·424
635	1 399·935	685	1 510·166	735	1 620·398	785	1 730·629
636	1 402·140	686	1 512·371	736	1 622·602	786	1 732·833
637	1 404·345	687	1 514·576	737	1 624·807	787	1 735·038
638	1 406·549	688	1 516·780	738	1 627·011	788	1 737·243
639	1 408·754	689	1 518·985	739	1 629·216	789	1 739·447
640	1 410·958	690	1 521·190	740	1 631·421	790	1 741·652
641	1 413·163	691	1 523·394	741	1 633·625	791	1 743·856
642	1 415·368	692	1 525·599	742	1 635·830	792	1 746·061
643	1 417·572	693	1 527·803	743	1 638·035	793	1 748·266
644	1 419·777	694	1 530·008	744	1 640·239	794	1 750·470
645	1 421·982	695	1 532·213	745	1 642·444	795	1 752·675
646	1 424·186	696	1 534·417	746	1 644·648	796	1 754·880
647	1 426·391	697	1 536·622	747	1 646·853	797	1 757·084
648	1 428·595	698	1 538·827	748	1 649·058	798	1 759·289
649	1 430·800	699	1 541·031	749	1 651·262	799	1 761·493
650	1 433·005	700	1 543·236	750	1 653·467	800	1 763·698

kg	lb	kg	lb	kg	lb	kg	lb
801	1 765 903	851	1 876·134	901	1 986·365	951	2 096·596
802	1 768·107	852	1 878·338	902	1 988·570	952	2 098·801
803	1 770·312	853	1 880·543	903	1 990·774	953	2 101·005
804	1 772·517	854	1 882·748	904	1 992·979	954	2 103·210
805	1 774·721	855	1 884·952	905	1 995·183	955	2 105·415
806	1 776·926	856	1 887·157	906	1 997·388	956	2 107·619
807	1 779·130	857	1 889·362	907	1 999·593	957	2 109·824
808	1 781·335	858	1 891·566	908	2 001·797	958	2 112·028
809	1 783·540	859	1 893·771	909	2 004·002	959	2 114·233
810	1 785·744	860	1 895·975	910	2 006·207	960	2 116·438
811	1 787·949	861	1 898·180	911	2 008·411	961	2 118·642
812	1 790·154	862	1 900·385	912	2 010·616	962	2 120·847
813	1 792·358	863	1 902·589	913	2 012·820	963	2 123·052
814	1 794·563	864	1 904·794	914	2 015·025	964	2 125·256
815	1 796·767	865	1 906·999	915	2 017·230	965	2 127·461
816	1 798·972	866	1 909·203	916	2 019·434	966	2 129·665
817	1 801·177	867	1 911·408	917	2 021·639	967	2 131·870
818	1 803·381	868	1 913·612	918	2 023·844	968	2 134·075
819	1 805·586	869	1 915·817	919	2 026·048	969	2 136·279
820	1 807·791	870	1 918·022	920	2 028·253	970	2 138·484
821	1 809·995	871	1 920·226	921	2 030·457	971	2 140·689
822	1 812·200	872	1 922·431	922	2 032·662	972	2 142·893
823	1 814·404	873	1 924·636	923	2 034·867	973	2 145·098
824	1 816·609	874	1 926·840	924	2 037·071	974	2 147·302
825	1 818·814	875	1 929·045	925	2 039·276	975	2 149·507
826	1 821·018	876	1 931·249	926	2 041·481	976	2 151·712
827	1 823·223	877	1 933·454	927	2 043·685	977	2 153·916
828	1 825·428	878	1 935·659	928	2 045·890	978	2 156·121
829	1 827·632	879	1 937·863	929	2 048·094	979	2 158·326
830	1 829·837	880	1 940·068	930	2 050·299	980	2 160·530
831	1 832·041	881	1 942·273	931	2 052·504	981	2 162·735
832	1 834·246	882	1 944·477	932	2 054·708	982	2 164·939
833	1 836·451	883	1 946·682	933	2 056·913	983	2 167·144
834	1 838·655	884	1 948·886	934	2 059·118	984	2 169·349
835	1 840·860	885	1 951·091	935	2 061·322	985	2 171·553
836	1 843·064	886	1 953·296	936	2 063·527	986	2 173·758
837	1 845·269	887	1 955·500	937	2 065·731	987	2 175·963
838	1 847·474	888	1 957·705	938	2 067·936	988	2 178·167
839	1 849·678	889	1 959·909	939	2 070·141	989	2 180·372
840	1 851·883	890	1 962·114	940	2 072·345	990	2 182·576
841	1 854·088	891	1 964·319	941	2 074·550	991	2 184·781
842	1 856·292	892	1 966·523	942	2 076·754	992	2 186·986
843	1 858·497	893	1 968·728	943	2 078·959	993	2 189·190
844	1 860·701	894	1 970·933	944	2 081·164	994	2 191·395
845	1 862·906	895	1 973·137	945	2 083·368	995	2 193·599
846	1 865·111	896	1 975·342	946	2 085·573	996	2 195·804
847	1 867·315	897	1 977·546	947	2 087·778	997	2 198·009
848	1 869·520	898	1 979·751	948	2 089·982	998	2 200·213
849	1 871·725	899	1 981·956	949	2 092·187	999	2 202·418
850	1 873·929	900	1 984·160	950	2 094·391	1 000	2 204·623

WEIGHT kilogrammes (kg) to hundredweight (cwt), stones, pounds (lb), ounces (oz)

kg	cwt	stones	lb	oz	kg	cwt	stones	lb	oz
1			2	3·274	51	1	0	0	6·972
2			4	6·548	52	1	0	2	10·246
3			6	9·822	53	1	0	4	13·520
4			8	13·096	54	1	0	7	0·794
5			11	0·370	55	1	0	9	4·068
6			13	3·644	56	1	0	11	7·342
7		1	1	6·918	57	1	0	13	10·616
8		1	3	10·192	58	1	1	1	13·890
9		1	5	13·466	59	1	1	4	1·164
10		1	8	0·740	60	1	1	6	4·438
11		1	10	4·014	61	1	1	8	7·712
12		1	12	7·288	62	1	1	10	10·986
13		2	0	10·562	63	1	1	12	14·260
14		2	2	13·835	64	1	2	1	1·534
15		2	5	1·109	65	1	2	3	4·808
16		2	7	4·383	66	1	2	5	8·081
17		2	9	7·657	67	1	2	7	11·355
18		2	11	10·931	68	1	2	9	14·629
19		2	13	14·205	69	1	2	12	1·903
20		3	2	1·479	70	1	3	0	5·177
21		3	4	4·753	71	1	3	2	8·451
22		3	6	8·027	72	1	3	4	11·725
23		3	8	11·301	73	1	3	6	14·999
24		3	10	14·575	74	1	3	9	2·273
25		3	13	1·849	75	1	3	11	5·547
26		4	1	5·123	76	1	3	13	8·821
27		4	3	8·397	77	1	4	1	12·095
28		4	5	11·671	78	1	4	3	15·369
29		4	7	14·945	79	1	4	6	2·643
30		4	10	2·219	80	1	4	8	5·917
31		4	12	5·493	81	1	4	10	9·191
32		5	0	8·767	82	1	4	12	12·465
33		5	2	12·041	83	1	5	0	15·739
34		5	4	15·315	84	1	5	3	3·013
35		5	7	2·589	85	1	5	5	6·287
36		5	9	5·863	86	1	5	7	9·561
37		5	11	9·137	87	1	5	9	12·835
38		5	13	12·411	88	1	5	12	0·109
39		6	1	15·685	89	1	6	0	3·383
40		6	4	2·958	90	1	6	2	6·657
41		6	6	6·232	91	1	6	4	9·931
42		6	8	9·506	92	1	6	6	13·204
43		6	10	12·780	93	1	6	9	0·478
44		6	13	0·054	94	1	6	11	3·752
45		7	1	3·328	95	1	6	13	7·026
46		7	3	6·602	96	1	7	1	10·300
47		7	5	9·876	97	1	7	3	13·574
48		7	7	13·150	98	1	7	6	0·848
49		7	10	0·424	99	1	7	8	4·122
50		7	12	3·698	100	1	7	10	7·396

kg	cwt	stones	lb	oz	kg	cwt	stones	lb	oz
101	1	7	12	10·670	151	2	7	10	14·368
102	2	0	0	13·944	152	2	7	13	1·642
103	2	0	3	1·218	153	3	0	1	4·916
104	2	0	5	4·492	154	3	0	3	8·190
105	2	0	7	7·766	155	3	0	5	11·464
106	2	0	9	11·040	156	3	0	7	14·738
107	2	0	11	14·314	157	3	0	10	2·012
108	2	1	0	1·588	158	3	0	12	5·286
109	2	1	2	4·862	159	3	1	0	8·560
110	2	1	4	8·136	160	3	1	2	11·834
111	2	1	6	11·410	161	3	1	4	15·108
112	2	1	8	14·684	162	3	1	7	2·382
113	2	1	11	1·958	163	3	1	9	5·656
114	2	1	13	5·232	164	3	1	11	8·930
115	2	2	1	8·506	165	3	1	13	12·204
116	2	2	3	11·780	166	3	2	1	15·478
117	2	2	5	15·054	167	3	2	4	2·752
118	2	2	8	2·328	168	3	2	6	6·026
119	2	2	10	5·601	169	3	2	8	9·300
120	2	2	12	8·875	170	3	2	10	12·574
121	2	3	0	12·149	171	3	2	12	15·847
122	2	3	2	15·423	172	3	3	1	3·121
123	2	3	5	2·697	173	3	3	3	6·395
124	2	3	7	5·971	174	3	3	5	9·669
125	2	3	9	9·245	175	3	3	7	12·943
126	2	3	11	12·519	176	3	3	10	0·217
127	2	3	13	15·793	177	3	3	12	3·491
128	2	4	2	3·067	178	3	4	0	6·765
129	2	4	4	6·341	179	3	4	2	10·039
130	2	4	6	9·615	180	3	4	4	13·313
131	2	4	8	12·889	181	3	4	7	0·587
132	2	4	11	0·163	182	3	4	9	3·861
133	2	4	13	3·437	183	3	4	11	7·135
134	2	5	1	6·711	184	3	4	13	10·409
135	2	5	3	9·985	185	3	5	1	13·683
136	2	5	5	13·259	186	3	5	4	0·957
137	2	5	8	0·533	187	3	5	6	4·231
138	2	5	10	3·807	188	3	5	8	7·505
139	2	5	12	7·081	189	3	5	10	10·779
140	2	6	0	10·355	190	3	5	12	14·053
141	2	6	2	13·629	191	3	6	1	1·327
142	2	6	5	0·903	192	3	6	3	4·601
143	2	6	7	4·177	193	3	6	5	7·875
144	2	6	9	7·451	194	3	6	7	11·149
145	2	6	11	10·724	195	3	6	9	14·423
146	2	6	13	13·998	196	3	6	12	1·697
147	2	7	2	1·272	197	3	7	0	4·970
148	2	7	4	4·546	198	3	7	2	8·244
149	2	7	6	7·820	199	3	7	4	11·518
150	2	7	8	11·094	200	3	7	6	14·792

kg	cwt	stones	lb	oz	kg	cwt	stones	lb	oz
201	3	7	9	2·066	251	4	7	7	5·764
202	3	7	11	5·340	252	4	7	9	9·038
203	3	7	13	8·614	253	4	7	11	12·312
204	4	0	1	11·888	254	4	7	13	15·586
205	4	0	3	15·162	255	5	0	2	2·860
206	4	0	6	2·436	256	5	0	4	6·134
207	4	0	8	5·710	257	5	0	6	9·408
208	4	0	10	8·984	258	5	0	8	12·682
209	4	0	12	12·258	259	5	0	10	15·956
210	4	1	0	15·532	260	5	0	13	3·230
211	4	1	3	2·806	261	5	1	1	6·504
212	4	1	5	6·080	262	5	1	3	9·778
213	4	1	7	9·354	263	5	1	5	13·052
214	4	1	9	12·628	264	5	1	8	0·326
215	4	1	11	15·902	265	5	1	10	3·600
216	4	2	0	3·176	266	5	1	12	6·874
217	4	2	2	6·450	267	5	2	0	10·148
218	4	2	4	9·724	268	5	2	2	13·422
219	4	2	6	12·998	269	5	2	5	0·696
220	4	2	9	0·272	270	5	2	7	3·970
221	4	2	11	3·546	271	5	2	9	7·244
222	4	2	13	6·820	272	5	2	11	10·518
223	4	3	1	10·094	273	5	2	13	13·792
224	4	3	3	13·367	274	5	3	2	1·066
225	4	3	6	0·641	275	5	3	4	4·340
226	4	3	8	3·915	276	5	3	6	7·613
227	4	3	10	7·189	277	5	3	8	10·887
228	4	3	12	10·463	278	5	3	10	14·161
229	4	4	0	13·737	279	5	3	13	1·435
230	4	4	3	1·011	280	5	4	1	4·709
231	4	4	5	4·285	281	5	4	3	7·983
232	4	4	7	7·559	282	5	4	5	11·257
233	4	4	9	10·833	283	5	4	7	14·531
234	4	4	11	14·107	284	5	4	10	1·805
235	4	5	0	1·381	285	5	4	12	5·079
236	4	5	2	4·655	286	5	5	0	8·353
237	4	5	4	7·929	287	5	5	2	11·627
238	4	5	6	11·203	288	5	5	4	14·901
239	4	5	8	14·477	289	5	5	7	2·175
240	4	5	11	1·751	290	5	5	9	5·449
241	4	5	13	5·025	291	5	5	11	8·723
242	4	6	1	8·299	292	5	5	13	11·997
243	4	6	3	11·573	293	5	6	1	15·271
244	4	6	5	14·847	294	5	6	4	2·545
245	4	6	8	2·121	295	5	6	6	5·819
246	4	6	10	5·395	296	5	6	8	9·093
247	4	6	12	8·669	297	5	6	10	12·367
248	4	7	0	11·943	298	5	6	12	15·641
249	4	7	2	15·217	299	5	7	1	2·915
250	4	7	5	2·490	300	5	7	3	6·189

kg	cwt	stones	lb	oz	kg	cwt	stones	lb	oz
301	5	7	5	9·463	351	6	7	3	13·161
302	5	7	7	12·736	352	6	7	6	0·435
303	5	7	10	0·010	353	6	7	8	3·709
304	5	7	12	3·284	354	6	7	10	6·983
305	6	0	0	6·558	355	6	7	12	10·256
306	6	0	2	9·832	356	7	0	0	13·530
307	6	0	4	13·106	357	7	0	3	0·804
308	6	0	7	0·380	358	7	0	5	4·078
309	6	0	9	3·654	359	7	0	7	7·352
310	6	0	11	6·928	360	7	0	9	10·626
311	6	0	13	10·202	361	7	0	11	13·900
312	6	1	1	13·476	362	7	1	0	1·174
313	6	1	4	0·750	363	7	1	2	4·448
314	6	1	6	4·024	364	7	1	4	7·722
315	6	1	8	7·298	365	7	1	6	10·996
316	6	1	10	10·572	366	7	1	8	14·270
317	6	1	12	13·846	367	7	1	11	1·544
318	6	2	1	1·120	368	7	1	13	4·818
319	6	2	3	4·394	369	7	2	1	8·092
320	6	2	5	7·668	370	7	2	3	11·366
321	6	2	7	10·942	371	7	2	5	14·640
322	6	2	9	14·216	372	7	2	8	1·914
323	6	2	12	1·490	373	7	2	10	5·188
324	6	3	0	4·764	374	7	2	12	8·462
325	6	3	2	8·038	375	7	3	0	11·736
326	6	3	4	11·312	376	7	3	2	15·010
327	6	3	6	14·586	377	7	3	5	2·284
328	6	3	9	1·860	378	7	3	7	5·558
329	6	3	11	5·133	379	7	3	9	8·832
330	6	3	13	8·407	380	7	3	11	12·106
331	6	4	1	11·681	381	7	3	13	15·379
332	6	4	3	14·955	382	7	4	2	2·653
333	6	4	6	2·229	383	7	4	4	5·927
334	6	4	8	5·503	384	7	4	6	9·201
335	6	4	10	8·777	385	7	4	8	12·475
336	6	4	12	12·051	386	7	4	10	15·749
337	6	5	0	15·325	387	7	4	13	3·023
338	6	5	3	2·599	388	7	5	1	6·297
339	6	5	5	5·873	389	7	5	3	9·571
340	6	5	7	9·147	390	7	5	5	12·845
341	6	5	9	12·421	391	7	5	8	0·119
342	6	5	11	15·695	392	7	5	10	3·393
343	6	6	0	2·969	393	7	5	12	6·667
344	6	6	2	6·243	394	7	6	0	9·941
345	6	6	4	9·517	395	7	6	2	13·215
346	6	6	6	12·791	396	7	6	5	0·489
347	6	6	9	0·065	397	7	6	7	3·763
348	6	6	11	3·339	398	7	6	9	7·037
349	6	6	13	6·613	399	7	6	11	10·311
350	6	7	1	9·887	400	7	6	13	13·585

WEIGHT   kilogrammes (kg) to hundredweight (cwt),
stones, pounds (lb), ounces (oz)

kg	cwt	stones	lb	oz	kg	cwt	stones	lb	oz
401	7	7	2	0·859	451	8	7	0	4·557
402	7	7	4	4·133	452	8	7	2	7·831
403	7	7	6	7·407	453	8	7	4	11·105
404	7	7	8	10·681	454	8	7	6	14·379
405	7	7	10	13·955	455	8	7	9	1·653
406	7	7	13	1·229	456	8	7	11	4·927
407	8	0	1	4·502	457	8	7	13	8·201
408	8	0	3	7·776	458	9	0	1	11·475
409	8	0	5	11·050	459	9	0	3	14·749
410	8	0	7	14·324	460	9	0	6	2·022
411	8	0	10	1·598	461	9	0	8	5·296
412	8	0	12	4·872	462	9	0	10	8·570
413	8	1	0	8·146	463	9	0	12	11·844
414	8	1	2	11·420	464	9	1	0	15·118
415	8	1	4	14·694	465	9	1	3	2·392
416	8	1	7	1·968	466	9	1	5	5·666
417	8	1	9	5·242	467	9	1	7	8·940
418	8	1	11	8·516	468	9	1	9	12·214
419	8	1	13	11·790	469	9	1	11	15·488
420	8	2	1	15·064	470	9	2	0	2·762
421	8	2	4	2·338	471	9	2	2	6·036
422	8	2	6	5·612	472	9	2	4	9·310
423	8	2	8	8·886	473	9	2	6	12·584
424	8	2	10	12·160	474	9	2	8	15·858
425	8	2	12	15·434	475	9	2	11	3·132
426	8	3	1	2·708	476	9	2	13	6·406
427	8	3	3	5·982	477	9	3	1	9·680
428	8	3	5	9·256	478	9	3	3	12·954
429	8	3	7	12·530	479	9	3	6	0·228
430	8	3	9	15·804	480	9	3	8	3·502
431	8	3	12	3·078	481	9	3	10	6·776
432	8	4	0	6·352	482	9	3	12	10·050
433	8	4	2	9·626	483	9	4	0	13·324
434	8	4	4	12·899	484	9	4	3	0·598
435	8	4	7	0·173	485	9	4	5	3·872
436	8	4	9	3·447	486	9	4	7	7·145
437	8	4	11	6·721	487	9	4	9	10·419
438	8	4	13	9·995	488	9	4	11	13·693
439	8	5	1	13·269	489	9	5	0	0·967
440	8	5	4	0·543	490	9	5	2	4·241
441	8	5	6	3·817	491	9	5	4	7·515
442	8	5	8	7·091	492	9	5	6	10·789
443	8	5	10	10·365	493	9	5	8	14·063
444	8	5	12	13·639	494	9	5	11	1·337
445	8	6	1	0·913	495	9	5	13	4·611
446	8	6	3	4·187	496	9	6	1	7·885
447	8	6	5	7·461	497	9	6	3	11·159
448	8	6	7	10·735	498	9	6	5	14·433
449	8	6	9	14·009	499	9	6	8	1·707
450	8	6	12	1·283	500	9	6	10	4·981

kg	cwt	stones	lb	oz	kg	cwt	stones	lb	oz
501	9	6	12	8·255	551	10	6	10	11·953
502	9	7	0	11·529	552	10	6	12	15·227
503	9	7	2	14·803	553	10	7	1	2·501
504	9	7	5	2·077	554	10	7	3	5·775
505	9	7	7	5·351	555	10	7	5	9·049
506	9	7	9	8·625	556	10	7	7	12·323
507	9	7	11	11·899	557	10	7	9	15·597
508	9	7	13	15·173	558	10	7	12	2·871
509	10	0	2	2·447	559	11	0	0	6·145
510	10	0	4	5·721	560	11	0	2	9·419
511	10	0	6	8·995	561	11	0	4	12·693
512	10	0	8	12·268	562	11	0	6	15·967
513	10	0	10	15·542	563	11	0	9	3·241
514	10	0	13	2·816	564	11	0	11	6·515
515	10	1	1	6·090	565	11	0	13	9·788
516	10	1	3	9·364	566	11	1	1	13·062
517	10	1	5	12·638	567	11	1	4	0·336
518	10	1	7	15·912	568	11	1	6	3·610
519	10	1	10	3·186	569	11	1	8	6·884
520	10	1	12	6·460	570	11	1	10	10·158
521	10	2	0	9·734	571	11	1	12	13·432
522	10	2	2	13·008	572	11	2	1	0·706
523	10	2	5	0·282	573	11	2	3	3·980
524	10	2	7	3·556	574	11	2	5	7·254
525	10	2	9	6·830	575	11	2	7	10·528
526	10	2	11	10·104	576	11	2	9	13·802
527	10	2	13	13·378	577	11	2	12	1·076
528	10	3	2	0·652	578	11	3	0	4·350
529	10	3	4	3·926	579	11	3	2	7·624
530	10	3	6	7·200	580	11	3	4	10·898
531	10	3	8	10·474	581	11	3	6	14·172
532	10	3	10	13·748	582	11	3	9	1·446
533	10	3	13	1·022	583	11	3	11	4·720
534	10	4	1	4·296	584	11	3	13	7·994
535	10	4	3	7·570	585	11	4	1	11·268
536	10	4	5	10·844	586	11	4	3	14·542
537	10	4	7	14·118	587	11	4	6	1·816
538	10	4	10	1·392	588	11	4	8	5·090
539	10	4	12	4·665	589	11	4	10	8·364
540	10	5	0	7·939	590	11	4	12	11·638
541	10	5	2	11·213	591	11	5	0	14·911
542	10	5	4	14·487	592	11	5	3	2·185
543	10	5	7	1·761	593	11	5	5	5·459
544	10	5	9	5·035	594	11	5	7	8·733
545	10	5	11	8·309	595	11	5	9	12·007
546	10	5	13	11·583	596	11	5	11	15·281
547	10	6	1	14·857	597	11	6	0	2·555
548	10	6	4	2·131	598	11	6	2	5·829
549	10	6	6	5·405	599	11	6	4	9·103
550	10	6	8	8·679	600	11	6	6	12·377

WEIGHT   kilogrammes (kg) to hundredweight (cwt),
stones, pounds (lb), ounces (oz)

kg	cwt	stones	lb	oz	kg	cwt	stones	lb	oz
601	11	6	8	15·651	651	12	6	7	3·349
602	11	6	11	2·925	652	12	6	9	6·623
603	11	6	13	6·199	653	12	6	11	9·897
604	11	7	1	9·473	654	12	6	13	13·171
605	11	7	3	12·747	655	12	7	2	0·445
606	11	7	6	0·021	656	12	7	4	3·719
607	11	7	8	3·295	657	12	7	6	6·993
608	11	7	10	6·569	658	12	7	8	10·267
609	11	7	12	9·843	659	12	7	10	13·541
610	12	0	0	13·117	660	12	7	13	0·815
611	12	0	3	0·391	661	13	0	1	4·089
612	12	0	5	3·665	662	13	0	3	7·363
613	12	0	7	6·939	663	13	0	5	10·637
614	12	0	9	10·213	664	13	0	7	13·911
615	12	0	11	13·487	665	13	0	10	1·185
616	12	1	0	0·761	666	13	0	12	4·459
617	12	1	2	4·034	667	13	1	0	7·733
618	12	1	4	7·308	668	13	1	2	11·007
619	12	1	6	10·582	669	13	1	4	14·281
620	12	1	8	13·856	670	13	1	7	1·554
621	12	1	11	1·130	671	13	1	9	4·828
622	12	1	13	4·404	672	13	1	11	8·102
623	12	2	1	7·678	673	13	1	13	11·376
624	12	2	3	10·952	674	13	2	1	14·650
625	12	2	5	14·226	675	13	2	4	1·924
626	12	2	8	1·500	676	13	2	6	5·198
627	12	2	10	4·774	677	13	2	8	8·472
628	12	2	12	8·048	678	13	2	10	11·746
629	12	3	0	11·322	679	13	2	12	15·020
630	12	3	2	14·596	680	13	3	1	2·294
631	12	3	5	1·870	681	13	3	3	5·568
632	12	3	7	5·144	682	13	3	5	8·842
633	12	3	9	8·418	683	13	3	7	12·116
634	12	3	11	11·692	684	13	3	9	15·390
635	12	3	13	14·966	685	13	3	12	2·664
636	12	4	2	2·240	686	13	4	0	5·938
637	12	4	4	5·514	687	13	4	2	9·212
638	12	4	6	8·788	688	13	4	4	12·486
639	12	4	8	12·062	689	13	4	6	15·760
640	12	4	10	15·336	690	13	4	9	3·034
641	12	4	13	2·610	691	13	4	11	6·308
642	12	5	1	5·884	692	13	4	13	9·582
643	12	5	3	9·158	693	13	5	1	12·856
644	12	5	5	12·431	694	13	5	4	0·130
645	12	5	7	15·705	695	13	5	6	3·404
646	12	5	10	2·979	696	13	5	8	6·677
647	12	5	12	6·253	697	13	5	10	9·951
648	12	6	0	9·527	698	13	5	12	13·225
649	12	6	2	12·801	699	13	6	1	0·499
650	12	6	5	0·075	700	13	6	3	3·773

kg	cwt	stones	lb	oz	kg	cwt	stones	lb	oz
701	13	6	5	7·047	751	14	6	3	10·745
702	13	6	7	10·321	752	14	6	5	14·019
703	13	6	9	13·595	753	14	6	8	1·293
704	13	6	12	0·869	754	14	6	10	4·567
705	13	7	0	4·143	755	14	6	12	7·841
706	13	7	2	7·417	756	14	7	0	11·115
707	13	7	4	10·691	757	14	7	2	14·389
708	13	7	6	13·965	758	14	7	5	1·663
709	13	7	9	1·239	759	14	7	7	4·937
710	13	7	11	4·513	760	14	7	9	8·211
711	13	7	13	7·787	761	14	7	11	11·485
712	14	0	1	11·061	762	14	7	13	14·759
713	14	0	3	14·335	763	15	0	2	2·033
714	14	0	6	1·609	764	15	0	4	5·307
715	14	0	8	4·883	765	15	0	6	8·581
716	14	0	10	8·157	766	15	0	8	11·855
717	14	0	12	11·431	767	15	0	10	15·129
718	14	1	0	14·705	768	15	0	13	2·403
719	14	1	3	1·979	769	15	1	1	5·677
720	14	1	5	5·253	770	15	1	3	8·951
721	14	1	7	8·527	771	15	1	5	12·225
722	14	1	9	11·800	772	15	1	7	15·499
723	14	1	11	15·074	773	15	1	10	2·773
724	14	2	0	2·348	774	15	1	12	6·047
725	14	2	2	5·622	775	15	2	0	9·320
726	14	2	4	8·896	776	15	2	2	12·594
727	14	2	6	12·170	777	15	2	4	15·868
728	14	2	8	15·444	778	15	2	7	3·142
729	14	2	11	2·718	779	15	2	9	6·416
730	14	2	13	5·992	780	15	2	11	9·690
731	14	3	1	9·266	781	15	2	13	12·964
732	14	3	3	12·540	782	15	3	2	0·238
733	14	3	5	15·814	783	15	3	4	3·512
734	14	3	8	3·088	784	15	3	6	6·786
735	14	3	10	6·362	785	15	3	8	10·060
736	14	3	12	9·636	786	15	3	10	13·334
737	14	4	0	12·910	787	15	3	13	0·608
738	14	4	3	0·184	788	15	4	1	3·882
739	14	4	5	3·458	789	15	4	3	7·156
740	14	4	7	6·732	790	15	4	5	10·430
741	14	4	9	10·006	791	15	4	7	13·704
742	14	4	11	13·280	792	15	4	10	0·978
743	14	5	0	0·554	793	15	4	12	4·252
744	14	5	2	3·828	794	15	5	0	7·526
745	14	5	4	7·102	795	15	5	2	10·800
746	14	5	6	10·376	796	15	5	4	14·074
747	14	5	8	13·650	797	15	5	7	1·348
748	14	5	11	0·924	798	15	5	9	4·622
749	14	5	13	4·197	799	15	5	11	7·896
750	14	6	1	7·471	800	15	5	13	11·170

kg	cwt	stones	lb	oz	kg	cwt	stones	lb	oz
801	15	6	1	14·443	851	16	6	0	2·142
802	15	6	4	1·717	852	16	6	2	5·416
803	15	6	6	4·991	853	16	6	4	8·690
804	15	6	8	8·265	854	16	6	6	11·963
805	15	6	10	11·539	855	16	6	8	15·237
806	15	6	12	14·813	856	16	6	11	2·511
807	15	7	1	2·087	857	16	6	13	5·785
808	15	7	3	5·361	858	16	7	1	9·059
809	15	7	5	8·635	859	16	7	3	12·333
810	15	7	7	11·909	860	16	7	5	15·607
811	15	7	9	15·183	861	16	7	8	2·881
812	15	7	12	2·457	862	16	7	10	6·155
813	16	0	0	5·731	863	16	7	12	9·429
814	16	0	2	9·005	864	17	0	0	12·703
815	16	0	4	12·279	865	17	0	2	15·977
816	16	0	6	15·553	866	17	0	5	3·251
817	16	0	9	2·827	867	17	0	7	6·525
818	16	0	11	6·101	868	17	0	9	9·799
819	16	0	13	9·375	869	17	0	11	13·073
820	16	1	1	12·649	870	17	1	0	0·347
821	16	1	3	15·923	871	17	1	2	3·621
822	16	1	6	3·197	872	17	1	4	6·895
823	16	1	8	6·471	873	17	1	6	10·169
824	16	1	10	9·745	874	17	1	8	13·443
825	16	1	12	13·019	875	17	1	11	0·717
826	16	2	1	0·293	876	17	1	13	3·991
827	16	2	3	3·566	877	17	2	1	7·265
828	16	2	5	6·840	878	17	2	3	10·539
829	16	2	7	10·114	879	17	2	5	13·813
830	16	2	9	13·388	880	17	2	8	1·086
831	16	2	12	0·662	881	17	2	10	4·360
832	16	3	0	3·936	882	17	2	12	7·634
833	16	3	2	7·210	883	17	3	0	10·908
834	16	3	4	10·484	884	17	3	2	14·182
835	16	3	6	13·758	885	17	3	5	1·456
836	16	3	9	1·032	886	17	3	7	4·730
837	16	3	11	4·306	887	17	3	9	8·004
838	16	3	13	7·580	888	17	3	11	11·278
839	16	4	1	10·854	889	17	3	13	14·552
840	16	4	3	14·128	890	17	4	2	1·826
841	16	4	6	1·402	891	17	4	4	5·100
842	16	4	8	4·676	892	17	4	6	8·374
843	16	4	10	7·950	893	17	4	8	11·648
844	16	4	12	11·224	894	17	4	10	14·922
845	16	5	0	14·498	895	17	4	13	2·196
846	16	5	3	1·772	896	17	5	1	5·470
847	16	5	5	5·046	897	17	5	3	8·744
848	16	5	7	8·320	898	17	5	5	12·018
849	16	5	9	11·594	899	17	5	7	15·292
850	16	5	11	14·868	900	17	5	10	2·566

kg	cwt	stones	lb	oz	kg	cwt	stones	lb	oz
901	17	5	12	5·840	951	18	5	10	9·538
902	17	6	0	9·114	952	18	5	12	12·812
903	17	6	2	12·388	953	18	6	1	0·086
904	17	6	4	15·662	954	18	6	3	3·360
905	17	6	7	2·936	955	18	6	5	6·634
906	17	6	9	6·209	956	18	6	7	9·908
907	17	6	11	9·483	957	18	6	9	13·182
908	17	6	13	12·757	958	18	6	12	0·456
909	17	7	2	0·031	959	18	7	0	3·729
910	17	7	4	3·305	960	18	7	2	7·003
911	17	7	6	6·579	961	18	7	4	10·277
912	17	7	8	9·853	962	18	7	6	13·551
913	17	7	10	13·127	963	18	7	9	0·825
914	17	7	13	0·401	964	18	7	11	4·099
915	18	0	1	3·675	965	18	7	13	7·373
916	18	0	3	6·949	966	19	0	1	10·647
917	18	0	5	10·223	967	19	0	3	13·921
918	18	0	7	13·497	968	19	0	6	1·195
919	18	0	10	0·771	969	19	0	8	4·469
920	18	0	12	4·045	970	19	0	10	7·743
921	18	1	0	7·319	971	19	0	12	11·017
922	18	1	2	10·593	972	19	1	0	14·291
923	18	1	4	13·867	973	19	1	3	1·565
924	18	1	7	1·141	974	19	1	5	4·839
925	18	1	9	4·415	975	19	1	7	8·113
926	18	1	11	7·689	976	19	1	9	11·387
927	18	1	13	10·963	977	19	1	11	14·661
928	18	2	1	14·237	978	19	2	0	1·935
929	18	2	4	1·511	979	19	2	2	5·209
930	18	2	6	4·785	980	19	2	4	8·483
931	18	2	8	8·059	981	19	2	6	11·757
932	18	2	10	11·332	982	19	2	8	15·031
933	18	2	12	14·606	983	19	2	11	2·305
934	18	3	1	1·880	984	19	2	13	5·579
935	18	3	3	5·154	985	19	3	1	8·852
936	18	3	5	8·428	986	19	3	3	12·126
937	18	3	7	11·702	987	19	3	5	15·400
938	18	3	9	14·976	988	19	3	8	2·674
939	18	3	12	2·250	989	19	3	10	5·948
940	18	4	0	5·524	990	19	3	12	9·222
941	18	4	2	8·798	991	19	4	0	12·496
942	18	4	4	12·072	992	19	4	2	15·770
943	18	4	6	15·346	993	19	4	5	3·044
944	18	4	9	2·620	994	19	4	7	6·318
945	18	4	11	5·894	995	19	4	9	9·592
946	18	4	13	9·168	996	19	4	11	12·866
947	18	5	1	12·442	997	19	5	0	0·140
948	18	5	3	15·716	998	19	5	2	3·414
949	18	5	6	2·990	999	19	5	4	6·688
950	18	5	8	6·264	1 000	19	5	6	9·962

t	tons	t	tons	t	tons	t	tons
0·5	0·4921	26	25·5894	76	74·7997	126	124·0101
1·0	0·9842	27	26·5736	77	75·7839	127	124·9943
1·5	1·4763	28	27·5578	78	76·7681	128	125·9785
2·0	1·9684	29	28·5420	79	77·7524	129	126·9627
2·5	2·4605	30	29·5262	80	78·7366	130	127·9469
3·0	2·9526						
3·5	3·4447	31	30·5104	81	79·7208	131	128·9311
4·0	3·9368	32	31·4946	82	80·7050	132	129·9153
4·5	4·4289	33	32·4788	83	81·6892	133	130·8995
5·0	4·9210	34	33·4630	84	82·6734	134	131·8837
		35	34·4472	85	83·6576	135	132·8679
5·5	5·4131						
6·0	5·9052	36	35·4315	86	84·6418	136	133·8522
6·5	6·3973	37	36·4157	87	85·6260	137	134·8364
7·0	6·8894	38	37·3999	88	86·6102	138	135·8206
7·5	7·3816	39	38·3841	89	87·5944	139	136·8048
8·0	7·8737	40	39·3683	90	88·5786	140	137·7890
8·5	8·3658						
9·0	8·8579	41	40·3525	91	89·5628	141	138·7732
9·5	9·3500	42	41·3367	92	90·5470	142	139·7574
10·0	9·8421	43	42·3209	93	91·5313	143	140·7416
		44	43·3051	94	92·5155	144	141·7258
10·5	10·3342	45	44·2893	95	93·4997	145	142·7100
11·0	10·8263						
11·5	11·3184	46	45·2735	96	94·4839	146	143·6942
12·0	11·8105	47	46·2577	97	95·4681	147	144·6784
12·5	12·3026	48	47·2419	98	96·4523	148	145·6626
13·0	12·7947	49	48·2261	99	97·4365	149	146·6468
13·5	13·2868	50	49·2104	100	98·4207	150	147·6311
14·0	13·7789						
14·5	14·2710	51	50·1946	101	99·4049	151	148·6153
15·0	14·7631	52	51·1788	102	100·3891	152	149·5995
		53	52·1630	103	101·3733	153	150·5837
15·5	15·2552	54	53·1472	104	102·3575	154	151·5679
16·0	15·7473	55	54·1314	105	103·3417	155	152·5521
16·5	16·2394						
17·0	16·7315	56	55·1156	106	104·3259	156	153·5363
17·5	17·2236	57	56·0998	107	105·3101	157	154·5205
18·0	17·7157	58	57·0840	108	106·2944	158	155·5047
18·5	18·2078	59	58·0682	109	107·2786	159	156·4889
19·0	18·6999	60	59·0524	110	108·2628	160	157·4731
19·5	19·1920						
20·0	19·6841	61	60·0366	111	109·2470	161	158·4573
		62	61·0208	112	110·2312	162	159·4415
20·5	20·1762	63	62·0050	113	111·2154	163	160·4257
21·0	20·6683	64	62·9892	114	112·1996	164	161·4099
21·5	21·1605	65	63·9735	115	113·1838	165	162·3942
22·0	21·6526						
22·5	22·1447	66	64·9577	116	114·1680	166	163·3784
23·0	22·6368	67	65·9419	117	115·1522	167	164·3626
23·5	23·1289	68	66·9261	118	116·1364	168	165·3468
24·0	23·6210	69	67·9103	119	117·1206	169	166·3310
24·5	24·1131	70	68·8945	120	118·1048	170	167·3152
25·0	24·6052						
		71	69·8787	121	119·0890	171	168·2994
		72	70·8629	122	120·0733	172	169·2836
		73	71·8471	123	121·0575	173	170·2678
		74	72·8313	124	122·0417	174	171·2520
		75	73·8155	125	123·0259	175	172·2362

t	tons	t	tons	t	tons	t	tons
176	173·2204	330	324·7883	580	570·8401	830	816·8918
177	174·2046	335	329·7093	585	575·7611	835	821·8128
178	175·1888	340	334·6304	590	580·6821	840	826·7339
179	176·1731	345	339·5514	595	585·6032	845	831·6549
180	177·1573	350	344·4725	600	590·5242	850	836·5760
181	178·1415	355	349·3935	605	595·4452	855	841·4970
182	179·1257	360	354·3145	610	600·3663	860	846·4180
183	180·1099	365	359·2356	615	605·2873	865	851·3391
184	181·0941	370	364·1566	620	610·2083	870	856·2601
185	182·0783	375	369·0776	625	615·1294	875	861·1811
186	183·0625	380	373·9987	630	620·0504	880	866·1022
187	184·0467	385	378·9197	635	624·9714	885	871·0232
188	185·0309	390	383·8407	640	629·8925	890	875·9442
189	186·0151	395	388·7618	645	634·8135	895	880·8653
190	186·9993	400	393·6828	650	639·7346	900	885·7863
191	187·9835	405	398·6038	655	644·6556	905	890·7073
192	188·9677	410	403·5249	660	649·5766	910	895·6284
193	189·9520	415	408·4459	665	654·4977	915	900·5494
194	190·9362	420	413·3669	670	659·4187	920	905·4704
195	191·9204	425	418·2880	675	664·3397	925	910·3915
196	192·9046	430	423·2090	680	669·2608	930	915·3125
197	193·8888	435	428·1300	685	674·1818	935	920·2335
198	194·8730	440	433·0511	690	679·1028	940	925·1546
199	195·8572	445	437·9721	695	684·0239	945	930·0756
200	196·8414	450	442·8932	700	688·9449	950	934·9967
205	201·7624	455	447·8142	705	693·8659	955	939·9177
210	206·6835	460	452·7352	710	698·7870	960	944·8387
215	211·6045	465	457·6563	715	703·7080	965	949·7598
220	216·5255	470	462·5773	720	708·6290	970	954·6808
225	221·4466	475	467·4983	725	713·5501	975	959·6018
230	226·3676	480	472·4194	730	718·4711	980	964·5229
235	231·2886	485	477·3404	735	723·3921	985	969·4439
240	236·2097	490	482·2614	740	728·3132	990	974·3649
245	241·1307	495	487·1825	745	733·2342	995	979·2860
250	246·0518	500	492·1035	750	738·1553	1 000	984·2070
255	250·9728	505	497·0245	755	743·0763	2 000	1 968·4140
260	255·8938	510	501·9456	760	747·9973	3 000	2 952·6210
265	260·8149	515	506·8666	765	752·9184	4 000	3 936·8280
270	265·7359	520	511·7876	770	757·8394	5 000	4 921·0350
275	270·6569	525	516·7087	775	762·7604	6 000	5 905·2420
						7 000	6 889·4490
						8 000	7 873·6560
280	275·5780	530	521·6297	780	767·6815	9 000	8 857·8630
285	280·4990	535	526·5507	785	772·6025		
290	285·4200	540	531·4718	790	777·5235	10 000	9 842·070
295	290·3411	545	536·3928	795	782·4446	15 000	14 763·105
300	295·2621	550	541·3139	800	787·3656	20 000	19 684·140
						25 000	24 605·175
305	300·1831	555	546·2349	805	792·2866	30 000	29 526·210
310	305·1042	560	551·1559	810	797·2077	35 000	34 447·245
315	310·0252	565	556·0770	815	802·1287	40 000	39 368·280
320	314·9462	570	560·9980	820	807·0497	45 000	44 289·315
325	319·8673	575	565·9190	825	811·9708	50 000	49 210·350

cwt	kg	cwt	kg	cwt	kg	cwt	kg
$\frac{1}{2}$	25·401 2	$25\frac{1}{2}$	1 295·460	$\frac{1}{2}$	22·679 6	$25\frac{1}{2}$	1 156·661
1	50·802 3	26	1 320·861	1	45·359 2	26	1 179·340
$1\frac{1}{2}$	76·203 5	$26\frac{1}{2}$	1 346·262	$1\frac{1}{2}$	68·038 9	$26\frac{1}{2}$	1 202·020
2	101·604 7	27	1 371·663	2	90·718 5	27	1 224·699
$2\frac{1}{2}$	127·005 9	$27\frac{1}{2}$	1 397·064	$2\frac{1}{2}$	113·398 1	$27\frac{1}{2}$	1 247·379
3	152·407 0	28	1 422·466	3	136·077 7	28	1 270·059
$3\frac{1}{2}$	177·808 2	$28\frac{1}{2}$	1 447·867	$3\frac{1}{2}$	158·757 3	$28\frac{1}{2}$	1 292·738
4	203·209 4	29	1 473·268	4	181·436 9	29	1 315·418
$4\frac{1}{2}$	228·610 6	$29\frac{1}{2}$	1 498·669	$4\frac{1}{2}$	204·116 6	$29\frac{1}{2}$	1 338·097
5	254·011 7	30	1 524·070	5	226·796 2	30	1 360·777
$5\frac{1}{2}$	279·412 9	$30\frac{1}{2}$	1 549·472	$5\frac{1}{2}$	249·475 8	$30\frac{1}{2}$	1 383·457
6	304·814 1	31	1 574·873	6	272·155 4	31	1 406·136
$6\frac{1}{2}$	330·215 2	$31\frac{1}{2}$	1 600·274	$6\frac{1}{2}$	294·835 0	$31\frac{1}{2}$	1 428·816
7	355·616 4	32	1 625·675	7	317·514 7	32	1 451·496
$7\frac{1}{2}$	381·017 6	$32\frac{1}{2}$	1 651·076	$7\frac{1}{2}$	340·194 3	$32\frac{1}{2}$	1 474·175
8	406·418 8	33	1 676·477	8	362·873 9	33	1 496·855
$8\frac{1}{2}$	431·819 9	$33\frac{1}{2}$	1 701·879	$8\frac{1}{2}$	385·553 5	$33\frac{1}{2}$	1 519·534
9	457·221 1	34	1 727·280	9	408·233 1	34	1 542·214
$9\frac{1}{2}$	482·622 3	$34\frac{1}{2}$	1 752·681	$9\frac{1}{2}$	430·912 8	$34\frac{1}{2}$	1 564·894
10	508·023 5	35	1 778·082	10	453·592 4	35	1 587·573
$10\frac{1}{2}$	533·424 6	$35\frac{1}{2}$	1 803·483	$10\frac{1}{2}$	476·272 0	$35\frac{1}{2}$	1 610·253
11	558·825 8	36	1 828·884	11	498·951 6	36	1 632·933
$11\frac{1}{2}$	584·227 0	$36\frac{1}{2}$	1 854·286	$11\frac{1}{2}$	521·631 2	$36\frac{1}{2}$	1 655·612
12	609·628 1	37	1 879·687	12	544·310 8	37	1 678·292
$12\frac{1}{2}$	635·029 3	$37\frac{1}{2}$	1 905·088	$12\frac{1}{2}$	566·990 5	$37\frac{1}{2}$	1 700·971
13	660·430 5	38	1 930·489	13	589·670 1	38	1 723·651
$13\frac{1}{2}$	685·831 7	$38\frac{1}{2}$	1 955·890	$13\frac{1}{2}$	612·349 7	$38\frac{1}{2}$	1 746·331
14	711·232 8	39	1 981·291	14	635·029 3	39	1 769·010
$14\frac{1}{2}$	736·634 0	$39\frac{1}{2}$	2 006·693	$14\frac{1}{2}$	657·708 9	$39\frac{1}{2}$	1 791·690
15	762·035 2	40	2 032·094	15	680·388 6	40	1 814·369
$15\frac{1}{2}$	787·436 4	$40\frac{1}{2}$	2 057·495	$15\frac{1}{2}$	703·068 2	$40\frac{1}{2}$	1 837·049
16	812·837 5	41	2 082·896	16	725·747 8	41	1 859·729
$16\frac{1}{2}$	838·238 7	$41\frac{1}{2}$	2 108·297	$16\frac{1}{2}$	748·427 4	$41\frac{1}{2}$	1 882·408
17	863·639 9	42	2 133·699	17	771·107 0	42	1 905·088
$17\frac{1}{2}$	889·041 0	$42\frac{1}{2}$	2 159·100	$17\frac{1}{2}$	793·786 6	$42\frac{1}{2}$	1 927·768
18	914·442 2	43	2 184·501	18	816·466 3	43	1 950·447
$18\frac{1}{2}$	939·843 4	$43\frac{1}{2}$	2 209·902	$18\frac{1}{2}$	839·145 9	$43\frac{1}{2}$	1 973·127
19	965·244 6	44	2 235·303	19	861·825 5	44	1 995·806
$19\frac{1}{2}$	990·645 7	$44\frac{1}{2}$	2 260·704	$19\frac{1}{2}$	884·505 1	$44\frac{1}{2}$	2 018·486
20	1 016·046 9	45	2 286·106	20	907·184 7	45	2 041·166
$20\frac{1}{2}$	1 041·448 1	$45\frac{1}{2}$	2 311·507	$20\frac{1}{2}$	929·864 4	$45\frac{1}{2}$	2 063·845
21	1 066·849 3	46	2 336·908	21	952·544 0	46	2 086·525
$21\frac{1}{2}$	1 092·250 4	$46\frac{1}{2}$	2 362·309	$21\frac{1}{2}$	975·223 6	$46\frac{1}{2}$	2 109·205
22	1 117·651 6	47	2 387·710	22	997·903 2	47	2 131·884
$22\frac{1}{2}$	1 143·052 8	$47\frac{1}{2}$	2 413·111	$22\frac{1}{2}$	1 020·582 8	$47\frac{1}{2}$	2 154·564
23	1 168·453 9	48	2 438·513	23	1 043·262 5	48	2 177·243
$23\frac{1}{2}$	1 193·855 1	$48\frac{1}{2}$	2 463·914	$23\frac{1}{2}$	1 065·942 1	$48\frac{1}{2}$	2 199·923
24	1 219·256 3	49	2 489·315	24	1 088·621 7	49	2 222·603
$24\frac{1}{2}$	1 244·657 5	$49\frac{1}{2}$	2 514·716	$24\frac{1}{2}$	1 111·301 3	$49\frac{1}{2}$	2 245·282
25	1 270·058 6	50	2 540·117	25	1 133·980 9	50	2 267·962

tons	t	tons	t	tons	t	tons	t
1	0·907 2	51	46·266 4	110	99·790 4	610	553·382 9
2	1·814 4	52	47·173 6	120	108·862 2	620	562·454 7
3	2·721 6	53	48·080 8	130	117·934 1	630	571·526 6
4	3·628 7	54	48·988 0	140	127·005 9	640	580·598 4
5	4·535 9	55	49·895 2	150	136·077 8	650	589·670 3
6	5·443 1	56	50·802 4	160	145·149 6	660	598·742 1
7	6·350 3	57	51·709 5	170	154·221 5	670	607·814 0
8	7·257 5	58	52·616 7	180	163·293 3	680	616·885 8
9	8·164 7	59	53·523 9	190	172·365 2	690	625·957 7
10	9·071 9	60	54·431 1	200	181·437 0	700	635·029 5
11	9·979 0	61	55·338 3	210	190·508 9	710	644·101 4
12	10·886 2	62	56·245 5	220	199·580 7	720	653·173 2
13	11·793 4	63	57·152 7	230	208·652 6	730	662·245 1
14	12·700 6	64	58·059 8	240	217·724 4	740	671·316 9
15	13·607 8	65	58·967 0	250	226·796 3	750	680·388 8
16	14·515 0	66	59·874 2	260	235·868 1	760	689·460 6
17	15·422 1	67	60·781 4	270	244·940 0	770	698·532 5
18	16·329 3	68	61·688 6	280	254·011 8	780	707·604 3
19	17·236 5	69	62·595 8	290	263·083 7	790	716·676 2
20	18·143 7	70	63·503 0	300	272·155 5	800	725·748 0
21	19·050 9	71	64·410 1	310	281·227 4	810	734·819 9
22	19·958 1	72	65·317 3	320	290·299 2	820	743·891 7
23	20·865 3	73	66·224 5	330	299·371 1	830	752·963 6
24	21·772 4	74	67·131 7	340	308·442 9	840	762·035 4
25	22·679 6	75	68·038 9	350	317·514 8	850	771·107 3
26	23·586 8	76	68·946 1	360	326·586 6	860	780·179 1
27	24·494 0	77	69·853 2	370	335·658 5	870	789·251 0
28	25·401 2	78	70·760 4	380	344·730 3	880	798·322 8
29	26·308 4	79	71·667 6	390	353·802 2	890	807·394 7
30	27·215 6	80	72·574 8	400	362·874 0	900	816·466 5
31	28·122 7	81	73·482 0	410	371·945 9	910	825·538 4
32	29·029 9	82	74·389 2	420	381·017 7	920	834·610 2
33	29·937 1	83	75·296 4	430	390·089 6	930	843·682 1
34	30·844 3	84	76·203 5	440	399·161 4	940	852·753 9
35	31·751 5	85	77·110 7	450	408·233 3	950	861·825 8
36	32·658 7	86	78·017 9	460	417·305 1	960	870·897 6
37	33·565 8	87	78·925 1	470	426·377 0	970	879·969 5
38	34·473 0	88	79·832 3	480	435·448 8	980	889·041 3
39	35·380 2	89	80·739 5	490	444·520 7	990	898·113 2
40	36·287 4	90	81·646 7	500	453·592 5	1 000	907·185 0
41	37·194 6	91	82·553 8	510	462·664 4	2 000	1 814·370 0
42	38·101 8	92	83·461 0	520	471·736 2	3 000	2 721·555 0
43	39·009 0	93	84·368 2	530	480·808 1	4 000	3 628·740 0
44	39·916 1	94	85·275 4	540	489·879 9	5 000	4 535·925 0
45	40·823 3	95	86·182 6	550	498·951 8	6 000	5 443·110 0
46	41·730 5	96	87·089 8	560	508·023 6	7 000	6 350·295 0
47	42·637 7	97	87·996 9	570	517·095 5	8 000	7 257·480 0
48	43·544 9	98	88·904 1	580	526·167 3	9 000	8 164·665 0
49	44·452 1	99	89·811 3	590	535·239 2	10 000	9 071·850 0
50	45·359 3	100	90·718 5	600	544·311 0		

kilogrammes (kg) to US cwt (centals), pounds (lb)

WEIGHT

tonnes (t) to US tons (short tons)

WEIGHT

kg	cwt	lb	kg	cwt	lb
10		22·046	510	11	24·359
20		44·093	520	11	46·405
30		66·139	530	11	68·451
40		88·185	540	11	90·498
50	1	10·231	550	12	12·544
60	1	32·278	560	12	34·590
70	1	54·324	570	12	56·636
80	1	76·370	580	12	78·683
90	1	98·416	590	13	0·729
100	2	20·463	600	13	22·775
110	2	42·509	610	13	44·821
120	2	64·555	620	13	66·868
130	2	86·601	630	13	88·914
140	3	8·648	640	14	10·960
150	3	30·694	650	14	33·006
160	3	52·740	660	14	55·053
170	3	74·786	670	14	77·099
180	3	96·833	680	14	99·145
190	4	18·879	690	15	21·191
200	4	40·925	700	15	43·238
210	4	62·971	710	15	65·284
220	4	85·018	720	15	87·330
230	5	7·064	730	16	9·376
240	5	29·110	740	16	31·423
250	5	51·156	750	16	53·469
260	5	73·203	760	16	75·515
270	5	95·249	770	16	97·561
280	6	17·295	780	17	19·608
290	6	39·341	790	17	41·654
300	6	61·388	800	17	63·700
310	6	83·434	810	17	85·746
320	7	5·480	820	18	7·793
330	7	27·526	830	18	29·839
340	7	49·573	840	18	51·885
350	7	71·619	850	18	73·931
360	7	93·665	860	18	95·978
370	8	15·711	870	19	18·024
380	8	37·758	880	19	40·070
390	8	59·804	890	19	62·116
400	8	81·850	900	19	84·163
410	9	3·896	910	20	6·209
420	9	25·943	920	20	28·255
430	9	47·989	930	20	50·301
440	9	70·035	940	20	72·348
450	9	92·081	950	20	94·394
460	10	14·128	960	21	16·440
470	10	36·174	970	21	38·486
480	10	58·220	980	21	60·533
490	10	80·266	990	21	82·579
500	11	2·313	1 000	22	4·625

t	tons	t	tons
1	1·102 3	51	56·218
2	2·204 6	52	57·320
3	3·306 9	53	58·422
4	4·409 2	54	59·525
5	5·511 6	55	60·627
6	6·613 9	56	61·729
7	7·716 2	57	62·832
8	8·818 5	58	63·934
9	9·920 8	59	65·036
10	11·023 1	60	66·139
11	12·125 4	61	67·241
12	13·227 7	62	68·343
13	14·330 0	63	69·446
14	15·432 3	64	70·548
15	16·534 7	65	71·650
16	17·637 0	66	72·752
17	18·739 3	67	73·855
18	19·841 6	68	74·957
19	20·943 9	69	76·059
20	22·046 2	70	77·162
21	23·148 5	71	78·264
22	24·250 8	72	79·366
23	25·353 1	73	80·469
24	26·455 4	74	81·571
25	27·557 8	75	82·673
26	28·660 1	76	83·776
27	29·762 4	77	84·878
28	30·864 7	78	85·980
29	31·967 0	79	87·082
30	33·069 3	80	88·185
31	34·171 6	81	89·287
32	35·273 9	82	90·389
33	36·376 2	83	91·492
34	37·478 5	84	92·594
35	38·580 9	85	93·696
36	39·683 2	86	94·799
37	40·785 5	87	95·901
38	41·887 8	88	97·003
39	42·990 1	89	98·106
40	44·092 4	90	99·208
41	45·194 7	91	100·310
42	46·297 0	92	101·413
43	47·399 3	93	102·515
44	48·501 6	94	103·617
45	49·604 0	95	104·719
46	50·706 3	96	105·822
47	51·808 6	97	106·924
48	52·910 9	98	108·026
49	54·013 2	99	109·129
50	55·115 5	100	110·231

Temperature

SI base-unit: **Kelvin** (K)

Degrees **Kelvin**, also known as degrees **Absolute**, are mainly used for scientific measurements. The customary international unit is the degree **Celsius** which is known as **Centigrade** (°C) in the United Kingdom. (In France, Centigrade is a unit of angular measure and the name Celsius is used for temperature.)

The zero of the Centigrade scale is the temperature of the ice-point (273·16°K). The units of the Centigrade and Kelvin temperature interval are the same. Another unit used in the United Kingdom is the degree Fahrenheit (°F).

	°C	°F
Ice point	0	32
Boiling point of water under standard pressure	100	212

To convert °F to °C, deduct 32 and multiply by $\frac{5}{9}$.
To convert °C to °F, multiply by $\frac{9}{5}$ and add 32.

TEMPERATURE degrees Fahrenheit (°F) to degrees Centigrade (°C)

°F	°C	°F	°C	°F	°C	°F	°C
−50	−45·556	1	−17·222	51	10·556	101	38·333
−49	−45·000	2	−16·667	52	11·111	102	38·889
−48	−44·444	3	−16·111	53	11·667	103	39·444
−47	−43·889	4	−15·556	54	12·222	104	40·000
−46	−43·333	5	−15·000	55	12·778	105	40·556
−45	−42·778	6	−14·444	56	13·333	106	41·111
−44	−42·222	7	−13·889	57	13·889	107	41·667
−43	−41·667	8	−13·333	58	14·444	108	42·222
−42	−41·111	9	−12·778	59	15·000	109	42·778
−41	−40·556	10	−12·222	60	15·556	110	43·333
−40	−40·000	11	−11·667	61	16·111	111	43·889
−39	−39·444	12	−11·111	62	16·667	112	44·444
−38	−38·889	13	−10·556	63	17·222	113	45·000
−37	−38·333	14	−10·000	64	17·778	114	45·556
−36	−37·778	15	−9·444	65	18·333	115	46·111
−35	−37·222	16	−8·889	66	18·889	116	46·667
−34	−36·667	17	−8·333	67	19·444	117	47·222
−33	−36·111	18	−7·778	68	20·000	118	47·778
−32	−35·556	19	−7·222	69	20·556	119	48·333
−31	−35·000	20	−6·667	70	21·111	120	48·889
−30	−34·444	21	−6·111	71	21·667	121	49·444
−29	−33·889	22	−5·556	72	22·222	122	50·000
−28	−33·333	23	−5·000	73	22·778	123	50·556
−27	−32·778	24	−4·444	74	23·333	124	51·111
−26	−32·222	25	−3·889	75	23·889	125	51·667
−25	−31·667	26	−3·333	76	24·444	126	52·222
−24	−31·111	27	−2·778	77	25·000	127	52·778
−23	−30·556	28	−2·222	78	25·556	128	53·333
−22	−30·000	29	−1·667	79	26·111	129	53·889
−21	−29·444	30	−1·111	80	26·667	130	54·444
−20	−28·889	31	−0·556	81	27·222	131	55·000
−19	−28·333	32	0·000	82	27·778	132	55·556
−18	−27·778	33	0·556	83	28·333	133	56·111
−17	−27·222	34	1·111	84	28·889	134	56·667
−16	−26·667	35	1·667	85	29·444	135	57·222
−15	−26·111	36	2·222	86	30·000	136	57·778
−14	−25·556	37	2·778	87	30·556	137	58·333
−13	−25·000	38	3·333	88	31·111	138	58·889
−12	−24·444	39	3·889	89	31·667	139	59·444
−11	−23·889	40	4·444	90	32·222	140	60·000
−10	−23·333	41	5·000	91	32·778	141	60·556
−9	−22·778	42	5·556	92	33·333	142	61·111
−8	−22·222	43	6·111	93	33·889	143	61·667
−7	−21·667	44	6·667	94	34·444	144	62·222
−6	−21·111	45	7·222	95	35·000	145	62·778
−5	−20·556	46	7·778	96	35·556	146	63·333
−4	−20·000	47	8·333	97	36·111	147	63·889
−3	−19·444	48	8·889	98	36·667	148	64·444
−2	−18·889	49	9·444	99	37·222	149	65·000
−1	−18·333	50	10·000	100	37·778	150	65·556
0	−17·778						

°F	°C	°F	°C	°F	°C	°F	°C
151	66·111	201	93·889	255	123·889	505	262·778
152	66·667	202	94·444	260	126·667	510	265·556
153	67·222	203	95·000	265	129·444	515	268·333
154	67·778	204	95·556	270	132·222	520	271·111
155	68·333	205	96·111	275	135·000	525	273·889
156	68·889	206	96·667	280	137·778	530	276·667
157	69·444	207	97·222	285	140·556	535	279·444
158	70·000	208	97·778	290	143·333	540	282·222
159	70·556	209	98·333	295	146·111	545	285·000
160	71·111	210	98·889	300	148·889	550	287·778
161	71·667	211	99·444	305	151·667	555	290·556
162	72·222	212	100·000	310	154·444	560	293·333
163	72·778	213	100·556	315	157·222	565	296·111
164	73·333	214	101·111	320	160·000	570	298·889
165	73·889	215	101·667	325	162·778	575	301·667
166	74·444	216	102·222	330	165·556	580	304·444
167	75·000	217	102·778	335	168·333	585	307·222
168	75·556	218	103·333	340	171·111	590	310·000
169	76·111	219	103·889	345	173·889	595	312·778
170	76·667	220	104·444	350	176·667	600	315·556
171	77·222	221	105·000	355	179·444	605	318·333
172	77·778	222	105·556	360	182·222	610	321·111
173	78·333	223	106·111	365	185·000	615	323·889
174	78·889	224	106·667	370	187·778	620	326·667
175	79·444	225	107·222	375	190·556	625	329·444
176	80·000	226	107·778	380	193·333	630	332·222
177	80·556	227	108·333	385	196·111	635	335·000
178	81·111	228	108·889	390	198·889	640	337·778
179	81·667	229	109·444	395	201·667	645	340·556
180	82·222	230	110·000	400	204·444	650	343·333
181	82·778	231	110·556	405	207·222	655	346·111
182	83·333	232	111·111	410	210·000	660	348·889
183	83·889	233	111·667	415	212·778	665	351·667
184	84·444	234	112·222	420	215·556	670	354·444
185	85·000	235	112·778	425	218·333	675	357·222
186	85·556	236	113·333	430	221·111	680	360·000
187	86·111	237	113·889	435	223·889	685	362·778
188	86·667	238	114·444	440	226·667	690	365·556
189	87·222	239	115·000	445	229·444	695	368·333
190	87·778	240	115·556	450	232·222	700	371·111
191	88·333	241	116·111	455	235·000	705	373·889
192	88·889	242	116·667	460	237·778	710	376·667
193	89·444	243	117·222	465	240·556	715	379·444
194	90·000	244	117·778	470	243·333	720	382·222
195	90·556	245	118·333	475	246·111	725	385·000
196	91·111	246	118·889	480	248·889	730	387·778
197	91·667	247	119·444	485	251·667	735	390·556
198	92·222	248	120·000	490	254·444	740	393·333
199	92·778	249	120·556	495	257·222	745	396·111
200	93·333	250	121·111	500	260·000	750	398·889

°C	°F	°C	°F	°C	°F	°C	°F
−50	−58·0	1	33·8	51	123·8	110	230·0
−49	−56·2	2	35·6	52	125·6	120	248·0
−48	−54·4	3	37·4	53	127·4	130	266·0
−47	−52·6	4	39·2	54	129·2	140	284·0
−46	−50·8	5	41·0	55	131·0	150	302·0
−45	−49·0	6	42·8	56	132·8	160	320·0
−44	−47·2	7	44·6	57	134·6	170	338·0
−43	−45·4	8	46·4	58	136·4	180	356·0
−42	−43·6	9	48·2	59	138·2	190	374·0
−41	−41·8	10	50·0	60	140·0	200	392·0
−40	−40·0	11	51·8	61	141·8	210	410·0
−39	−38·2	12	53·6	62	143·6	220	428·0
−38	−36·4	13	55·4	63	145·4	230	446·0
−37	−34·6	14	57·2	64	147·2	240	464·0
−36	−32·8	15	59·0	65	149·0	250	482·0
−35	−31·0	16	60·8	66	150·8	260	500·0
−34	−29·2	17	62·6	67	152·6	270	518·0
−33	−27·4	18	64·4	68	154·4	280	536·0
−32	−25·6	19	66·2	69	156·2	290	554·0
−31	−23·8	20	68·0	70	158·0	300	572·0
−30	−22·0	21	69·8	71	159·8	310	590·0
−29	−20·2	22	71·6	72	161·6	320	608·0
−28	−18·4	23	73·4	73	163·4	330	626·0
−27	−16·6	24	75·2	74	165·2	340	644·0
−26	−14·8	25	77·0	75	167·0	350	662·0
−25	−13·0	26	78·8	76	168·8	360	680·0
−24	−11·2	27	80·6	77	170·6	370	698·0
−23	−9·4	28	82·4	78	172·4	380	716·0
−22	−7·6	29	84·2	79	174·2	390	734·0
−21	−5·8	30	86·0	80	176·0	400	752·0
−20	−4·0	31	87·8	81	177·8	410	770·0
−19	−2·2	32	89·6	82	179·6	420	788·0
−18	−0·4	33	91·4	83	181·4	430	806·0
−17	1·4	34	93·2	84	183·2	440	824·0
−16	3·2	35	95·0	85	185·0	450	842·0
−15	5·0	36	96·8	86	186·8	460	860·0
−14	6·8	37	98·6	87	188·6	470	878·0
−13	8·6	38	100·4	88	190·4	480	896·0
−12	10·4	39	102·2	89	192·2	490	914·0
−11	12·2	40	104·0	90	194·0	500	932·0
−10	14·0	41	105·8	91	195·8	510	950·0
−9	15·8	42	107·6	92	197·6	520	968·0
−8	17·6	43	109·4	93	199·4	530	986·0
−7	19·4	44	111·2	94	201·2	540	1 004·0
−6	21·2	45	113·0	95	203·0	550	1 022·0
−5	23·0	46	114·8	96	204·8	560	1 040·0
−4	24·8	47	116·6	97	206·6	570	1 058·0
−3	26·6	48	118·4	98	208·4	580	1 076·0
−2	28·4	49	120·2	99	210·2	590	1 094·0
−1	30·2	50	122·0	100	212·0	600	1 112·0
0	32·0						